Matisse

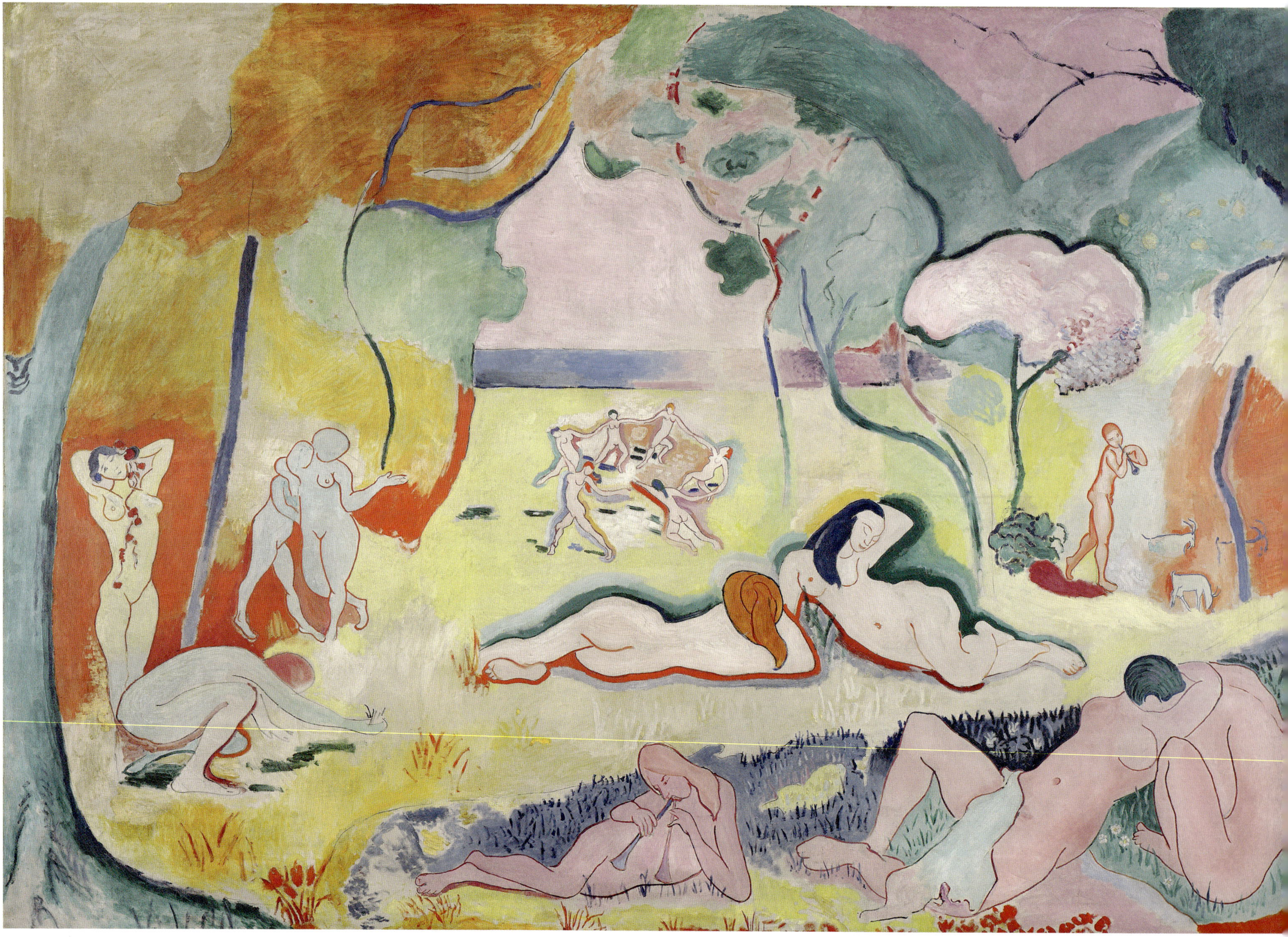

Henri Matisse, *Le Bonheur de vivre (The Joy of Life)*, (Barnes Foundation, Philadelphia)

JOHN CAUMAN

Matisse

IN 50 WORKS

PAVILION

CONTENTS

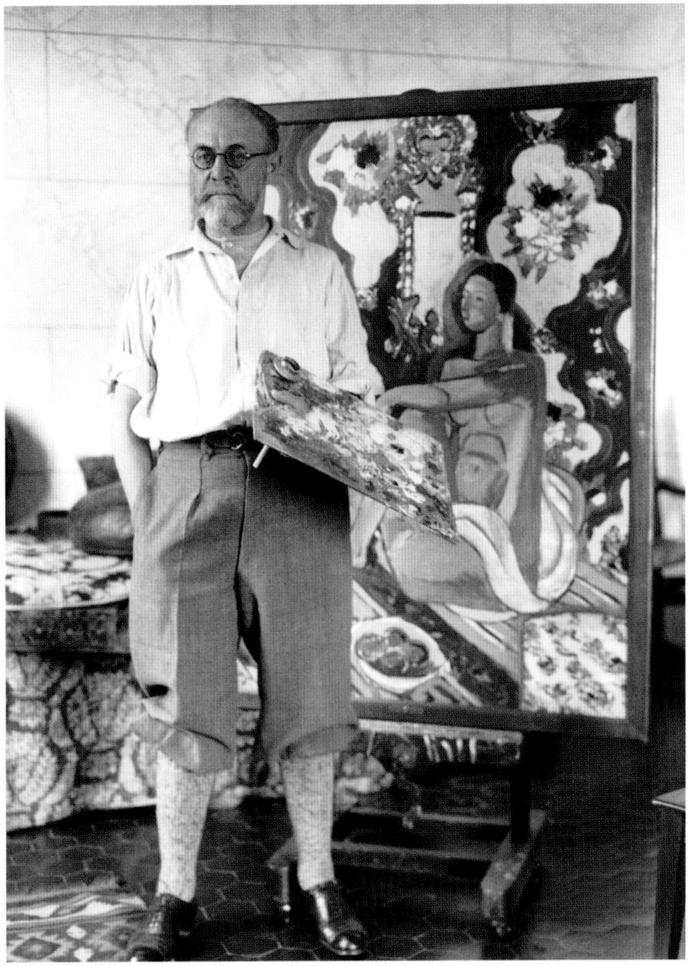

Henri Matisse in his studio, place Charles-Félix, Nice, c. 1926–7

I just saw in Paris the latest show of Matisse's chez Bernheim ... My word, they were lovely. He seems to go on inventing one melody after another and each more exactly right and unexpected than the last. He's a kind of Mozart in colour.

– Roger Fry to Vanessa Bell, 2 May 1923[1]

Matisse made his first coloured pictures at the age of 19. Stricken with a severe intestinal ailment, he was bedridden for several months. In the course of his recovery his mother gave him a set of colours with 'chromos', reproductions to be copied. This was the beginning of his life as a painter. Henceforth he would associate art-making with a restoration to physical and spiritual health, of his own and of others; he would, for example, lend his paintings to friends who were recovering from illness, or totally immerse himself in his work to alleviate stress. In the final years of his life, as he became infirm and bedridden, he worked still more diligently and tirelessly, as for him making art had become a therapeutic – indeed transcendent – experience.

Henri-Émile-Benoît Matisse was born on 31 December 1869, at the home of his maternal grandparents, in Le Cateau-Cambrésis in the north of France, near the Belgian border. The region, cold, dark and rainy, is known for textiles and weaving. His formative years were spent with his family in nearby Bohain-en-Vermandois, until 1882, when he boarded at the Lycée Henri-Martin, in the larger town of Saint-Quentin; as a student there he discovered that he had an innate talent for drawing. His father, Émile-Hippolyte-Henri Matisse, who owned a grain and hardware store, intended him to be a lawyer. His mother, née Anna Héloise Gérard, who was artistically inclined, worked as a milliner and painted porcelain as a hobby; it was she who would introduce her son Henri to painting.

Following his graduation from the lycée, Matisse went to Paris to study law. After passing the examination, he returned to his native region to work as a clerk at a law office in Saint-Quentin. As relief from the monotony of his job, he took drawing classes at a municipal art school, which also offered classes in tapestry and textile design. In 1891 he won his father's reluctant acceptance of his artistic ambitions. Provided with a small allowance, he went to Paris to study at the Académie Julian under the supervision of the conservative academic painter William-Adolphe Bouguereau, in preparation for the entrance examination at the

École des Beaux-Arts. He would not be inspired by the master's teachings, which largely involved by-rote copying, nor would the master be impressed with him.

The following year Matisse, having failed the entrance examination, retreated briefly to his home region. In the course of a visit to the Palais des Beaux-Arts de Lille, he encountered paintings by Goya and Chardin, which reaffirmed his choice of vocation. Back in Paris, he began to work independently at the Cours Yvon, the glass-enclosed courtyard of the École des Beaux-Arts, where he attracted the attention of a newly appointed instructor, Symbolist painter Gustave Moreau, who invited him to join his studio, at first informally. In 1895, he would be officially admitted to the school and to the Moreau class.

Matisse would be forever grateful to the master; in 1942, at the age of seventy-two, he told a radio interviewer that of all his teachers, 'only one among them counts for me: Gustave Moreau'.[2] Matisse had little interest in painting like Moreau, nor did Moreau encourage his students to do so. Not only did his students draw and paint from live models in the studio, he often brought them to copy artworks at the Louvre – not then a common practice – and to sketch in the streets of Paris. Matisse made lifelong friends among his fellow students of Moreau's studio, among them Charles Camoin, Henri Manguin and Albert Marquet.

Moreau was early to see Matisse's gifts as an artist, and Matisse never forgot his master's prophetic words, 'You are going to simplify painting.'[3] It was another elder, however – not an official teacher, but a mentor – who helped open his eyes to modern art: Camille Pissarro. Three decades earlier, Pissarro had accompanied Cézanne to paint *en plein air* in the French countryside; now, in 1897, he brought Matisse to see the Caillebotte bequest of Cézanne and the Impressionists at the Musée de Luxembourg.

Matisse was living at 19, quai Saint-Michel, on the left bank of Paris near the River Seine, across from the Notre-Dame Cathedral. His companion of these years was Caroline Joblaud, known as Camille, a fashionable Parisienne who (like the artist's mother and his future wife, Amélie Parayre) worked in a hat shop. In 1894 Camille gave birth to Matisse's daughter, Marguerite. In autumn-winter 1896–7 Matisse undertook *The Dinner Table* (pp. 33), a large interior which was in effect his diploma picture as a student of Moreau, marking his debut as a mature artist. The model in the painting, posing as a housekeeper, was Camille Joblaud.

Matisse's relationship with Camille ended in 1897. In the autumn of that year, at the wedding of mutual friends, he met Amélie Parayre, an idealistic young woman from Toulouse two years his junior. The artist would later describe Amélie as 'a very lovely Toulousaine, erect, with a good carriage and the possessor of beautiful dark hair … She gave the impression, despite the fact that she was timid and reserved, of a person of great kindness, force and gentleness'.[4] After a brief courtship, they married in 1898. *The Invalid* (pp. 35), painted in 1899 at her parents' home near Toulouse, depicts Amélie at the time of the birth of Jean, their first son. Amélie would provide moral support for her husband's artistic endeavours, and in the early years of their marriage financial support as well, when she opened a hat shop to aid their struggling family.

Matisse often visited Ambroise Vollard's small art gallery on the rue Lafitte, where he viewed works by Van Gogh, Gauguin and Cézanne. In 1899 he purchased from Vollard a small Cézanne, *Three Bathers* (1876–7) (opposite). Despite his family's straitened circumstances in years ahead, he would refrain from selling it. In 1925 he told an interviewer, 'In moments of doubt, when I was still searching for myself, frightened sometimes by my discoveries, I thought: "If Cézanne is right, I am right."'[5] The structural influence of Cézanne is apparent in Matisse's work in such paintings as *Male Model* of 1900 and *Carmelina* of 1903 (pp. 37 and 38), and the Aix master would continue to be an inspiration in the decades that followed.

Matisse's young family was growing. Camille Joblaud, as a single mother in turn-of-the-century Paris, with the social stigma attached to this status, was ill-equipped to raise a daughter on her own. She felt she had little choice but to accept when Amélie offered to adopt Marguerite, who would grow close to her adoptive mother. In the spring of 1900, Pierre, a second son, was born to Amélie.

Another early influence on Matisse was the Neo-Impressionism of Paul Signac. Following the premature death of Georges Seurat, who died in 1891 at the age of 31, Signac became the chief practitioner of this style, which he articulated in three articles for *La Revue Blanche* in 1898 – published the following year as the treatise *From Eugène Delacroix to Neo-Impressionism* – which Matisse read with great interest. Matisse was seeking ways to intensify his colour, and Signac offered a method: to juxtapose small dots of pure colour, which are blended not on the canvas, but in the viewer's eye. As early as 1899, Matisse was applying this technique to still-life compositions.

In the winter of 1903–04 Matisse met Signac, who was vice president of the Société des Artistes Indepéndants, which every spring presented the non-juried Salon des Indépendants. Signac spent summers in St Tropez on the Côte d'Azur and encouraged

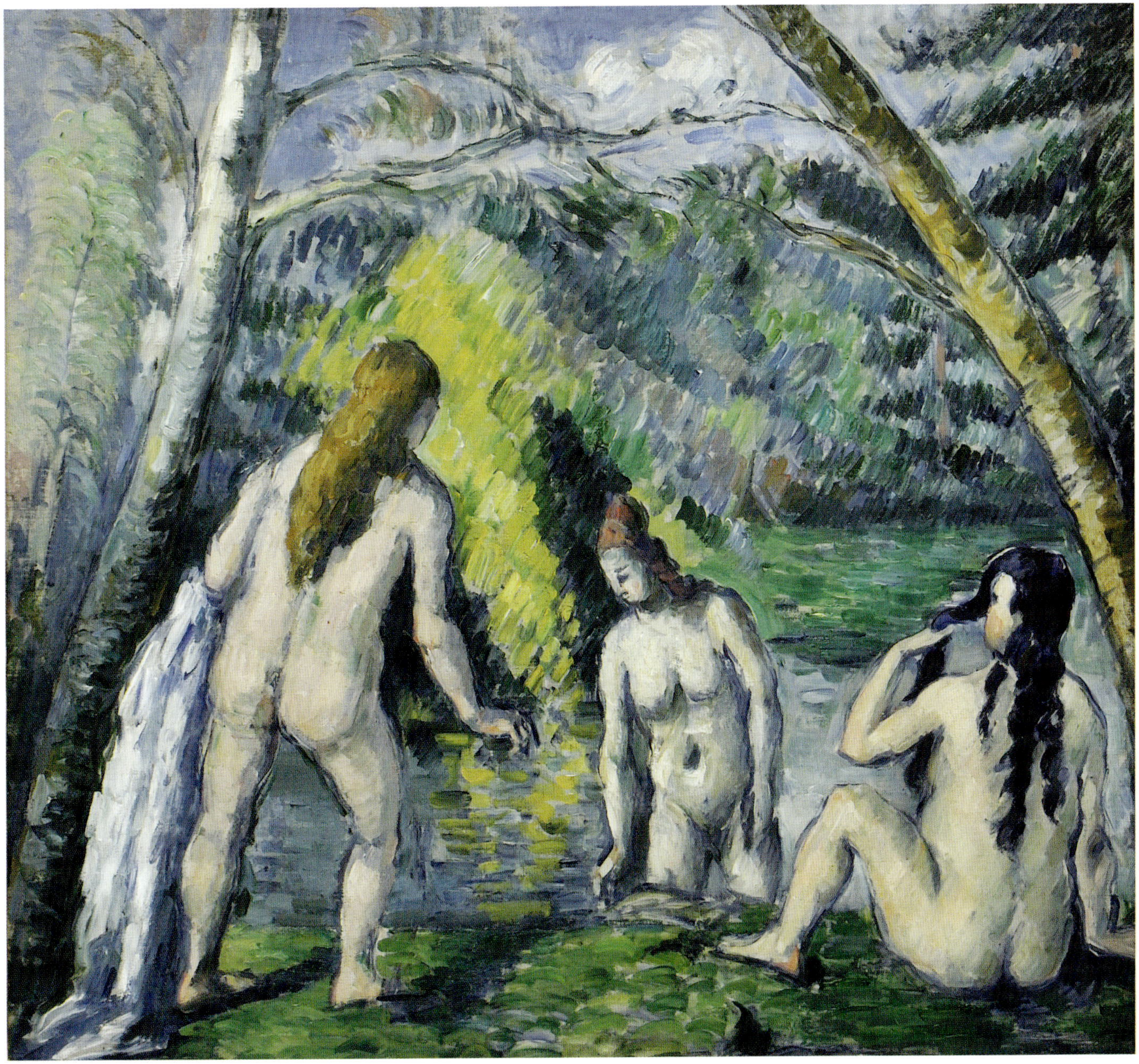

Paul Cézanne, *Three Bathers,* 1876–7
Oil on canvas | 52 × 54.5cm (20½ × 21⅜in), Musée du Petit Palais, Paris (Gift of Henri Matisse)

younger artists to join him there for painting excursions. This suited Matisse, who was temperamentally attracted to sunlight and warm climates (and, conversely, depressed by cold, rainy and overcast weather). That summer Signac found him an inexpensive rental property and Matisse travelled there with Amélie and their son Pierre, aged four. During the following autumn and winter of 1904, Matisse produced a major work, *Luxe, calme et volupté* (pp. 41) based on sketches from the previous summer. Inspired in part by Baudelaire's poem *L'invitation au voyage*, he employed the technique of Neo-Impressionism to create an imaginary figure and landscape composition.

In his appearance and demeanour, Matisse did not convey the air of 'bohemian'; with his gold-rimmed spectacles, neatly trimmed beard and tweedy attire, he embodied more the persona of a British gentleman. While he was still a student, his friends gave him the nickname 'The Professor'. When the parents of his friend the painter André Derain (who was his junior by ten years) balked at their son's choice of career, Derain asked Matisse to intervene on his behalf. Matisse, with Amélie, paid them a call, and the visit was a success. In summer 1905 Derain joined Matisse to paint in Collioure, a coastal village in the south of France. In years to come, Matisse would continue the practice of following the sun and going south to paint.

That summer Matisse abandoned Neo-Impressionism for a less scientific, more intuitive technique. Often working out of doors alongside Derain, Matisse created loosely painted, intensely coloured compositions. Among his paintings of this summer was *Open Window, Collioure* (pp. 43), in which a window joins interior and exterior, a frequent theme in his work.

At summer's end Matisse returned to Paris, where he painted *Woman with a Hat* (pp. 45), a portrait of his wife, in complementary colours of red and green, blue and

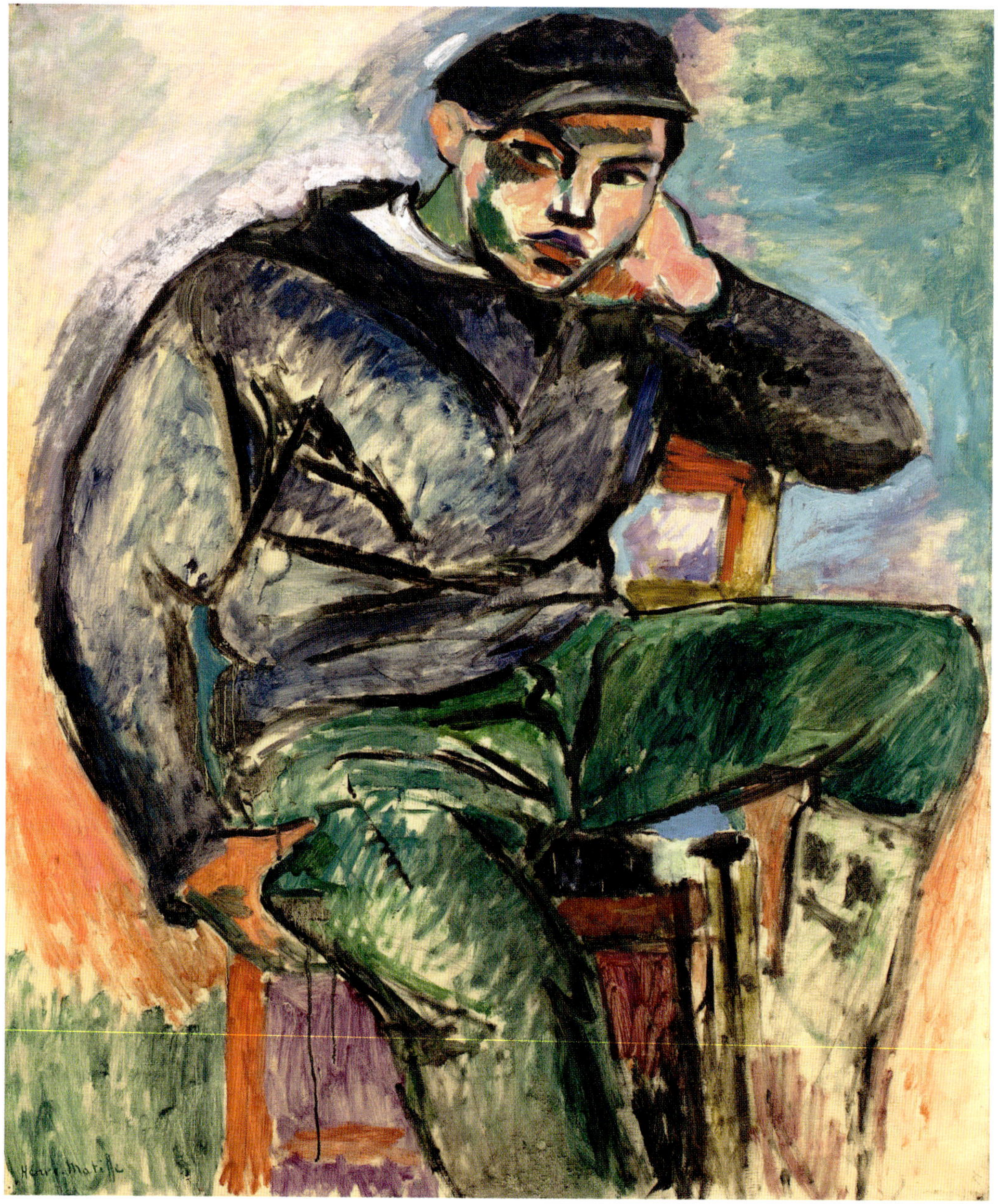

Henri Matisse, *Young Sailor I*, 1906
Oil on canvas | 99.7 × 81.3cm (39¼ × 32in), Collection Sheldon H. Solow, New York

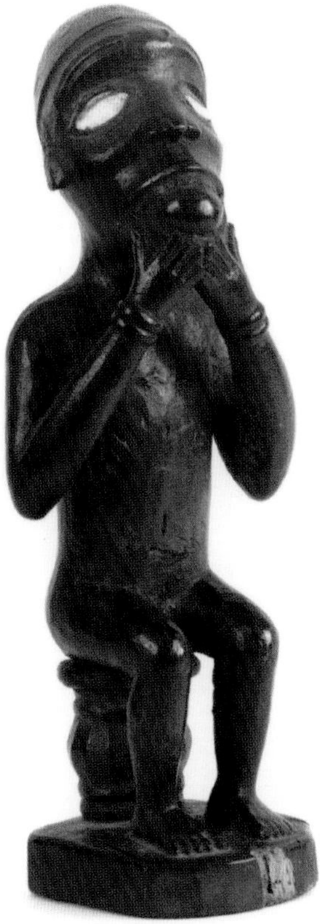

Vili Figure, Democratic Republic of Congo
24cm (9⅝in) tall. Private Collection (formerly collection Henri Matisse)

orange, yellow and violet. With *Open Window, Collioure,* it was among his ten submissions to the Salon d'Automne, held in the glass and metal structure of the Grand Palais. Also taking part in the exhibition were his colleagues Derain, Maurice de Vlaminck, Charles Camoin, Henri Manguin, Albert Marquet and Georges Rouault, who along with Matisse were dubbed 'Fauves' (wild beasts) by the critic Louis Vauxcelles; Matisse was immediately identified as their leader.

On the opening day of the Salon, *Woman with a Hat* aroused the interest of the collector Leo Stein, who brought it to the attention of his sister Gertrude, his brother Michael and his sister-in-law Sarah. On the Salon's closing day, Leo bought the painting (with the agreement of Gertrude, with whom he shared household expenses). These four expatriate Americans, who lived at two separate residences on the Left Bank of Paris, would become Matisse's first patrons, and, in today's parlance, would provide both 'networking' and 'a scene'. Sarah Stein would become a lifelong friend and confidante. In 1906 she and Michael purchased a second portrait of Amélie, *Madame Matisse: The Green Line* (pp. 47), painted at the time of the 1905 Autumn Salon. At weekly gatherings at the two Stein households, Matisse would meet an international roster of artists, writers and future collectors; among the collectors were two sisters from Baltimore, Claribel and Etta Cone, who in annual excursions to Paris would continue to purchase his work when the Steins no longer had the wherewithal to do so. Through the Steins, Matisse met Pablo Picasso, twelve years his junior, whose lifelong friendship and rivalry would be beneficial for both artists; each would go on to recognize the other as his only true artistic peer.

In late 1905 Matisse rented a large studio in an abandoned monastery, the Couvent du Sacré-Cœur, where he undertook *Le Bonheur de vivre (The Joy of Life)*, an ambitious Arcadian figure-and-landscape composition (pp. 53). The painting – expressive rather than descriptive in its colour – contained within it motifs that he would further explore in years to come. He was gradually moving away from the modelled Cézannian form and space, and jarring complementary colours of Fauvism, towards a flattened, decorative style. In spring 1906 it was his sole entry in the Salon des Indépendants, where it was purchased by Leo Stein.

Later that spring Matisse returned to Collioure, and after a two-week sojourn in Algeria, North Africa, he remained in the Midi for summer and part of autumn. He painted two versions of a portrait of a young fisherman, *Young Sailor I and II* (opposite and pp. 49). The first version, painted in a Fauve style, conveyed a likeness of the sitter; the second version was painted in a more abstract, decorative style, closer to that of *Le Bonheur de vivre*. (Matisse would often follow this protocol of working in series, in which the first version is closer to observed reality, the second more synthesized and abstract.) That summer he also painted *Self-Portrait in a Striped Shirt* (pp. 51), similar in style to *Young Sailor I,* in which he depicts himself in the garb of a Collioure fisherman.

Blue Nude (Memory of Biskra) of early 1907 (pp. 55) was Matisse's first painting to incorporate the influence of African tribal sculpture. The previous spring he had purchased an African statuette, the *Vili Figure*, and had shown it to Picasso; later that spring he had visited Biskra in Algeria. The visual dialogue between the two artists, both of whom were synthesizing tribal art and Cézanne in their work, was instrumental both in the development of Matisse's art and in the evolution of Picasso's Cubism (see *Nude with Drapery*, right). In autumn 1907 Matisse viewed the proto-Cubist painting *Demoiselles d'Avignon* (1907, The Museum of Modern Art, New York) in Picasso's studio; in early 1908 he painted *Bathers with a Turtle* (pp. 61), a work comparable in size and proportions and in its incorporation of facial features found in tribal art.

Matisse, who had grown up in a textile town, was aware of fabric designs before he was exposed to the fine arts. The interplay of decorative patterns was a dominant feature of his art, and is evident in his portrait of his wife, *Red Madras Headdress* (pp. 57), painted in early summer 1907. Later that summer he travelled to Italy and was impressed by the monumentality and simplicity of the frescoes of Giotto and Piero della Francesca. When he returned to Collioure, he began a series of two paintings with an Arcadian theme, *Le Luxe I*, completed by *Le Luxe II* (pp. 59), painted in Paris in the autumn and winter of 1907–8. *Red Madras Headdress* and *Le Luxe II* exemplify the polarities of Matisse's decorative style circa 1907–13: on the one hand, contrapuntal patterning; on the other, simplified compositions of flattened colour areas.

Matisse valued Sarah Stein's criticism of his work, and he, in turn, advised her on her own painting. She found him to be a gifted teacher, and she and her husband Michael encouraged him to take on more students. In early 1908, with financial help from the Steins, he opened his own school, the Académie Matisse, in the abandoned convent where he already had a studio. It began as an international group of approximately ten students, including the German Hans Purrmann and the Americans Max Weber and Patrick Henry Bruce. Matisse's curriculum was based on the beaux-arts instruction of Gustave Moreau, supplemented by the examples of Cézanne's paintings and of African tribal carvings. At this time Matisse was formulating a treatise on the practice of art, which he would publish at the year's end as 'Notes of a Painter'. Teaching at the academy was an opportunity to refine his ideas and apply them beyond the scope of his own work. In spring 1908 the Academy moved to larger quarters in another abandoned convent, located at the Hôtel Biron, an eighteenth-century mansion in a 7 hectare (17 acre) park (site of the present-day Rodin Museum). Matisse moved his studio and family quarters to the mansion and adjacent buildings. By the time the school closed in early 1912, over eighty students had been in attendance; of them, most were Scandinavians; about twenty per cent were women; only three were known to be French.

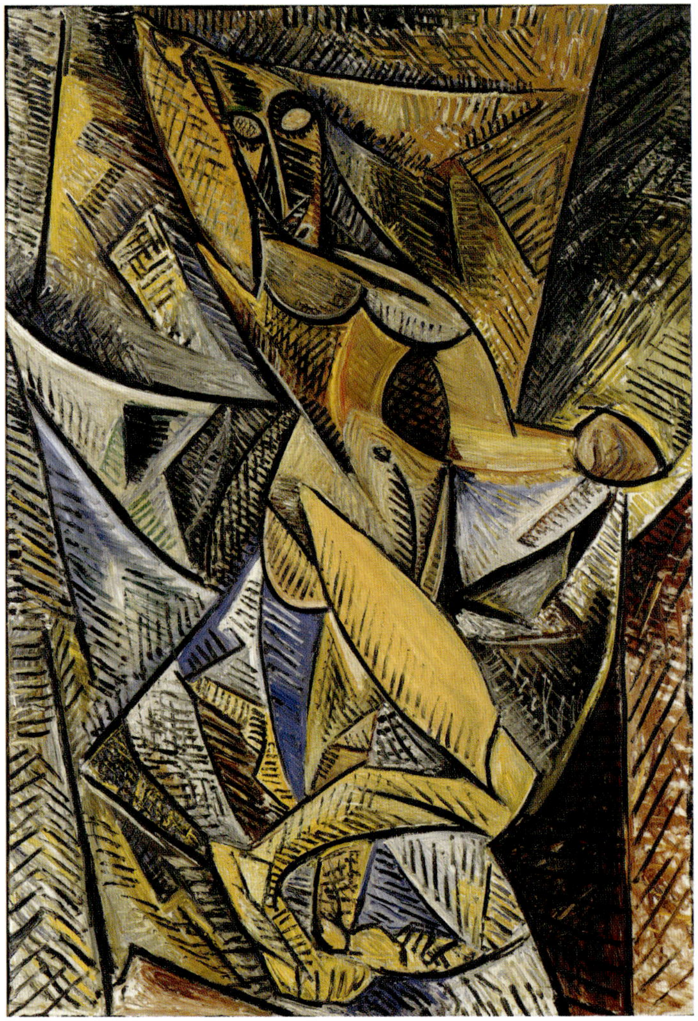

Pablo Picasso, *Nude with Drapery* (also called *Dance of the Veils)*, 1907
Oil on canvas | 150 × 100cm (59¾ × 39¾in)
The State Hermitage Museum, St Petersburg

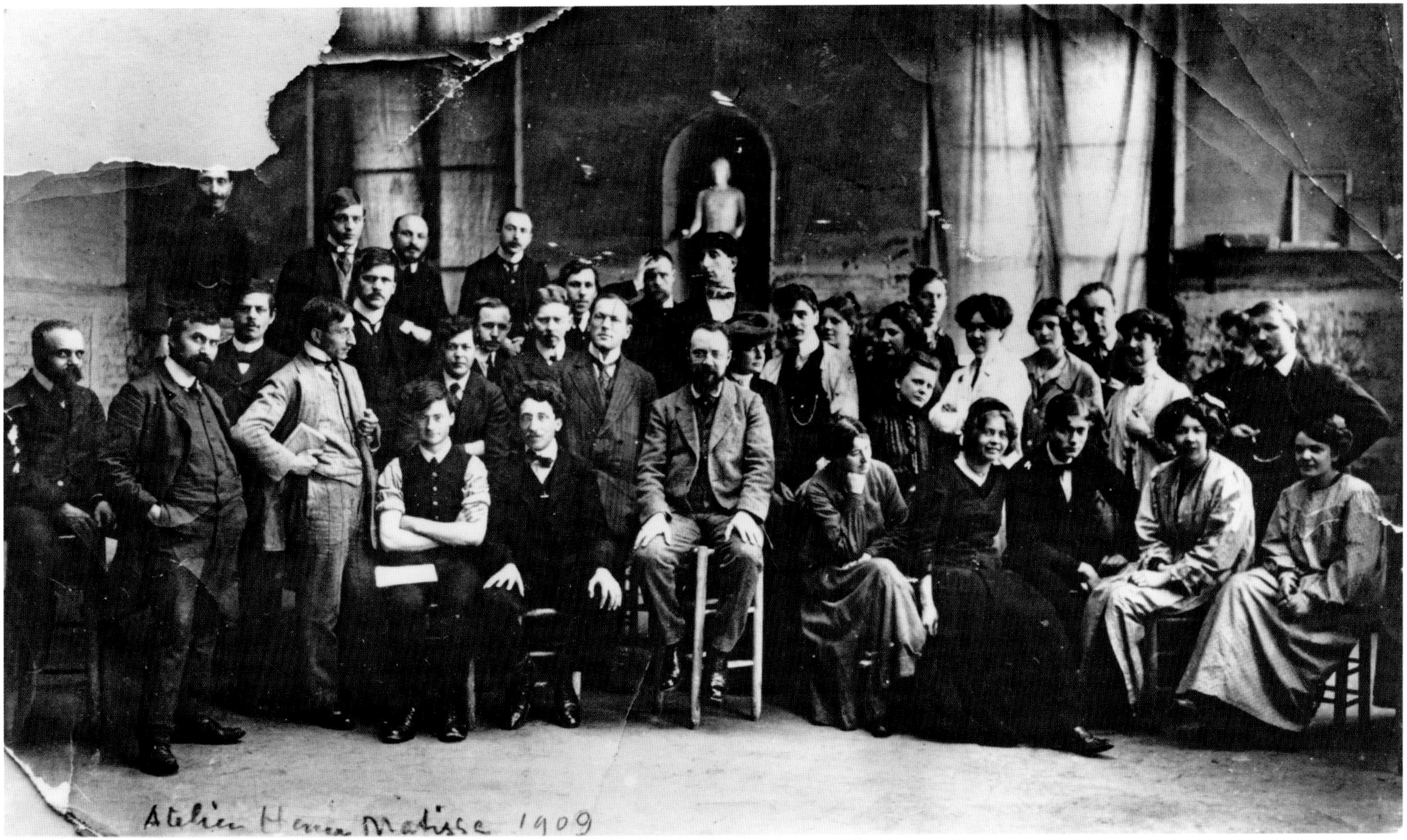

Matisse and his students, Hôtel Biron, Paris, 1910

In his essay 'Notes of a Painter', published in *La Grande Revue* in December 1908, Matisse writes, 'What I am after, above all, is expression'. Matisse goes on to say, 'Expression, for me, does not reside in passions glowing in a human face or manifested by violent movement. The entire arrangement of my picture is expressive: the place occupied by the figures, the empty spaces around them, the proportions, everything has its share.'[6] His goal is not to imitate nature, but to condense the sensations he receives from nature and produce an equivalent that realizes the essential character of what is portrayed. The total effect is meant to have a soothing, spiritually uplifting influence on the mind.

Harmony in Red (pp. 63), painted from Matisse's studio at the Hôtel Biron, juxtaposes interior and exterior views, presenting images of dynamic organic growth: the blossoming trees and flowers of the park, the fruit and flower still life of the table, and the flowerpot and arabesque patterning of the wallpaper and tablecloth. The subject is a revisiting of *The Dinner Table* of 1896–7, painted in his current decorative style. Matisse had been inspired by Vincent Van Gogh's use of arabesque and floral patterns in the backgrounds of such works as *La Berceuse*, a portrait series of 1889. *Harmony in Red* was purchased by the Russian textile merchant Sergei Shchukin, who, along with Russian textile manufacturer Ivan Morosov, would supplant the Steins as Matisse's principal patrons.

In early 1909 Shchukin commissioned Matisse to paint a mural-sized decorative panel for his mansion in Moscow. The artist rapidly composed a full-scale oil sketch, *Dance I*, a composition of five female nudes on a green hillside set against a blue sky (pp. 65). An Arcadian scene in the style of *Le Luxe II*, it ultimately descends from the ring of six dancers in *Le Bonheur de vivre*. Shchukin, delighted with the preparatory panel, agreed to this commission; in addition, he agreed to a second decorative panel, signifying music. (Shchukin would not agree to a third proposed panel, of five bathers by a waterfall, which Matisse would later rework as *Bathers by a River* (pp. 106-7).

In autumn 1909 Matisse and family moved to a home in the suburb Issy-les-Moulineaux, southwest of Paris; in the garden he had a studio built, a large prefabricated glass structure. There he undertook *Still Life with 'Dance'* (pp. 65 and 67), an interior of the studio with *Dance I* in the background; the painting would later be purchased by Ivan Morosov. In 1910 he completed *Dance II* and its companion panel, *Music* (pp. 71 and 69); the theme of 'music' is embodied by five nude male figures on a hill, singing or playing instruments.

Matisse's post-Fauve style of 1907–13 fluctuated between polarities of monumental simplicity, as in *Music* and *Dance*, and complex patterning, as in *Harmony in Red*. His fascination with the decorative qualities of the art of the Near East was intensified by his visit to Munich in late 1910, where he viewed a major exhibition of Islamic art. He was particularly interested in the implications for his own work of Persian miniatures, which, unlike the carpets and other textiles, were representational as well as intricately patterned.

The decorative patterning of Persian miniatures had a major influence on the four paintings of 1911 that Alfred Barr later dubbed 'symphonic interiors'.[7] (This is a felicitous term, given that Matisse, an amateur violinist, often sought to evoke through his art a response in the viewer analogous to effects of music.) The four symphonic interiors are *The Pink Studio*, *The Painter's Family*, *Interior with Aubergines*, and *The Red Studio* (pp. 73, 75, 77 and 79). Compare Matisse's *The Painter's Family* to Cézanne's *Girl at the Piano* (opposite). These works are autobiographical in nature, given that they depict either the artist's studio or

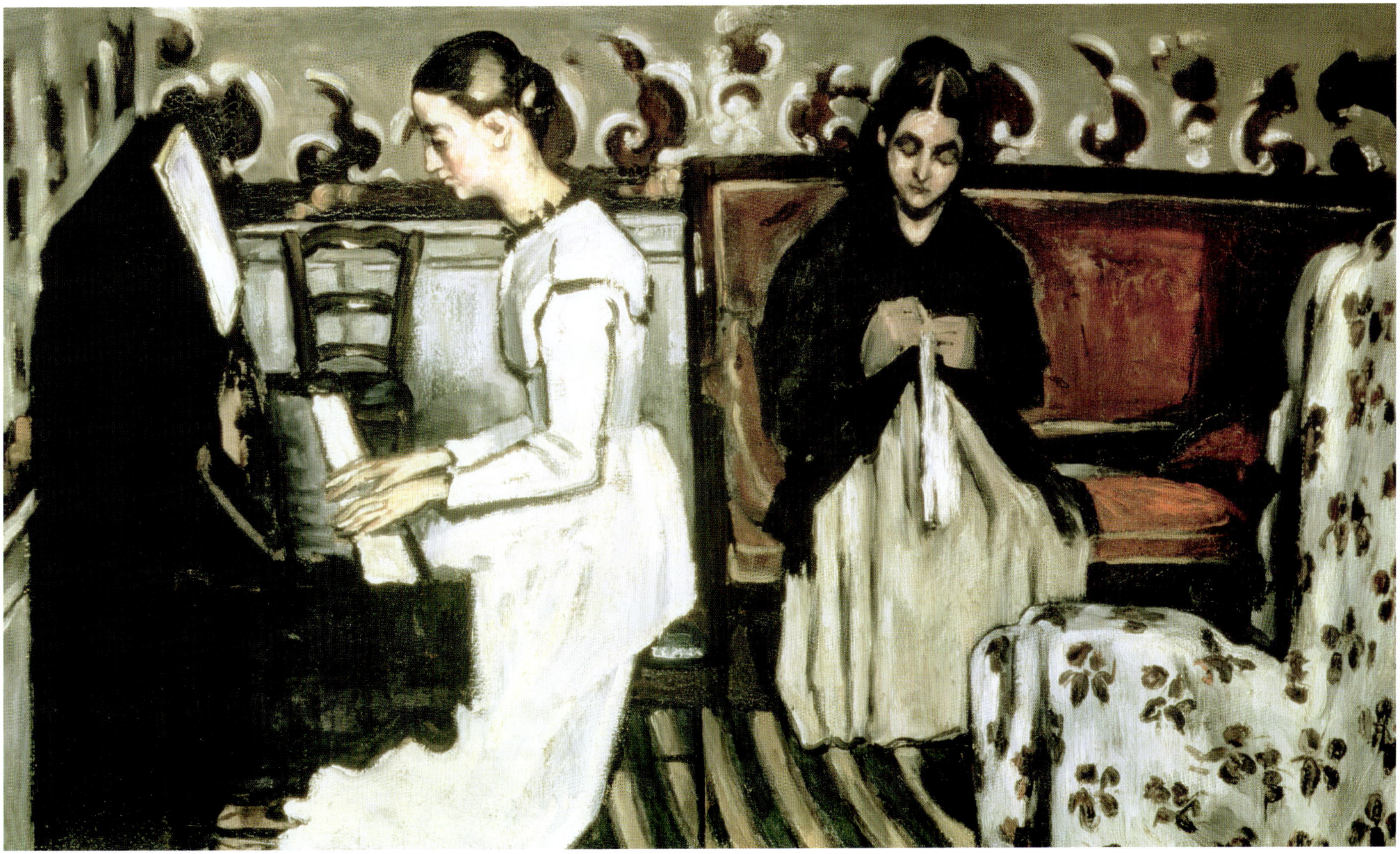

Paul Cézanne, *Girl at the Piano (Overture to Tannhäuser)*, 1869–70
Oil on canvas | 57 × 92cm (22⅜ × 36³⁄₁₆in)
The State Hermitage Museum, St Petersburg

the family quarters of his home. *The Pink Studio* and *The Red Studio* are interiors of the studio in Issy with inventories of his recent paintings and sculpture, and hence of his life as an artist. *The Painter's Family* presents his wife, daughter and two sons in the living room of their home in Issy (the artist in absentia is represented by his sculpture *The Serf* on the mantle). *Interior with Aubergines* shows the living room of the family home in Collioure

of that summer. With its segmented patterning, it is the work among the four in which the impact of Persian miniatures is most apparent. It is believed to have had an influence on the Cubist collages and Synthetic Cubist paintings of Picasso and Braque.

The Conversation (pp. 85), begun at Matisse's Paris studio at the Hôtel Biron, was completed after the family's move to Issy. (It would be purchased by Shchukin in 1913.) It depicts the artist and his wife in profile – he, standing and she, seated – facing each other across an open window that looks out on the garden and studio. The figures are painted in a simplified, geometrical style, their faces modelled in light and shadow, revealing the influence of the *Stele of Hammurabi*, an Ancient Babylonian relief sculpture which the artist had seen at the Louvre. As in many of his paintings, Matisse allowed pentimenti to be visible, revealing the artist's process before arriving at the final result. In this case, alteration of the positioning of the figures may indicate some anguish on the artist's part related to the subject of the work, underlying tensions in his and Amélie's marriage. Having been so close a decade earlier, when she was directly involved in his work, they now seemed to be drifting apart.

The patronage of the Steins and of Shchukin and Morosov contributed to Matisse's growing international reputation. In 1908 he exhibited five paintings at the first Salon de la Toison d'Or (Salon of the Golden Fleece) in Moscow, which also included works by (among others) Cézanne, Signac, Matisse's fellow Fauves, and contemporary Russian artists. He exhibited four paintings at the second Salon de la Toison d'Or in 1909. Matisse had solo exhibitions in New York in 1908, 1910 and 1912, held at Alfred Stieglitz's Little Galleries of the Photo-Secession, known as '291' for its address on Fifth Avenue. The painter-photographer Edward Steichen, who was acting as Stieglitz's scout in Europe, had met Matisse through Sarah Stein. Although the exhibitions were mostly of works on paper and included only one painting, the exhibition of 1912 was the artist's first anywhere devoted primarily to his sculpture. In 1910 the painter and critic Roger Fry, a member of the Bloomsbury Group of writers and artists, presented a grand survey of modern French art at the Grafton Galleries, London, under the title *Manet and the Post-Impressionists*. While the three 'old masters' of the modern movement – Cézanne, Van Gogh and

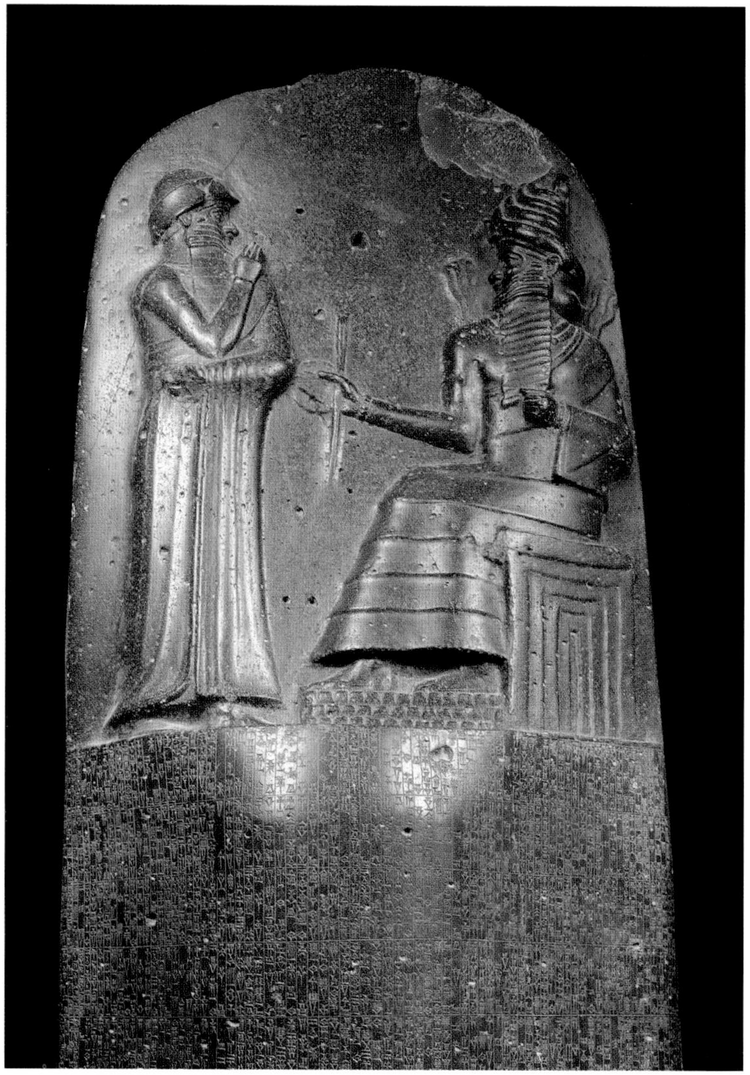

Upper portion of the *Stele of Hammurabi*, c. 1792–50 BC
Diorite | Height of stele 225cm (88½in), height of relief 71cm (28in), Louvre, Paris

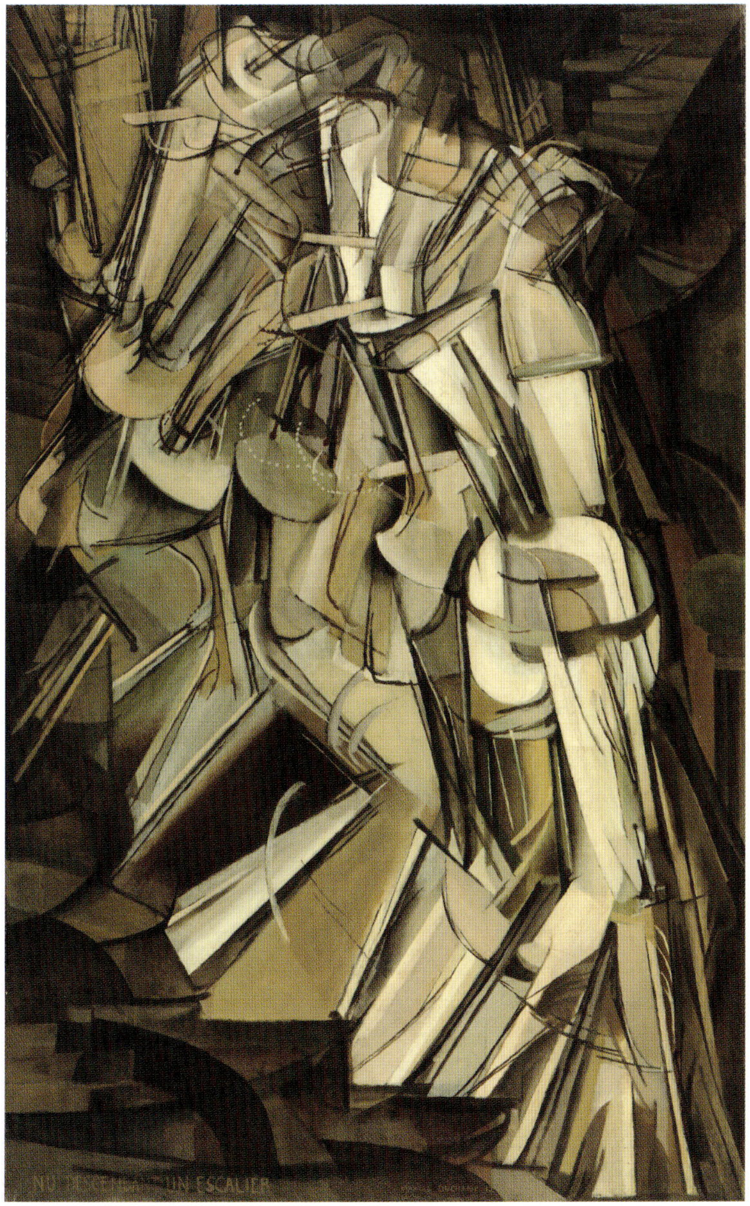

Marcel Duchamp, *Nude Descending a Staircase,* 1912
Oil on canvas | 147 × 89.2cm (57⅞ × 35⅛in)
Philadelphia Museum of Art

Gauguin – were the focus of the exhibition, three paintings by Matisse were included, along with sculptures, works on paper and a ceramic vase.

In 1912–13 Matisse was a central figure in three major international exhibitions, in both Europe and the United States. In 1912 the *Sonderbund Exhibition* in Cologne, organized by Karl Osthaus, presented, among others, Cézanne, Van Gogh, Gauguin and Signac, in addition to a room devoted to Edvard Munch, sixteen works by Picasso, and five by Matisse. The *Second Post-Impressionist Exhibition*, which, like *Manet and the Post-Impressionists*, was organized by Roger Fry and held at the Grafton Galleries, London, focused on the younger generation of artists; of the previous generation, only Cézanne was included. (In the UK and the United States, where the word 'Fauve' was nearly unknown, Matisse was initially known as a 'Post-Impressionist', a term coined by Fry.) Matisse was represented by nineteen paintings, in addition to sculpture and works on paper. Among the paintings were *Young Sailor II*, *Le Luxe II*, *Dance I*, *The Red Studio*, *The Conversation*, and *Goldfish and Sculpture* (pp. 83).

The *International Exhibition of Modern Art*, better known as The Armory Show, was held at the 69th Regiment Armory, New York, in 1913. (A scaled-down version of the exhibition would subsequently travel to Chicago and to Boston.) In contrast with the thirteen paintings Matisse had in the show, Picasso had five. Of the Post-Impressionist 'old masters', only Van Gogh was a bigger presence than Matisse, with seventeen paintings; Cézanne matched Matisse, with thirteen; while Gauguin showed just eight paintings. In addition to seven works secured from the Grafton show – among them *Young Sailor II*, *Le Luxe II*, *The Red Studio* and *Goldfish and Sculpture* – Leo Stein lent *Blue Nude*, and Sarah and Michael Stein lent *Red Madras Headdress*. It was the greater American public's first exposure to modern art. *Red Madras Headdress* was lampooned mercilessly in the press, second only to Marcel Duchamp's notorious *Nude Descending a Staircase* (see opposite).

In addition to his participation in international exhibitions during these years, Matisse made several excursions abroad. In November 1911 he travelled to St Petersburg and to Moscow, where he was a guest in Shchukin's home and viewed the Russian icons in the collection of the artist and collector Ilya Ostroukhov. He made two visits to Tangier,

Morocco – from January to April 1912 and from October 1912 to February 1913. During these visits he completed 23 paintings, and his impressions of Morocco – its light, its architecture, and the appearance and dress of its residents – continued to affect his later work. In Tangier bowls of goldfish were used as objects of contemplation, and upon his return to Issy he acquired goldfish and a cylindrical bowl for his studio. The motif would appear in many of his paintings, among them *Goldfish* (1912, pp. 81), *Goldfish and Sculpture* (1912), and *Goldfish and Palette* (1914–15, pp. 99). In 1913 an exhibition of the Moroccan paintings was held at the Bernheim-Jeune Gallery; included in the exhibition were *Seated Riffian* (pp. 87) and *Entrance to the Casbah* (pp. 89).

In the period between Matisse's return from Morocco in 1913 and his departure for Nice in 1917, years corresponding to World War I and the months leading up to it, his art moved into a new phase. His paintings of this period were often uncharacteristically subdued in their use of colour and characterized by architectonic severity. To a greater degree than before, he would allow the process by which he arrived at his final result to be visible, with underpainting and scratches evident on the pictorial surface. Rather than presenting a bold contrast with Cubism, his art in these years often found common cause with the Cubists. Matisse himself would characterize his techniques of this period as 'the methods of modern construction'.[8] As in the Cubist output of Braque, Picasso and Juan Gris, the works, though always grounded in nature, would sometimes approach pure abstraction. Matisse would now find a strong supporter in the critic and poet Guillaume Apollinaire, author of *The Cubist Painters* (1913).

Matisse and Picasso grew personally closer during this period. In July 1913 Picasso was in Paris, suffering from a fever and from emotional distress due to the recent death of his father. Matisse visited him at his sickbed, bringing flowers and oranges; Picasso would later acquire Matisse's painting *Still Life with Oranges* (1912, Musée Picasso, Paris), symbolic of their friendship. In August Picasso visited Matisse in Issy; together they went horseback riding and, while going for walks, exchanged ideas on painting.

'The methods of modern construction' are evident in two of Matisse's portraits of the period, those of *Madame Matisse* (1913, pp. 91) and *Yvonne Landsberg* (1914, pp. 95). In the case of the portrait of his wife Amélie, Matisse began depicting her representationally, but as he reworked the painting, it became increasingly abstract. While Mme Matisse, elegantly attired, sits gracefully in her chair, she seems absent rather than present; her facial features resemble a Fang mask from Gabon, central Africa, that belonged to Matisse's collection (opposite). She is said to have wept when she saw the final painting, presumably because she interpreted it as signifying her estrangement from her husband.[9]

Similarly, the portrait of Yvonne Landsberg became increasingly abstract as work proceeded, the young sitter's facial features replaced by a masklike countenance. The painting is nearly monochrome, with the artist's process visible on the surface, and lines etched in as paint is scratched away. These lines seem to emanate from the sitter like the force lines used by the Italian Futurists. The sitter's brother Bertie,

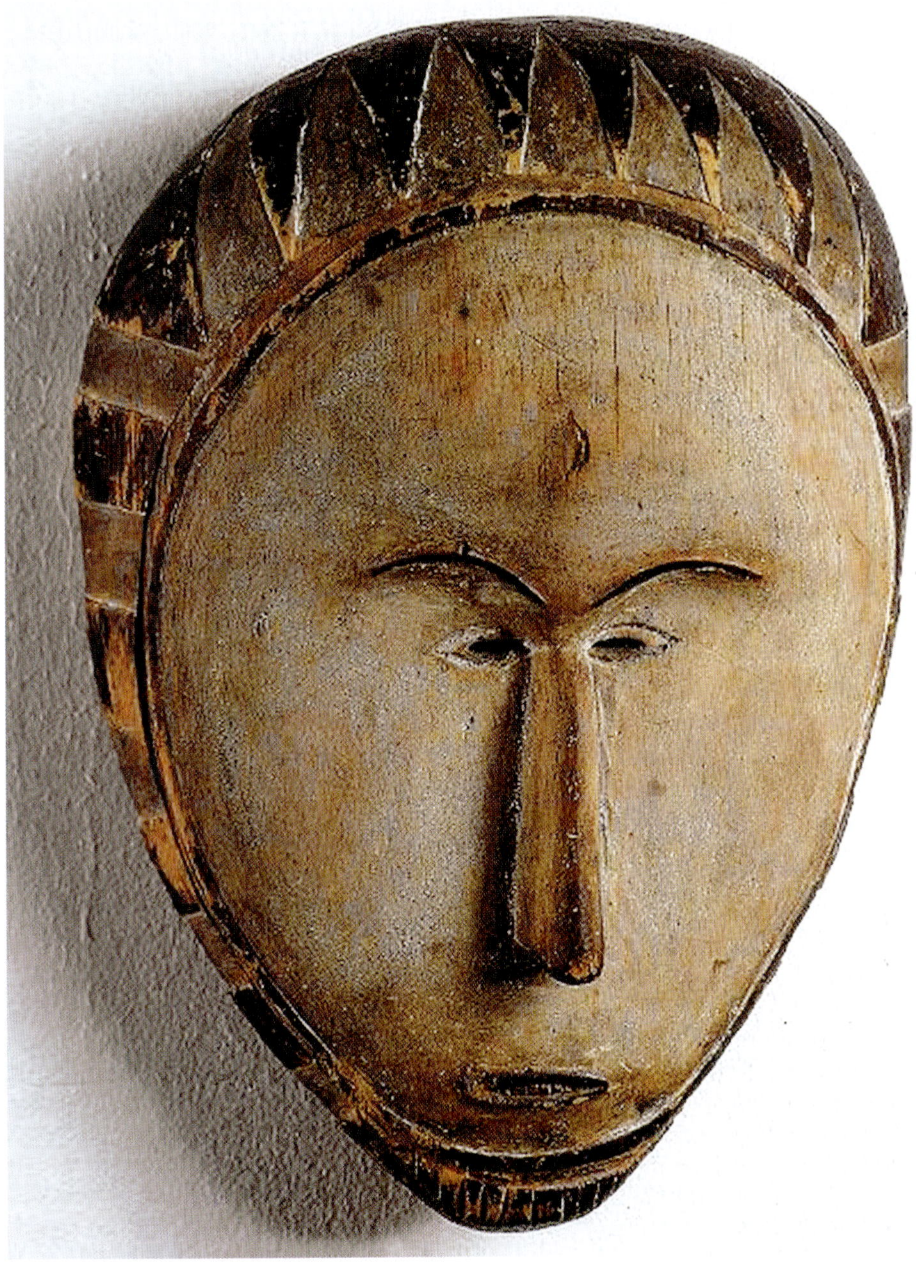

Fang mask, Gabon
Painted wood | Height of mask 48cm (18⅞in), Centre Pompidou, Paris

who chaperoned the posing sessions and was a supporter of modernism, had a response quite opposite to that of Mme Matisse à propos her own portrait: he later recalled that as the work progressed, it 'became *less* physically but – possibly – *more* spiritually like my sister.'[10] The portrait was shown at Matisse's exhibition held at the Montross Gallery, New York in 1915, where it was bought by the American collector Walter Conrad Arensberg, who would later purchase Marcel Duchamp's *Nude Descending a Staircase* (see p. 17), with which it shares a similar size, format, and Futurist influence.

Two of Matisse's paintings of 1914, painted in a colouristically restricted, geometric style that verges on pure abstraction, were not publicly exhibited in his lifetime. They are *View of Notre-Dame* (pp. 93), painted on the eve of World War I, and *French Window at Collioure* (pp. 97), painted just after the war's outbreak. *View of Notre-Dame* is based on the vista seen from the artist's studio on quai Saint-Michel (the first version of the painting appears opposite). *French Window at Collioure* depicts the *porte-fenêtre* of Matisse's home in the Midi, where he was joined by his old friend Albert Marquet, and often visited the Cubist artist Juan Gris, with whom he had animated discussions about art. The work, with its window panes in opaque black, is uncharacteristically pessimistic, reflecting his uncertainty about the future. (He had tried to enlist in the French army, but had been rejected due to age.)

Matisse's continuing dialogue with Cubism is evident in his interiors and still lifes in the years that followed. *Goldfish and Palette* (1914-1915, pp. 98-9), set in his quai Saint-Michel studio, began as a portrayal of a figure holding a palette, but as work proceeded, the figure became increasingly fragmented, to the point where the goldfish become the most vivid presence in the painting. (Goldfish, like violins and violin cases, are surrogates for the artist.) *Gourds* (1916, pp. 103), is a frontal still-life composition in a shallow relief space, like the simulated collage of a Synthetic Cubist painting.

The years 1915–17 were a highly productive period for Matisse. Working in his architectonic, constructive style, he produced, in addition to numerous easel pictures and the relief sculpture *Back III*, three ambitious mural-sized paintings. *The Moroccans* (pp. 101), which verges on pure abstraction, was based on memories of his recent visits to Tangier. It was done in tandem with *Gourds*, with which it shares compositional traits, including the use of black as a colour. *Bathers by a River* had a long gestation period; originally conceived as a vision of Arcadia, it was initially related to the Shchukin *Music* and *Dance II* panels. As it evolved, it became, like *The Moroccans*, a memory image of the artist's visits to Morocco. It would later be influential for the post-World War II generation of American painters. The third of these large-scale paintings was *The Piano Lesson* (1916,

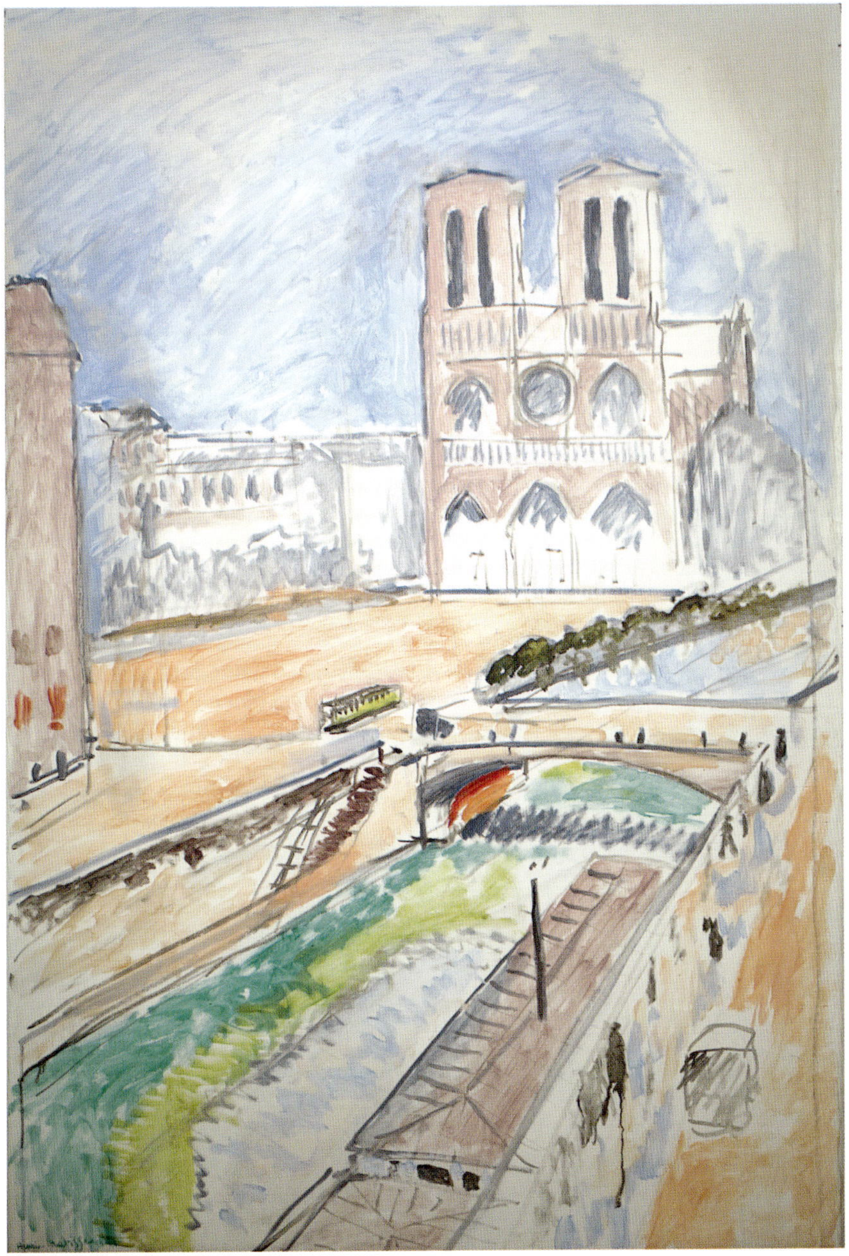

Henri Matisse, *View of Notre-Dame*, first version, 1914
Oil on canvas | 147 × 98cm (57⅞ × 38⅝in), Kunstmuseum Solothurn, Switzerland

pp. 105), an interior in a nearly square format, featuring the artist's son Pierre (then aged 16, reconceived as a child of 9 or 10) at the centre of competing forces; it is a metaphor of artistic and musical creation.

In late 1917, Matisse moved to Nice – alone – where he would spend the greater part of each year (usually winter and part of spring) for most of the remaining years of his life. His wife, sons and daughter would occasionally join him there, and he would return to Paris and Issy, or travel, during the summer months. Initially, he would live in hotel rooms, first at the Hôtel Beau-Rivage, then at the Hôtel Méditerranée; in 1921 he found more permanent quarters in an apartment block at 1, place Charles Félix.

Matisse's relocation to the south corresponded to a shift in the direction of his art, away from both the geometric austerity of 1913–17, and from the decorative style of 1907–12 which preceded it, towards a return to sensuality and to nature. Matisse's 'Nice period' refers to the work of the artist's early years in Nice, from 1917 through the 1920s. Now colouristic intensity is subordinated to effects of light, and there is a restoration of three-dimensionality and illusionistic perspective. The interest in decorative pattern persists, but primarily when such patterning is found in the actual motif. Nice-period works were no longer cutting-edge avant-garde, although as the 1920s progressed, the artist showed renewed interest in sculptural simplicity. The prototype for the Nice period was no longer to be found in Islamic art, in Cézanne or in Cubism; now Matisse looked again to Impressionism. He had never met Cézanne, whom he considered a 'god of painting', and who died in 1906.[11] Soon upon his move to Nice, however, he visited Renoir, who lived in nearby Cagnes-sur-Mer, and he would call on him on numerous occasions, sometimes bringing his own pictures, before the older artist's death in late 1919.

Interior with a Violin Case of 1918–19 (pp. 109) is a Nice-period interior of Matisse's room at the Hôtel Méditerranée. The composition, with its open window and decorative patterning of walls, wall hanging, floor, ceiling and balustrade, is characteristically Matissean, but the boundaries of exterior and interior are respected, the decorative patterns have counterparts in the actual motif, and the three-dimensional space of the room is affirmed by perspectival devices. As in an Impressionist painting, convincing effects of sunlight stream into the room through the window.

Pianist and Checker Players of 1924 (pp. 111) presents a musical counterpoint of patterns of walls, floor, tablecloth and checkerboard within the perspectival space of Matisse's apartment on place Charles-Félix in Nice. The painting is an imaginative reconstruction of *The Painter's Family* of 1911, now rendered in the Nice-period style and with the artist's model Henriette Darricarrère and her brothers as stand-ins for the artist's family in Issy. To a still greater degree than the earlier work, *Pianist and Checker Players* reveals the influence of Cézanne's *Girl at the Piano (Overture to Tannhäuser)* of 1869 (see p. 15).

Decorative Figure on an Ornamental Ground of 1925–6 (pp. 113) presents a favourite subject of Matisse during the Nice period, the odalisque. Odalisques – or harem women of the Near East and North Africa – either nude or in costume, belong to the tradition of orientalism in French art, going back to the eighteenth century. In an interview with his friend Tériade, publisher of the art journal *Verve*, Matisse declared, 'I do odalisques in order to do nudes. But how does one do nudes without it being artificial? And then, because I know that they exist. I was in Morocco. I have seen them.'[12] Henriette Darricarrère, model for the odalisque, was simultaneously posing for Matisse's sculpture (opposite) from which he derived the pose. The power of the work derives from the tension between the sculptural presence of the figure and the vivid patterning of the background. With this work, the artist is moving away from the sensuous, relaxed naturalism of the Nice period towards a more monumental style. An inspiration for this evolution was the great sculptor of the High Renaissance, Michelangelo, whose work preoccupied Matisse at this time.

The portrait *Woman with a Veil* (1927, pp. 115) was Matisse's last painting to feature Henriette. With its masklike face, geometric composition, scratchings into the pictorial surface and melancholy air, the artist has evolved, to a still greater degree, away from Nice-period naturalism and towards the cutting-edge avant-gardism that marked his earlier years.

Between 1930 and 1933, Matisse made four visits to the United States. For most of the year of 1930, he was in transit. Beginning in March, he crossed country by train, en route to Tahiti, where Gauguin had painted three decades earlier. Matisse was treated as a visiting

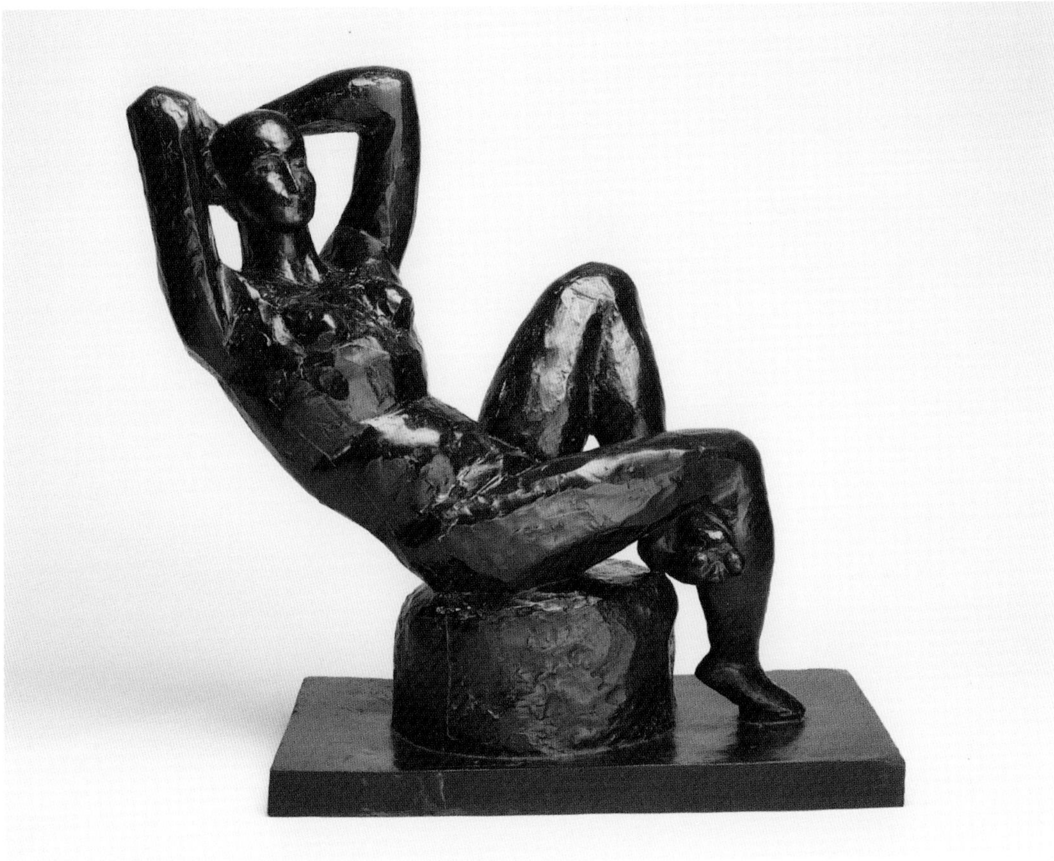

Henri Matisse, *Large Seated Nude*, 1922–9
Bronze | 76.7 × 80.3 × 35.6cm (30³⁄₁₆ × 31⅝ × 14in),
Baltimore Museum of Art

dignitary by the American press, and his letters home to his wife were an exuberant travelogue. He first met with the press at the Valentine Gallery in New York, where his son Pierre was a partner (Pierre would open his own gallery in 1931). On his way to San Francisco, he visited Chicago, Las Vegas and Los Angeles. On 21 March he boarded the *Tahiti* from San Francisco. He spent nearly three months in the South Seas, where his output comprised numerous drawings and one small painting, but his travels there would find their fullest expression two decades later, in his cut-out compositions (see *The Swimming Pool* and *Memory of Oceania*, pp. 132–3 and 129).

Matisse returned to France via the Panama Canal, bypassing the United States, but was back in New York harbour in September. The official purpose of this visit was to serve on the Carnegie International jury, which gave first prize to Picasso (Matisse had been awarded the Carnegie prize in 1927). After two days of official duties in Pittsburgh, he had a busy public schedule in New York, Washington and Philadelphia. Whatever the intent of his hosts, for Matisse the main attraction was the Barnes Foundation in Merion, Pennsylvania (a Philadelphia suburb).

Dr Albert Barnes, the pre-eminent collector of Matisse in the United States, continued to be an active buyer of his paintings at the time of the Great Depression. His collection, rich in works by Picasso, Cézanne and Renoir as well as Matisse, was on view at the Foundation, which was an educational institution, and not then a public museum. Visiting the Foundation gave Matisse the opportunity to reunite with his works of the Stein years, such as *Bonheur de vivre* and *Red Madras Headdress*. When Matisse arrived in Merion, Barnes offered him a commission to paint a mural for the lunettes of the main hall of the Foundation; Matisse agreed to consider the project.

In October Matisse was back in France. He visited Sarah and Michael Stein at their villa Les Terrasses in Vaucresson just outside Paris. He talked with them about his impressions of the United States and about their mutual friends the Cone sisters, who had been, since the end the war, second only to Barnes as collectors of his work. He spoke warmly of Claribel Cone, who had died the previous year, and of his intention to do a memorial drawing of her. Later that month he met with Barnes in Paris, and agreed to the mural project. In December he returned to the United States, where he visited Etta Cone and her collection in Baltimore and went to Merion to take measurements for the mural.

The subject Matisse chose for the Barnes mural was the dance. After working on the mural for more than a year, he discovered – to his horror – a discrepancy in the measurements of the painting and the architectural site. The error was soon confirmed, and Matisse elected to redo the project from the beginning; the first version is now in the Musée d'Art Moderne de la Ville de Paris. As Alfred Barr noted, a less conscientious artist, rather than starting over with new canvases, would have 'made a few minor adjustments and passed on to some less tedious undertaking'.[13]

Matisse developed a technique of composing the decoration with cut pieces of coloured paper; in the final stage of composition, he removed the papers and applied paint in their place. This method allowed him to work full-scale, while making rapid changes that would have been more difficult with pigment or charcoal alone. A decade and a half later, he would employ this paper cut-out technique as an independent medium.

In May 1933 Matisse installed the mural in Merion (pp. 118–19), in the course of which he collapsed in nervous exhaustion. He soon recovered, however, later telling an interviewer, 'As soon as I saw the decoration in place I felt that it … took on a meaning quite different from what it had had in my studio, where it was only a painted canvas.' Matisse added that in the Barnes Foundation 'It became a rigid thing, heavy as stone, and one that seemed to have been spontaneously created at the same time with the building.'[14] The theme of the dance is here configured within an architectural framework. Matisse arrived at a simplified, flattened style of dancing figures whose poses sometimes rhyme with their framework, at times defy its limitations. Colour is restricted to grey, black, blue and pink.

Matisse left Merion and arrived in New York, where a heated controversy concerning public art was in progress. The Mexican artist Diego Rivera had been commissioned to paint a mural in the lobby of the RCA building in Rockefeller Center. His inclusion of a figure of Lenin had been deemed unacceptable by the Rockefeller family. When he refused to remove the figure, work was halted, and the mural was boarded up. Artists and intellectuals protested; marchers picketed Rockefeller Center. On the eve of sailing back to France, Matisse met with the press at Pierre's gallery. Asked by a reporter for a comment on the Rivera controversy, he replied: 'Propaganda has no place in art. Art should rise above politics ... There was a time for that, back in the Middle Ages. Then there were no newspapers ... and images painted or engraved were the chief source of expression and entertainment. Art can afford to rise above this now.'[15]

With *Large Reclining Nude (The Pink Nude)* of 1935 (pp. 121), Matisse applied the simplified, flattened style and colour harmonies of the dancers of the Barnes mural to an easel painting of a reclining nude, comparable to the pose of the *Blue Nude* of 1907. He arrived at this finished work after a long process, by which it underwent a transformation from representation to near abstraction – his method spanning many years. The critic Charles Caffin, writing for Alfred Stieglitz's *Camera Work* in 1909, had written: 'He shows me a series of drawings from the nude. In the first, he explains that he has drawn "what exists"; and the drawing shows the knowledge and skill, characteristic of French academic art. Then others follow in which he has sought for further and further "simplification," until finally the figure, as he expressed it, was *organisé*.'[16] It was this process of 'organisation' by which the model for *Large Reclining Nude* became transformed in pictorial style from representational to the near abstraction of the Barnes mural.

The model for *Large Reclining Nude* was a young Russian émigré, Lydia Delectorskaya, whom Matisse had hired as an assistant while he was at work on the Barnes mural. Lydia would continue by his side for the remaining years of his life, as an invaluable personal assistant, secretary, model and companion.

In the 1940s Matisse's art returned to the bold, decorative modernism of the post-Fauve years 1907–13. This output was often produced at times of great personal stress, both physical and emotional. Matisse had moved to the Hôtel Régina in Cimiez, just outside Nice, in 1938. The Germans occupied Paris in June 1940; throughout the war Matisse would live in unoccupied Vichy France. Many French artists who were too old to be mobilized left the country; Matisse did not, though he had opportunities to do so. In autumn he declined an invitation for a teaching position at Mills College in California, and that winter he refused an offer from Varian Fry of the Emergency Rescue Committee for safe passage to the United States. As he had written to his son Pierre, 'If everyone who has any value leaves France, what remains of France?'[17]

In 1940 Matisse and his wife Amélie became legally separated, causing great tension within the family. When Matisse completed *The Dream* (pp. 123), he wrote to Pierre, 'I won't say that this painting made me forget everything else, but at least it brought me some relief'.[18] The painting bears a remarkable stylistic similarity to Picasso's portrait of the sleeping Marie-Thérèse Walter, painted in the previous decade (opposite). Picasso, like Matisse, remained in France throughout the war. When Matisse left his collection of artworks in Paris at the Banque de France for safekeeping, he left Picasso in charge, and Picasso was able to assure him that they were indeed safe.

In that same winter of 1940 Matisse was diagnosed with duodenal cancer. Surgery was performed in Lyon in January 1941, and he remained in Lyon, convalescing at the Grand Nouvel Hôtel until May, at which time he returned to Nice-Cimiez and resumed painting. He had first picked up a paintbrush as a youth of 19, while recovering from an intestinal ailment. Now, at the age of 71, art-making was a means of restoring his physical and spiritual health. He produced a series of self-portraits and still lifes, culminating in *Still Life with Magnolia* (pp. 125). With its objects of green, blue, yellow and violet, with patterns and images that suggest growth, on a brilliant red ground, it recalls such decorative works as *Harmony in Red* of 1908. Like the tympanum of a Romanesque church portal, it evokes an entry into a spiritual realm. As Matisse would write, in the text of his illustrated book *Jazz* (1947): 'Do I believe in God? Yes, when I am working.'[19]

Due to the risk in coastal Nice of aerial bombardment by the Allies, in 1943 Matisse moved to the Villa le Rêve in the nearby town of Vence. It was there that he painted *Interior with an Egyptian Curtain* (1948, pp. 127), which belongs to a series of great interiors of 1947–8, his final major statements in the medium of oil on canvas. It is a remarkably life-affirming work, inundated with light and colour, presenting some of the artist's favourite motifs and themes: a window, patterned fabric, the analogies of growth in trees, fruit and textile design. It is perhaps his most effective use of black as a luminous, unifying colour.

When Matisse was recovering from surgery in 1941, he was attended by a young nurse, Monique Bourgeois. She would soon join a Dominican convent, and as Sister Jacques, she became his assistant on an undertaking that consumed much of his energy between 1948 and 1951, the decoration of the Chapel of the Rosary in Vence. This project fulfilled an ambition that he had long held: to decorate an interior space, in the footsteps of Giotto and other Italian masters of the fourteenth and fifteenth centuries. No doubt the mosques he had visited in Tangier were an influence, for the Vence chapel, unlike most Christian churches, is suffused with brilliant sunlight. The light of the chapel is filtered through stained-glass windows of floral design in yellow, green and blue, signifying the Tree of Life in Genesis. As he had for the figures of the Barnes *Dance* (pp. 118–19), he created the window compositions using cut and pasted paper. The murals for the Vence chapel are in

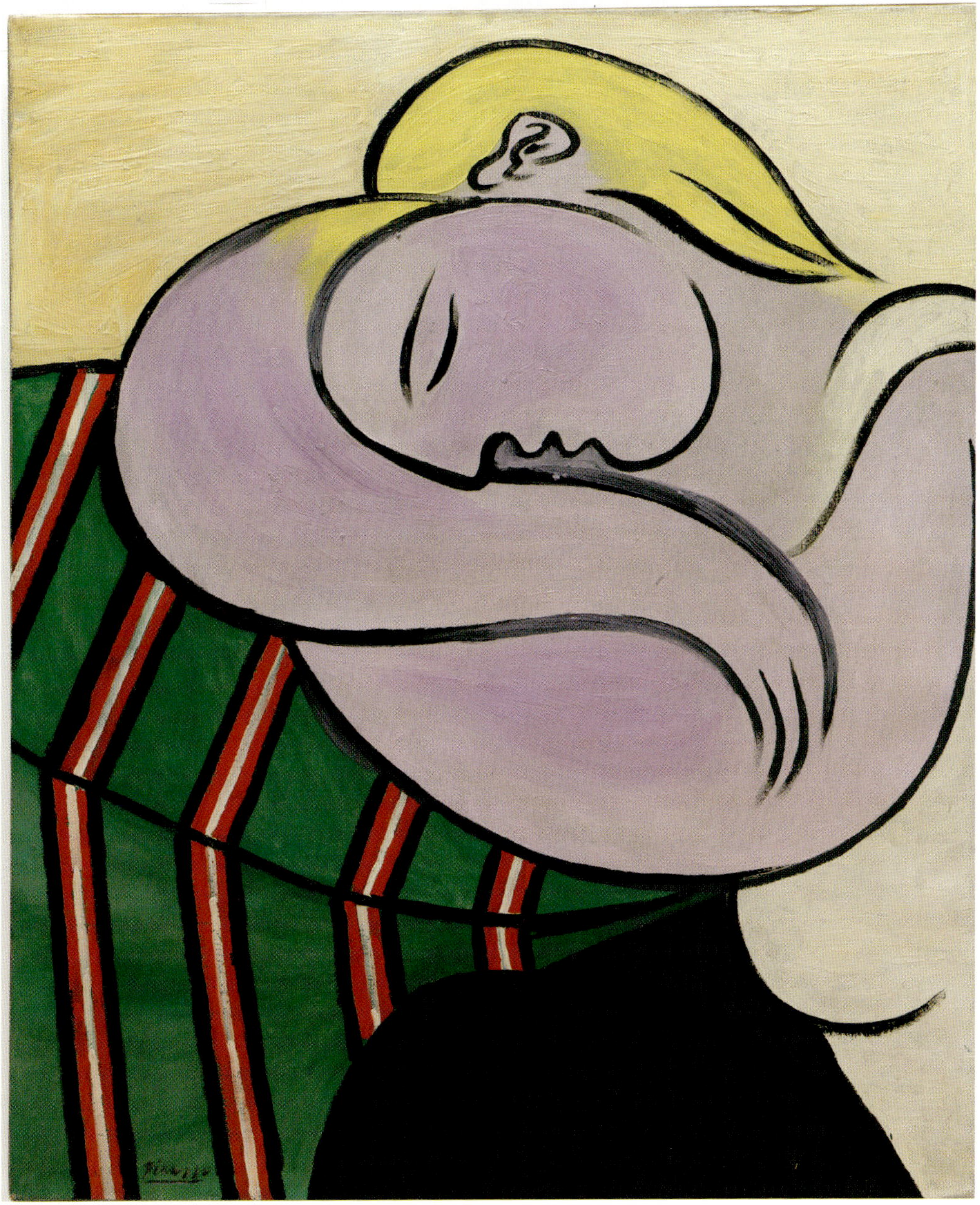

Pablo Picasso, *Woman with Yellow Hair,* 1931
Oil on canvas | 100 × 81cm (39⅜ × 31⅞in), Guggenheim Museum, New York

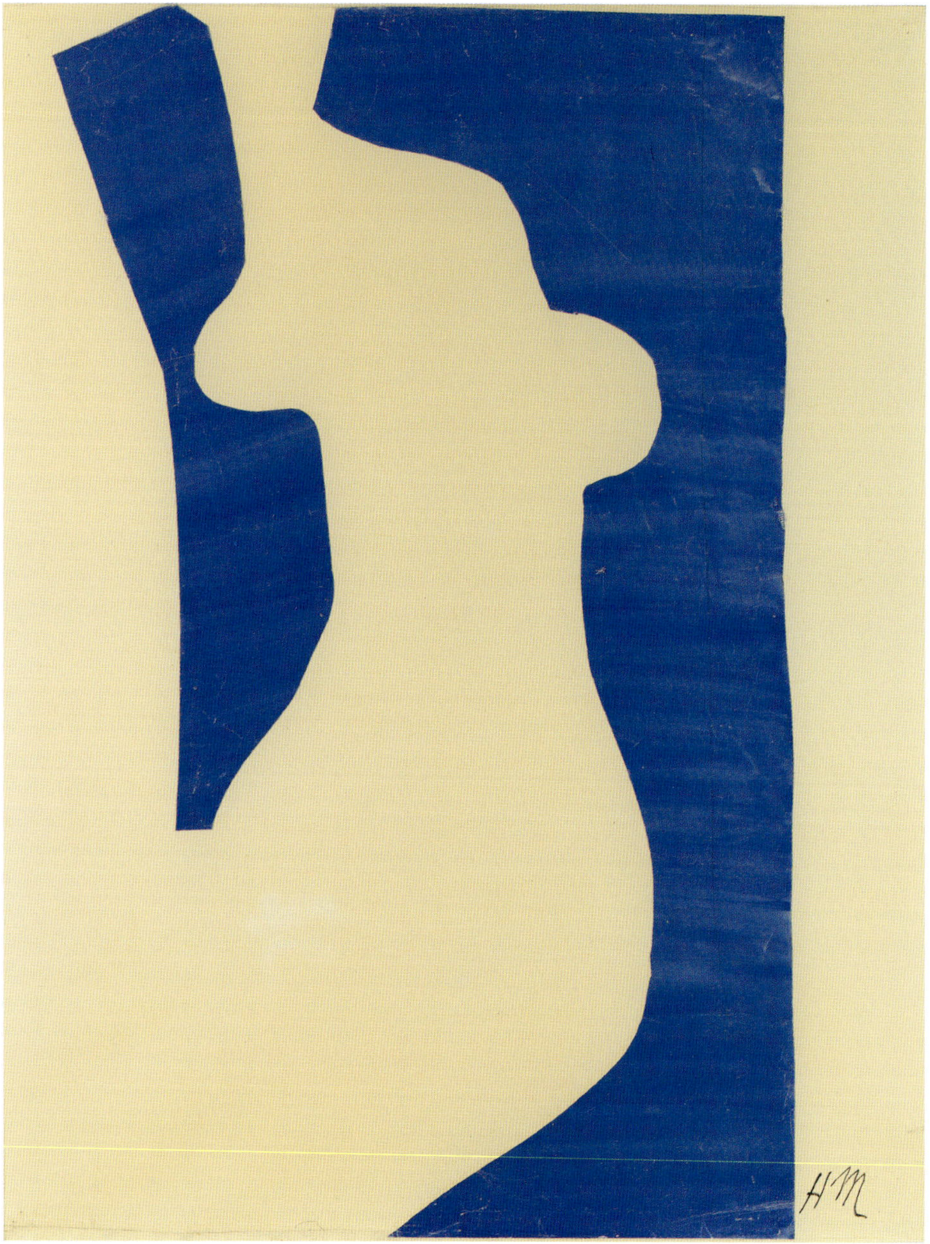

Henri Matisse, *Venus,* 1952
Gouache on cut-and-pasted paper, mounted on paper panel | 101.2 × 76.5cm (39⅞ × 30⅛in)
National Gallery of Art, Washington, DC

black outline on white ceramic tile, representing St Dominic, the Madonna and Child, and the Stations of the Cross. Matisse also designed vestments for the priests and liturgical objects for Mass.

While Matisse was at work on the Vence Chapel, he returned the larger working and living space of his apartment at the Hôtel Régina in Nice-Cimiez, which would be his primary residence for the remainder of his life. Henceforth the cut-out technique, now as an independent medium, would be his primary artistic means. He was making a virtue of necessity, as he was no longer physically able to stand for the intervals necessary to paint with a brush. He would instead instruct assistants to paint the paper with gouache in his desired colours. He referred to the cut-out technique as 'gouache découpée' and likened it to carving in colour.[20]

The cut-out composition *The Swimming Pool* originally decorated the walls of Matisse's dining room in Nice-Cimiez. Its aquatic imagery, a cavalcade of swimmers and marine life in motion, was inspired by memories of his two-and-a-half months in Tahiti in spring–summer 1930. The colour scheme is restricted to blue forms on a white ground, and the final image in the composition resembles the cut-out of *Venus* (opposite). Like the dancers of the Barnes mural, the pool inhabitants are unimpeded by the boundaries that frame them. A more explicit evocation of the artist's Tahitian sojourn is *Memory of Oceania* (pp. 129), a mural-sized cut-out composition in a square format in a range of warm and cool colours of blue, yellow, red, orange, ochre and black. It was inspired by Matisse's recollection of the window view from his hotel room in Tahiti, which looked out on the beach and sea.

To a greater degree than any of the previous evolutions of Matisse's style, the cut-outs included works that approached pure abstraction. A case in point is *The Snail* (p. 135), which, significantly, had the alternate title *Chromatic Composition*. Whereas the artist produced paintings at the time of his architectonic, Cubist-influenced period of 1913–17 that were nearly abstract – see pp. 92–3 and 96–7, *View of Notre-Dame* and *French Window at Collioure* – they originated in direct observation, becoming more abstract as he reworked the pictorial surface. *The Snail*, by contrast, is a reversal of his previous process; it is based not on his *perception*, but rather on his *conception* of the subject. The snail that is evoked is not restricted to a mollusc in a spiral shell, but, by extension, signifies the idea of spiralling motion – motion conveyed by both the arrangement of geometric shapes on the pictorial field and by the juxtaposition of complementary colours.

Now in the ninth decade of his life, Matisse was producing work of extraordinary originality and contemporaneity. With his late cut-outs he was – to a greater degree any other European artist of his generation – creating artworks that inspired a younger generation of painters in Europe and the United States. In the years following his death, the art of Henri Matisse would continue to serve as an influential force among countless painters inspired by his ingeniously harmonious compositions, affirming a remark made by the English critic Roger Fry, who designated him 'Mozart in colour'.[21]

THE PAINTINGS

1896–7 THE DINNER TABLE

Private Collection
Oil on canvas | 100 × 131cm (39⅜ × 51½in)

By autumn 1896 Henri Matisse had been studying with the Symbolist painter Gustave Moreau for nearly five years. Moreau had confidence in his pupil's abilities and encouraged him to demonstrate his mastery with an ambitious work. The result, completed the following winter, features a light-filled interior with a richly coloured, opulently laden dessert table attended by a housekeeper in a crimson blouse. Matisse's previous paintings had been copies of old masters from the Louvre and landscapes and interiors in the muted tonalities of seventeenth-century Dutch painters.

Matisse's new awareness of colour had been incubated the previous summer, during a stay in Belle-Île-en-Mer, Brittany, spent with his companion Caroline Joblaud and their young daughter Marguerite, born two years earlier. In Belle-Île he painted *en plein air* in the company of fellow artist Émile Wéry, their Paris neighbour from 19 quai Saint-Michel. Matisse later recalled, 'Working next to him I noticed that he could get more luminosity from his primary colors than I could with my old-master palette. This was the first stage in my evolution, and I went back to Paris free of the Louvre's influence and heading towards color.'[22] This search for colour did not involve the study of paintings, but rather the observation of light in nature.

A stream of light from the window at the centre floods the room. It creates reflections in the crystal decanters, and illuminates the warm colours and rich textures of the fruit, flowers and tablecloth, along with the housekeeper's face, hand, arm and shoulder. The high vantage point of the viewer, at the housekeeper's eye level, assures the domination of the visual field by the objects spread across the table. The window frames the flower arrangement and the ministrations of the housekeeper. The model for this figure was the aforementioned Caroline Joblaud, known as Camille. Matisse's wife Amélie would often play a comparable role in forthcoming works.

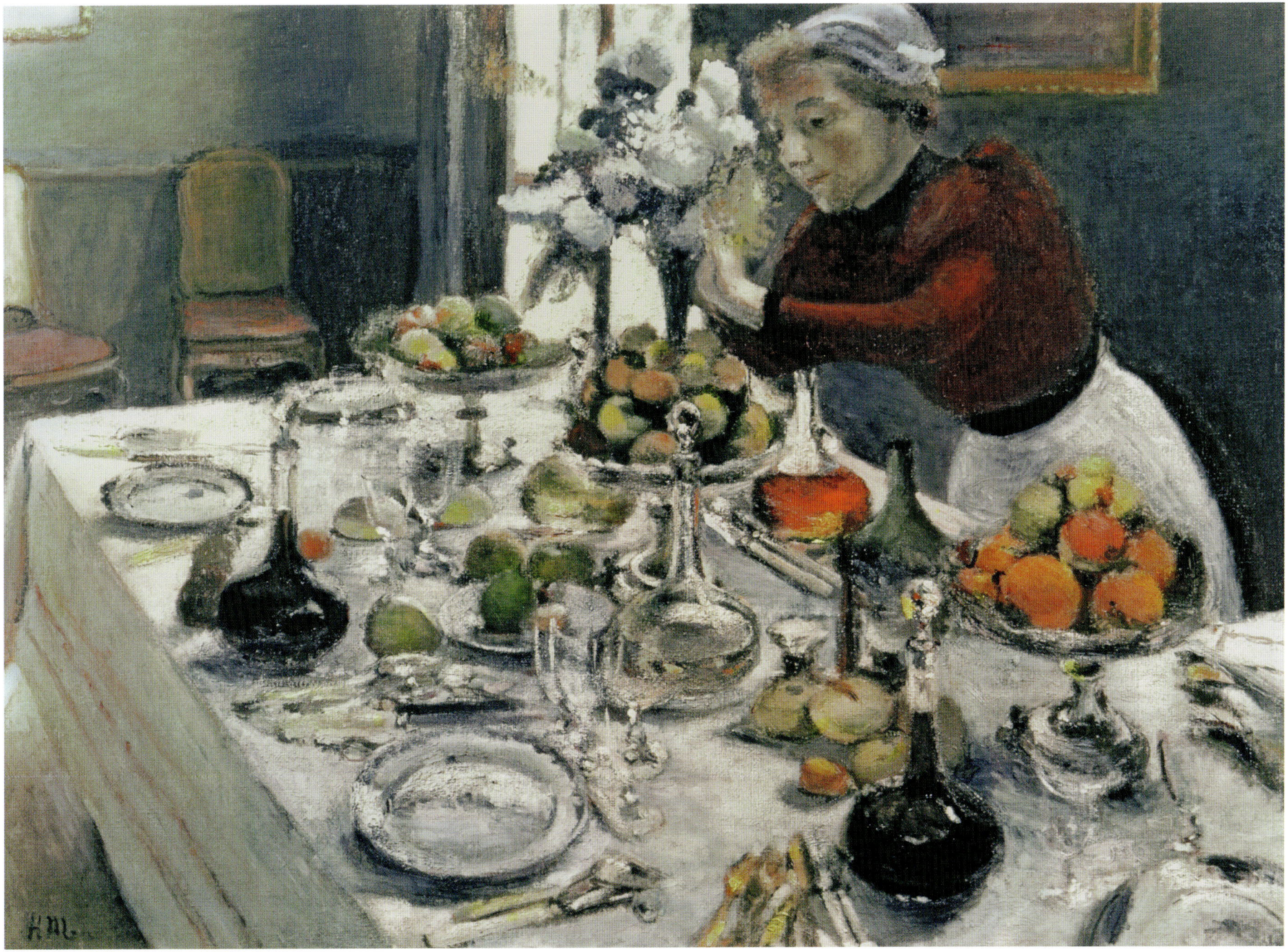

1899 THE INVALID

The Baltimore Museum of Art
Oil on canvas | 46 × 38cm (18½ × 15in)

Matisse, like Cézanne but unlike Picasso, was a late bloomer as an artist. Following his marriage to Amélie Parayre in 1898, the couple travelled to Corsica, where he was first exposed to the light of the Mediterranean Sea, which would so greatly affect him throughout his life. 'I decided to take a year off, avoid all hindrances, and paint the way I wanted to,' he later recalled. 'I worked only for myself … I felt a passion for color developing within me.'[23]

The Invalid was painted in early 1899 in the home of Matisse's in-laws near the city of Toulouse in the south of France, where the couple stayed following their return to the mainland. It depicts Mme Matisse, bedridden, at the time of the birth of Jean, their first son. It is small in format, rendered with broad brushstrokes of paint, thickly applied, in vibrant, intense colours. Luminosity and spatial depth are evoked by complementary colours of red and green, yellow and violet, and orange and blue. The depth of the interior is intensified by the device of the armchair at the lower left, turned on its axis toward the background, leading the viewer's eye into the space of the room and to the dark curtain and the lighted window at the rear. Some details, such as the still-life objects on the table and the facial features of the reclining figure, are indeterminate; others, such as the triangle of white, blue and pink to the lower right, seem to have no counterpart in the visible world. For Matisse, representation had become secondary to the celebration of colour and his freedom to use it.

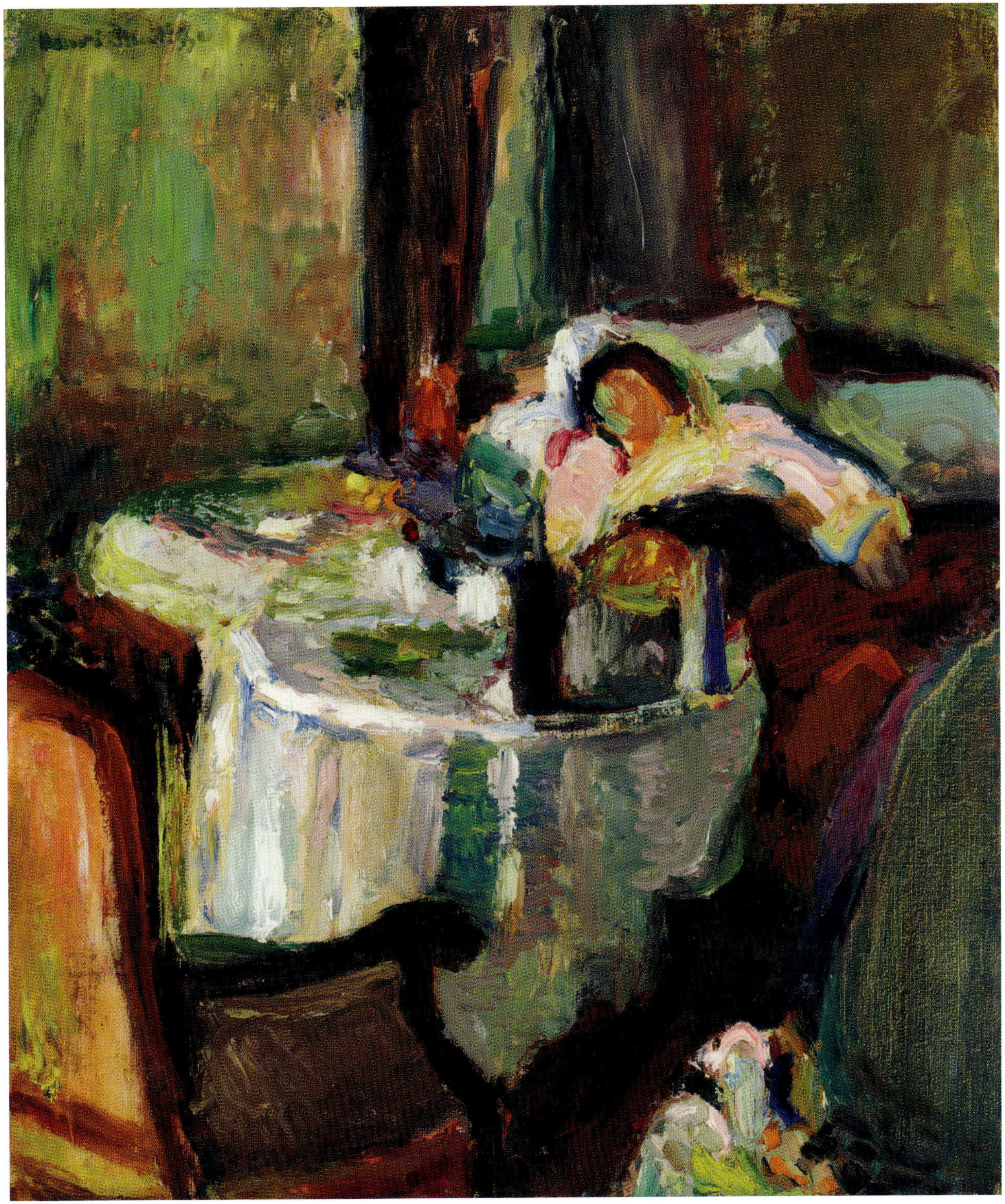

1900

MALE MODEL

The Museum of Modern Art, New York
Oil on canvas | 99.3 × 72.7cm (39⅛ × 28⅝in)

Male Model belongs to a series of studio nudes that Matisse painted in 1900. 'What interests me most,' he would write in his essay 'Notes of a Painter' (1908), 'is neither still life nor landscape, but the human figure.'[24] Yet before 1900 the human figure – to say nothing of the nude – was rarely to be found in his work.

Matisse's circumstances at the turn of the century were financially and emotionally strained. Desperate to support his young family, he briefly entered the employ of a studio that built set decorations for the Exposition Universelle, the Paris World's Fair of 1900. It was his first and only exposure, art historian Jack Flam has noted, to the 'backbreaking labor of the working class.'[25] Despite these difficulties, he resisted the temptation to sell his prized possession, Cézanne's *Three Bathers* (p. 9), purchased the previous year.

The male model of this painting was a stocky, bearded Italian known as Bevilacqua. Matisse universalizes his model without idealizing him, portraying his common humanity rather than his individual psychology.

Matisse makes no effort to disguise the dingy reality of the studio in which the model poses. Bevilacqua stands on a bare platform; the blue tonality of the walls behind him implies the coldness of the room, whose only heat is provided by the stove on the right, behind the translucent curtain. The contrasting warm and cold tonalities – of pink and brown versus blue, green and violet – which Matisse would employ in the decorative paintings of his Fauve period five years hence, is here used to structural and luminous, rather than decorative, effect. This is a Cézannian device, as are the broad generalizations of the face and the use of *passage* to ease transitions between the planes of the body and between the ambiguous contours of the figure, the voids surrounding it, and the walls in the background. As this painting makes evident, Matisse preceded Picasso and Braque by several years as an assimilator of Cézanne.

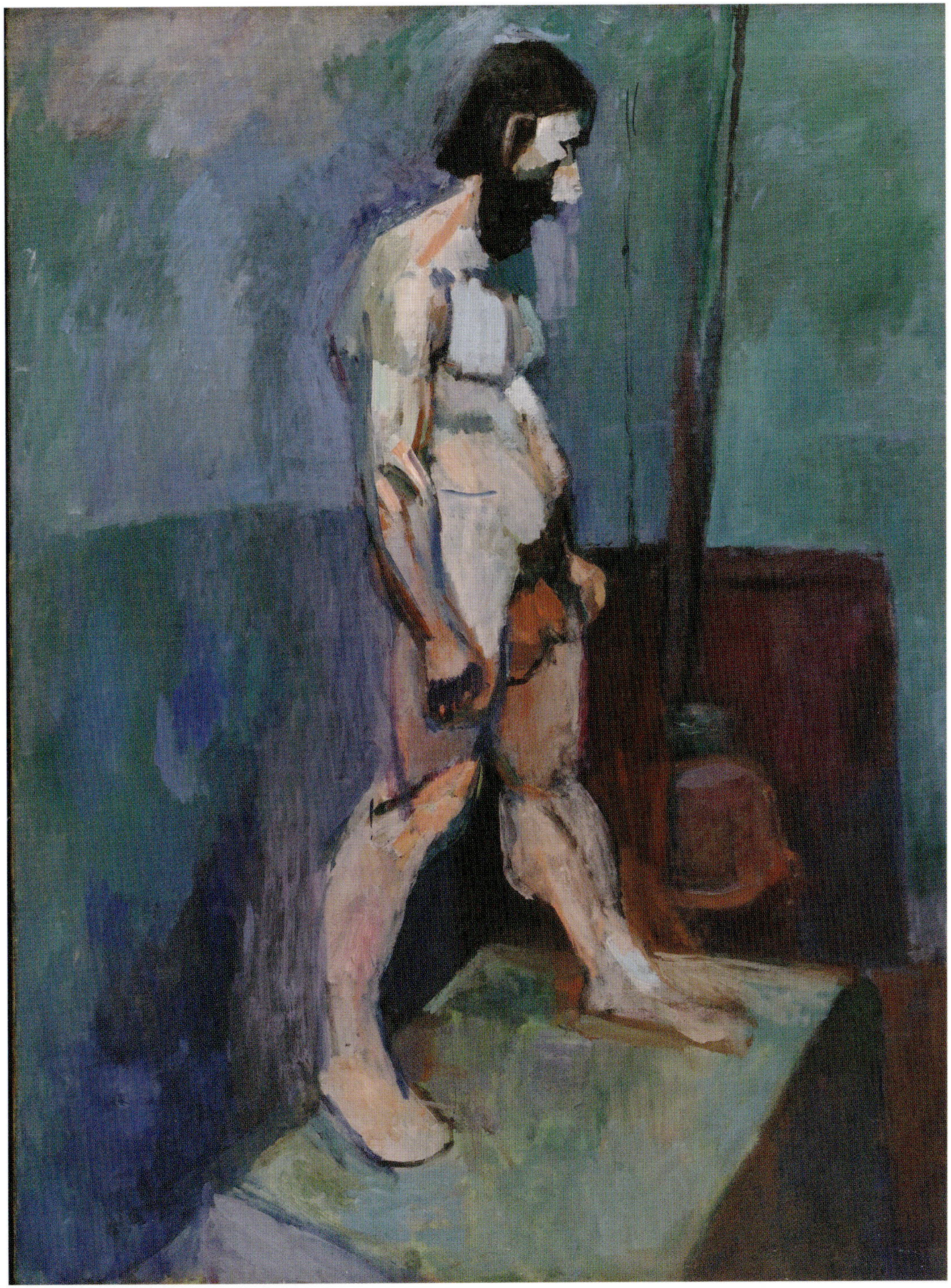

1903

CARMELINA

Museum of Fine Arts, Boston
Oil on canvas | 81.3 × 59cm (32 × 23¼in)

In December 1899, at great financial sacrifice, Matisse purchased *Three Bathers* (p. 9), a small painting by Cézanne, from the dealer Ambroise Vollard. In the years immediately following, he would maintain possession of it, despite his family's strained economic circumstances. In 1936 he donated the work to the Museum of the City of Paris at the Petit Palais, writing to the museum's director: 'It has sustained me morally in the critical moments of my venture as an artist; I have drawn from it my faith and my perseverance.'[26]

As we have seen, Matisse utilized Cézannian devices of light and structure in the roughly painted *Male Model* of 1900 (p. 37). Three years later, with *Carmelina*, he placed a female model at the centre in a balanced, frontal composition and in a more bourgeois setting. Neither her figure nor her facial features are idealized. Whereas blues are dominant in the earlier painting, ochres prevail here. The composition is built from a series of rectangular forms. Cézanne's influence is evident in the construction of the figure with unblended patches of pigment. As with Cézanne, positive and negative spaces are given equal emphasis, as are foreground and background. John Elderfield has commented that within three years after Matisse's purchase of *Three Bathers* 'he had painted a model named Carmelina as if the left-hand figure of *Three Bathers* had come into his quai Saint-Michel studio, bringing her towel with her.'[27]

A rectangular mirror in the background reveals a rear view of the upper body of the model and, to her left, a self-portrait of the bearded artist wearing a shirt of an intense red that contrasts with the subdued reds elsewhere in the painting. Both artist and model look outward, meeting the gaze of the spectator as well as of each other. This painting is an early instance in Matisse's work of the theme of the artist and his model, a subject that recurs in many of his paintings in decades to come.

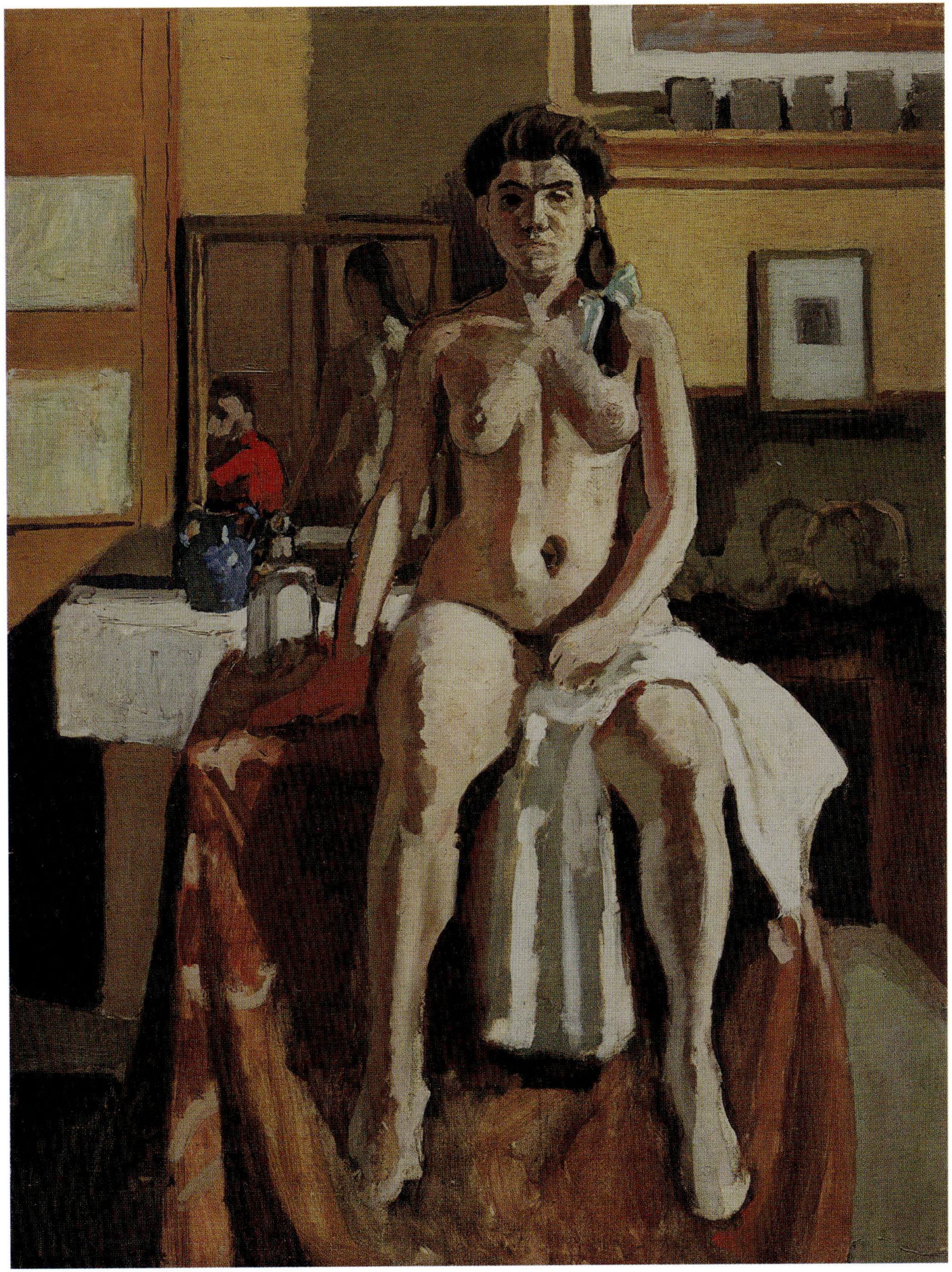

1904

LUXE, CALME ET VOLUPTÉ

Musée d'Orsay, Paris
Oil on canvas | 98.5 × 118.5cm (38¾ × 46⅝in)

Luxe, calme et volupté, completed in autumn–winter 1904, was Matisse's first painting made not directly from life, but from imagination. Its point of departure was *Gulf of Saint-Tropez* (Kunstsammlung Nordrhein-Westfalen, Düsseldorf), a smaller work, created the previous summer, depicting his wife Amélie and four-year-old son Pierre seated on the shore amidst a colourful landscape.

That summer Matisse, seeking the inspiration of the Mediterranean sun, had rented a cottage in Saint-Tropez. Paul Signac, who owned a summer home in the coastal town, had encouraged him to make the excursion. Signac, who, with Georges Seurat, had founded Neo-Impressionism – also known as Divisionism or Pointillism – was a forceful advocate of the style.

With *Luxe, calme et volupté* Matisse adapts Divisionist points of colour to his own needs: brushstrokes are larger and freer than those of orthodox Divisionism. In the foreground is a beach, which recedes to the left, with a bay to the right, a range of mountains in the distance, and a luminous, multi-coloured twilit sky. In the foreground to the right is a tree which is parallel to the mast of a moored boat in the middle distance. On the beach a woman in contemporary dress is seated before a blanket with the trappings of a picnic; behind her and to her left stands a child, draped in a blanket. In attendance are five female bathers in a variety of poses. The bathers seem to inhabit a mythological realm, rather than the naturalistic realm of the woman and child. Landscape elements frame the bathers in a manner suggesting the influence on Matisse of Cézanne's *Three Bathers* (p. 9) in his private collection.

The painting's title derives from a refrain in Baudelaire's poem *L'invitation au voyage* (1857):

> *Là, tout n'est qu'ordre et beauté,*
> *Luxe, calme et volupté.*
>
> There all is order and beauty,
> Luxury, peace and pleasure.

Matisse does not seek to illustrate Baudelaire's poem, but rather to create a metaphorical equivalent. His painting evokes a Golden Age, not of a mythical past, but of an idealized present.

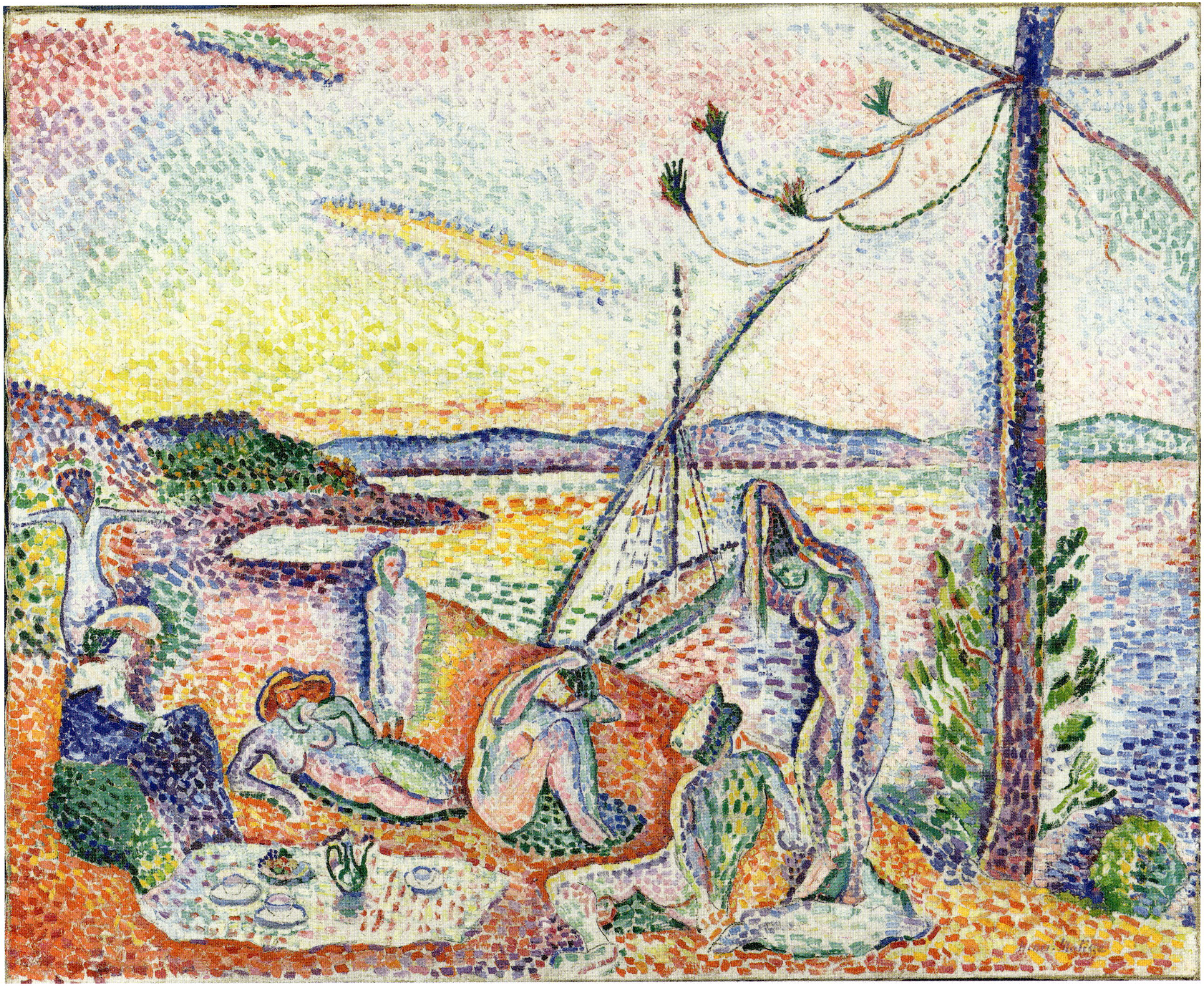

1905

OPEN WINDOW, COLLIOURE

National Gallery of Art, Washington, DC
Oil on canvas | 55.3 × 46cm (21¾ × 18⅛in)

Matisse spent the summer months of 1905 in the Mediterranean fishing village of Collioure. He was joined by André Derain, and the two, often working outdoors, produced their first canvases in the style later known as Fauvism.

Open Window, Collioure, painted from a room above the Port d'Avall harbour, joins interior and exterior views. The composition is unified by interlocking rectangles and highly keyed colour. The harbour and the room are differentiated not by luminosity or colour intensity, but by type of brushstroke. The green and violet walls of the room, and the orange and crimson doors of the French window, are painted in flat areas, with the white of the canvas allowed to show through. The intermediate space of the windowsill, with potted flowering plants and framing ivy, is rendered in swirling arabesques of red, green, pink and blue. The harbour view of water, sky, docked boats and their masts – in pink, blue and violet – is rendered with wavy brushstrokes that evoke the rhythm of the sea. The absence of shadow results in a nearly flat composition, with the harbour, windowsill and open doors all in close proximity to the picture plane.

This small but intense painting is an early instance of the window motif in Matisse's work. Late in his life he told an interviewer: 'Windows have always interested me because they are a passageway between the exterior and the interior.'[28]

If the terms 'exterior' and 'interior' are considered as signifiers not only of physical space but of consciousness, the window can be seen as a metaphor for the art of painting, a means by which the artist conveys his interior life to the exterior world.

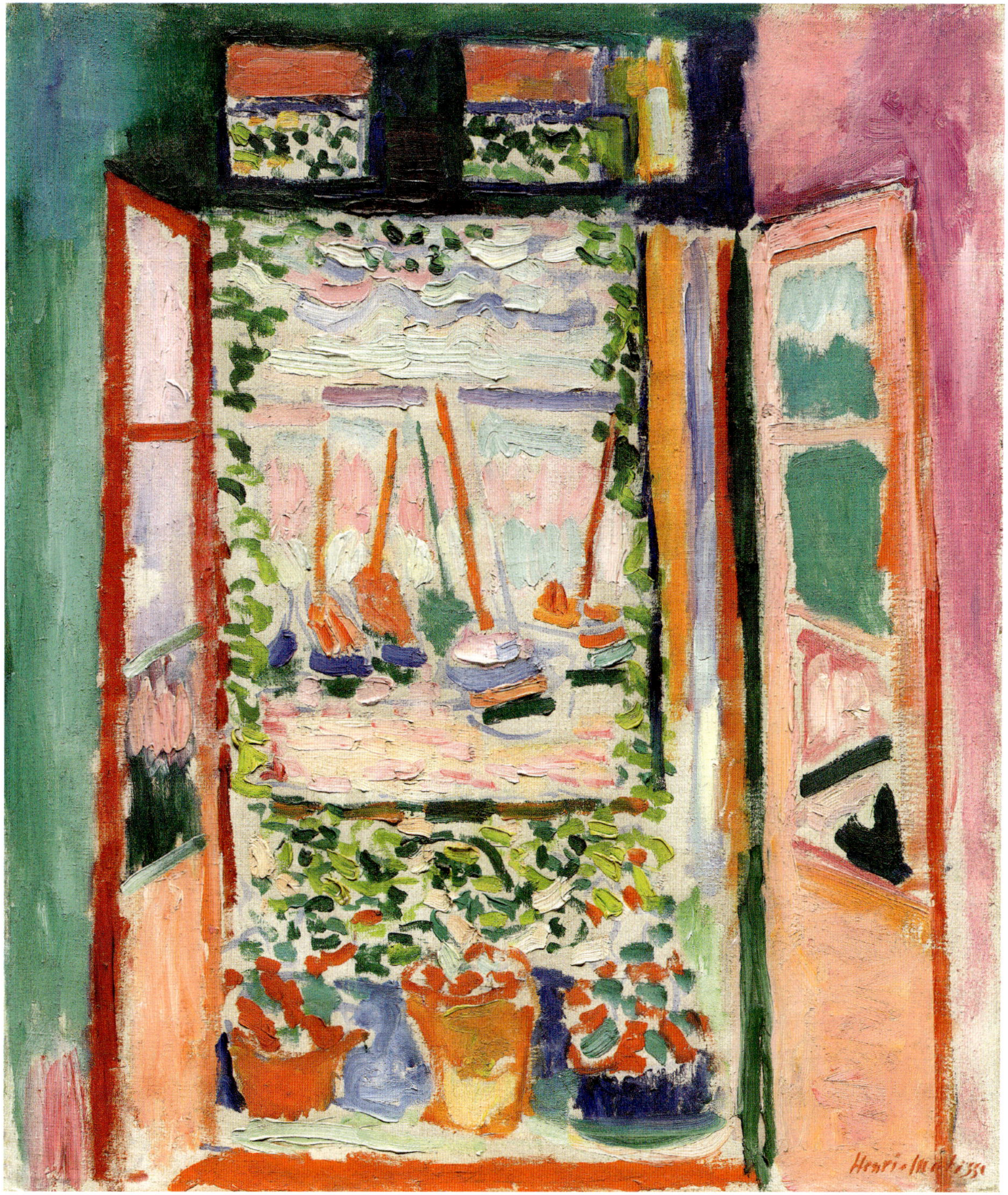

1905 WOMAN WITH A HAT

San Francisco Museum of Modern Art
Oil on canvas | 80.65 × 59.69cm (31¾ × 23½in)

'Brilliant and powerful, but the nastiest smear of paint I had ever seen.'[29] Such was the initial reaction of the collector Leo Stein when he viewed Matisse's *Woman with a Hat* on the opening day of the Paris Salon d'Automne of 1905. Stein's memorable phrase eloquently evokes the disquieting ambivalence that a sensitive viewer often experiences before a new and challenging work of art – what the critic Robert Hughes would later designate 'the shock of the new'. Stein would go on to purchase the painting and initiate his family into their role as friends and collectors of Matisse.

Woman with a Hat, a portrait of the artist's wife Amélie, presents the subject in a traditional pose: she is seated at half-length, her body in three-quarter view, her head turned towards the viewer. Her gloved arm rests on the arm of the chair and holds an elaborate fan, hiding her upper body; still more elaborate is the plumed hat that occupies the upper third of the picture.

The greatest departure from tradition is the bold, bright, and seemingly arbitrary colour. No longer applied in the discrete dots of Neo-Impressionism, as in *Luxe, calme et volupté* (p. 41), colour now appears as splotches, scumbles and impasto. As in the paintings of Cézanne, shifts in planes are indicated by shifts in colour; but unlike Cézanne, Matisse chooses his colours not for their fidelity to nature but for their status as complementaries. Thus, for example, he paints the face in red and green, as well as yellow, with violet patches in the background; and he paints the hair in an intense red which is balanced against the green in the hat. The background is indeterminate and virtually abstract; it is densely applied in the lower-third, less densely in the upper two-thirds, but throughout in brilliant complementary contrasts.

The new style which Matisse presents in this painting would come to be called Fauvism. The term originated in a humorous comment by the critic Louis Vauxcelles, who, reviewing the Salon d'Automne in the journal *Gil Blas*, compared the shocking paintings by Matisse and his colleagues (among them André Derain and Maurice de Vlaminck), to two traditional busts by the sculptor Albert Marque: 'Donatello among the wild beasts [*fauves*].'

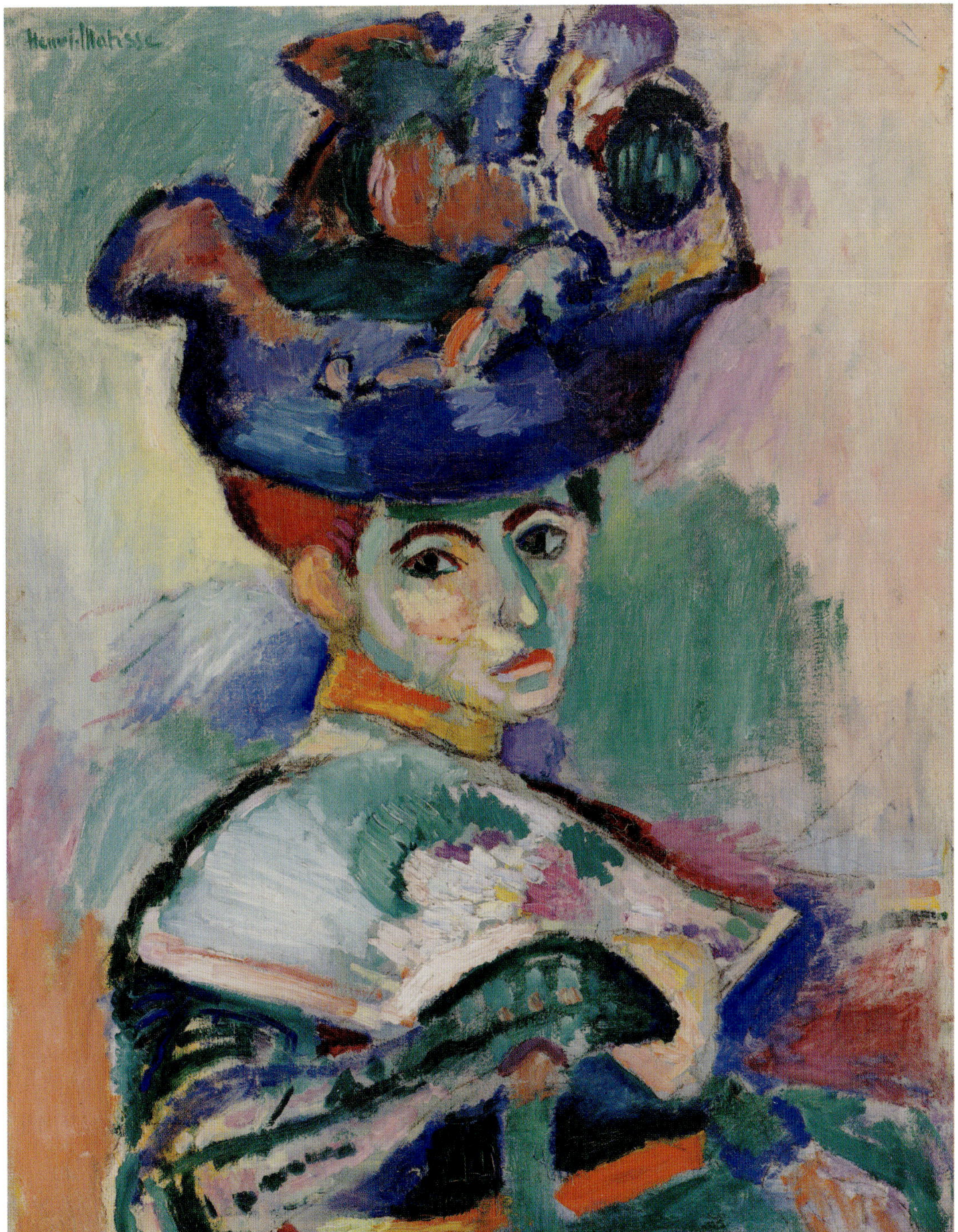
Henri-Matisse

1905

MADAME MATISSE: THE GREEN LINE

Statens Museum for Kunst, Copenhagen
Oil on canvas | 40.5 × 32.5cm (16 × 12¾in)

Matisse's first patrons were the Stein family – Leo and his sister Gertrude, Michael and his wife Sarah – American expatriates in Paris in the early years of the twentieth century. Among the four, it was Sarah Stein who would be personally closest to the artist, as his friend and student. By contrast with Leo, there was no ambivalence in her initial reaction to *Woman with a Hat* (p. 45) at the 1905 Salon d'Automne. She was immediately drawn to the picture and later regretted having deferred to him regarding its purchase.

In late winter of that year or early spring 1906 Sarah and Michael Stein bought *Madame Matisse: The Green Line* from the Galerie Druet, Paris. No doubt their failure to acquire the earlier work was a motivating factor in the purchase. Though one-fourth the size of *Woman with a Hat*, it is comparably daring. Like the larger picture, it is a portrait of Amélie Matisse, with bold juxtapositions of exaggerated colour. The title refers to the vertical green shadow that bifurcates the head, mediating between complementary regions of cool and warm flesh tones. By contrast with the larger portrait, it is bold and simple in composition, and it reveals, rather than conceals, its subject.

The viewer's attention focuses on Amélie's face, which occupies nearly the entire pictorial field, unmediated by the distractions of an elaborate hat and concealing fan. Her pose is frontal; her gaze meets that of the viewer. The composition is made up of broad planes of colour: violet, green and orange background, deep blue coiffure, red and orange dress, pale blue brocaded collar. Light and shade are primarily conveyed by these colour planes, rather than by modelling, producing an overall flattening effect. The stern gaze and partitioned face suggest the psychological dimension of the subject, conflicted yet confident.

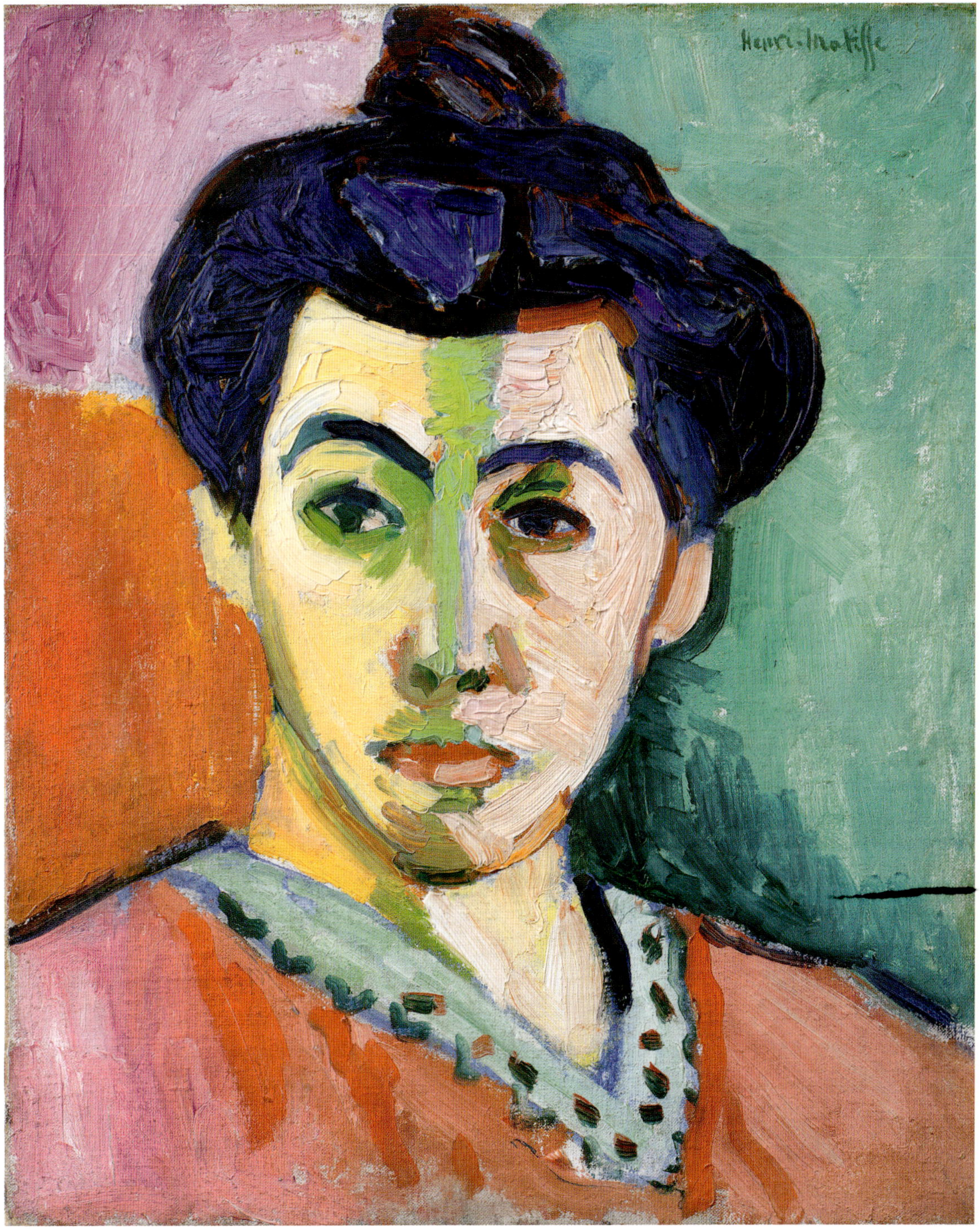
Henri-Matisse

1906

YOUNG SAILOR II

The Metropolitan Museum of Art, New York
Oil on canvas | 101.3 x 82.9cm (39⅞ x 32⅝in)

In 1906 Matisse was back in Collioure, where he painted a portrait of a neighbour, Camille Calmon, a 16-year-old youth from a fisherman's family. The portrait appeared as a series of two, *Young Sailor I* (p. 10) and *Young Sailor II*. The first version was the product of direct observation; the second version was derived from the earlier painting, apart from the model.

Leo Stein later recalled that Matisse 'brought back from the country a study of a young fisherman, and also a free copy of it with extreme deformations. At first he pretended that this had been made by the letter-carrier of Collioure, but finally admitted that it was an experiment of his own. It was the first thing he did with forced deformations.'[30]

Young Sailor I, set against a multi-coloured, thinly painted indeterminate background like that of *Woman with a Hat* (p. 45), is rendered in a linear, sculptural manner, evoking Cézanne in its three-dimensionality and visible brushstrokes. The face and hands are painted in Fauve colours of complementary green, red and pink.

Young Sailor II, by contrast, is rendered in a flat, decorative, primitive manner. There is no longer an effort to convey a likeness of the sitter. The shirt and trousers, in brilliant blue and green, are flowing and graceful; the face, with its rounded triangular shape and elliptical eyes, has a mask-like quality; and the background is a flat field of pink. The artist's words to Leo Stein, initially disclaiming responsibility for the work, indicate that Matisse himself was at first uneasy about these 'forced deformations'. In temporarily shifting responsibility to a fictional 'letter-carrier of Collioure', he may have had in mind the modern primitive Henri Rousseau, who exhibited with the Fauve painters at the 1905 Salon d'Automne (Rousseau, nicknamed 'Le Douanier' – 'the customs officer' – was a toll collector in Paris).

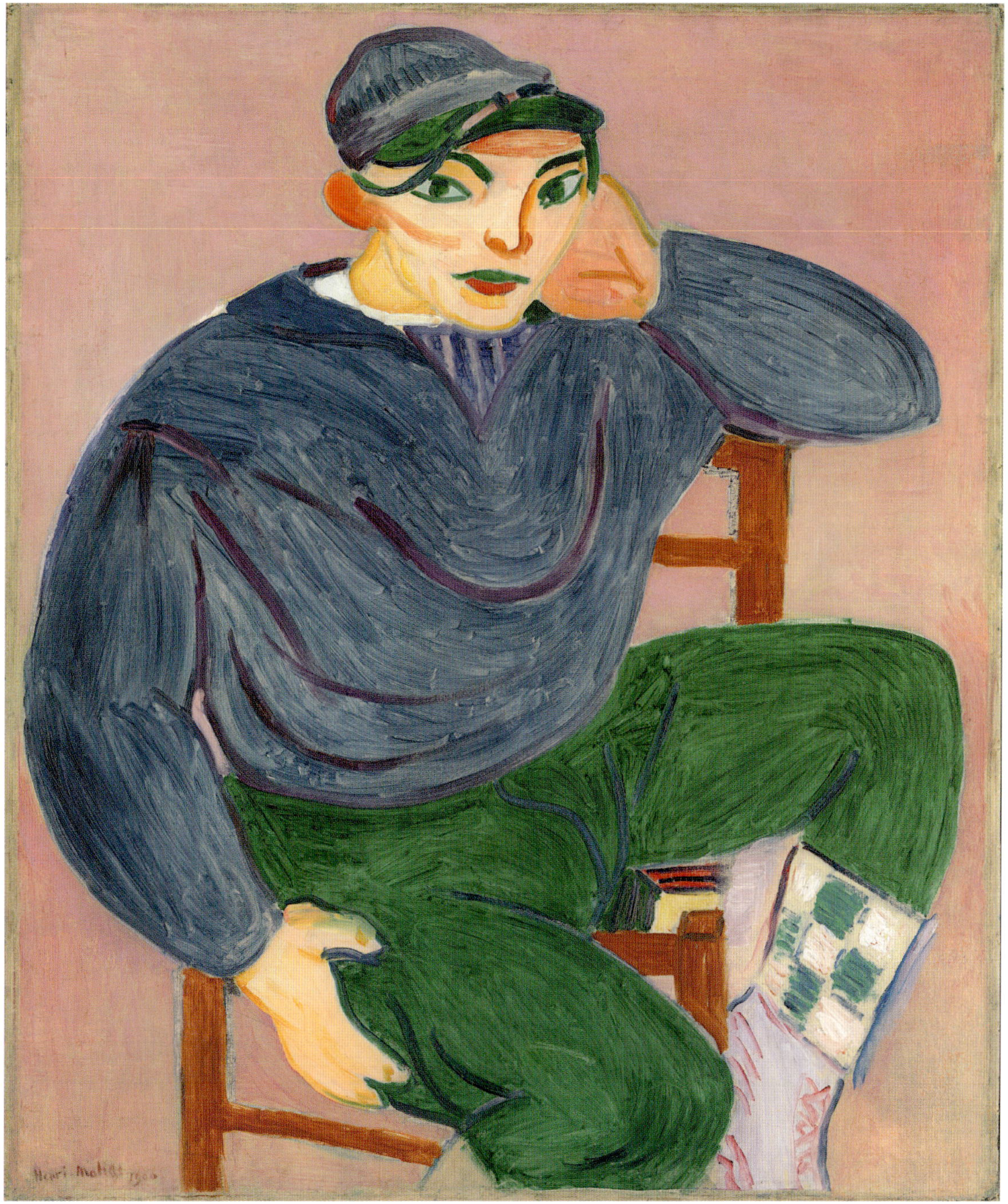

1906

SELF-PORTRAIT IN A STRIPED SHIRT

Statens Museum for Kunst, Copenhagen
Oil on canvas | 55 × 46cm (21⅝ × 18⅛in)

In her memoir *Picasso and His Friends,* Fernande Olivier – Picasso's companion at the time he and Matisse first met – wrote that 'There was something very sympathetic about Matisse.' She added that with 'his thick, golden beard, he really looked like a grand old man of art. He seemed to be hiding, though, behind his thick spectacles, and his expression was opaque, gave nothing away.'[31]

Notwithstanding the astuteness of Fernande's portrayal, it is quite the opposite of the persona presented in *Self-Portrait in a Striped Shirt.* In this over-life-size painting, the subject, having divested himself of spectacles, confronts the viewer with a penetrating gaze. The artist presented here is not a discursive intellectual, but a labourer at his craft with an affinity for the Collioure fisherman whose garb he has appropriated. (His striped *marinière* would later become an attribute of his friend and rival Picasso.)

Matisse employs Cézannian devices of structure and brushwork to capture his own likeness. With the exception of the multi-coloured shirt, colour is relatively subdued, with Fauve complementaries of blue and pink modelling the face. The usual attributes of an artist – such as smock, beret, easel, paintbrush or model – are not present here. What signifies the subject's profession is the heightened facture of the painting itself, with its variously scumbled, impastoed and unfinished background, and the freedom and variety of paint application and brushstroke on the face, neck, hair, beard and shirt.

Self-Portrait in a Striped Shirt sets itself apart from Matisse's other self-portraits – indeed, from his other works – in its psychological intimacy and candour. Its first owners were Michael and Sarah Stein. Michael's sister Gertrude reportedly deemed it too intimate to be publicly exhibited – advice that was ignored by Michael and Sarah and by the artist himself.[32]

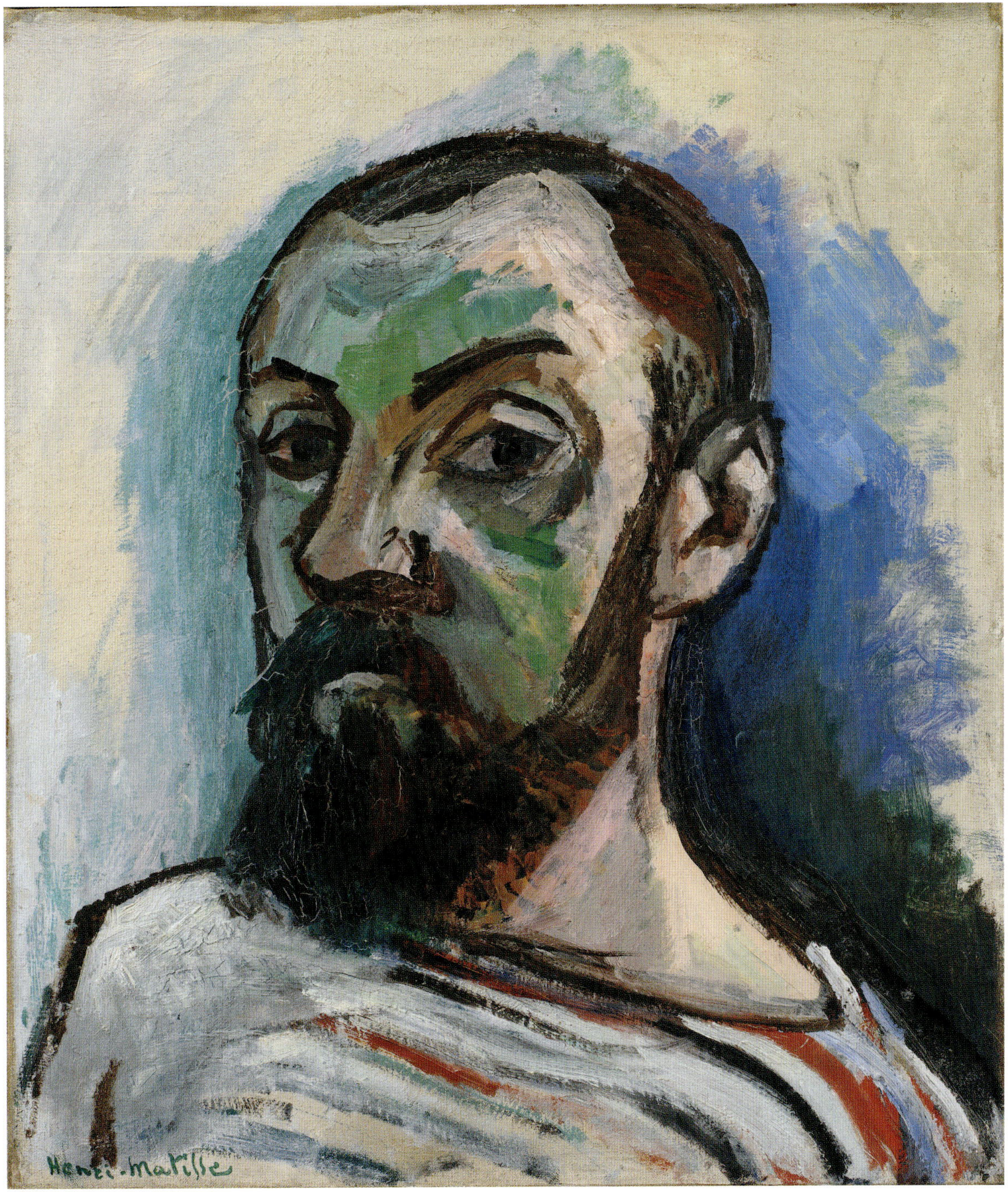
Henri-Matisse

1905–06 LE BONHEUR DE VIVRE (THE JOY OF LIFE)

Barnes Foundation, Philadelphia
Oil on canvas | 176.5 × 240.7cm (69½ × 94¾in)

At the time of its creation, *Le Bonheur de vivre* was the largest and most ambitious work of Matisse's career. Like its predecessor, *Luxe, calme et volupté* (p. 41) it is an Arcadian landscape depicting a Golden Age. As in the earlier picture, the figures derive from the artist's imagination, while the landscape itself was based on observation from nature: in this case, his prototype was *Landscape near Collioure* (1905, Statens Museum for Kunst, Copenhagen), with its arch-like grove of trees at the centre.

Matisse later told the interviewer Pierre Courthion that *Le Bonheur de vivre* 'was made by juxtaposition: things conceived independently of each other that I arranged together'.[33] Indeed, the figures, all nude, are depicted without consistency of scale. In the right foreground is a pair of embracing lovers: a crouching man and a reclining woman, their bodies merged to resemble a one-headed being. In the centre foreground, smaller in scale than the lovers, is the reclining figure of a female pipe-player. In the middle ground, left, are a standing and a crouching woman; behind them, two women embrace, one's head resting on the other's shoulder. In the centre are two reclining female figures, large in scale; one, eyes closed, turns towards the viewer, while the other, back turned, faces a ring of six female dancers in the background. On the right, a male pipe-player accompanies three goats that resemble prehistoric wall images from the caves of Lascaux.

What is most stunning about *Le Bonheur de vivre* is the powerful and revolutionary colour. A luminous yellow radiates from the centre outwards; it turns to pink above the horizon, and throughout the picture is juxtaposed with pink, blue, red, green and violet. Compatible rather than complementary colours are often adjoining – an exception being the green and red outlines of the central reclining figures. Colour is often expressive, rather than descriptive, as in the yellow and green bodies on the left and of the cavalcade of colours of the trees, foliage and lawn.

Le Bonheur de vivre, Matisse's sole entry in the 1906 Salon des Indépendants, was a visual manifesto of his views on art. Two years hence, he would publish *Notes of a Painter*, in which he would write: 'What I am after, above all, is expression … The entire arrangement of my picture is expressive: the place occupied by the figures, the empty spaces around them, the proportions, everything has its share.'[34] The painting is strikingly prescient. Seeds of his future works, among them *Blue Nude* (p. 55), *Le Luxe I* and *II* (p. 59), and *Dance I* and *II* (pp. 65 and 71) are already present in sections of *Le Bonheur de vivre*.

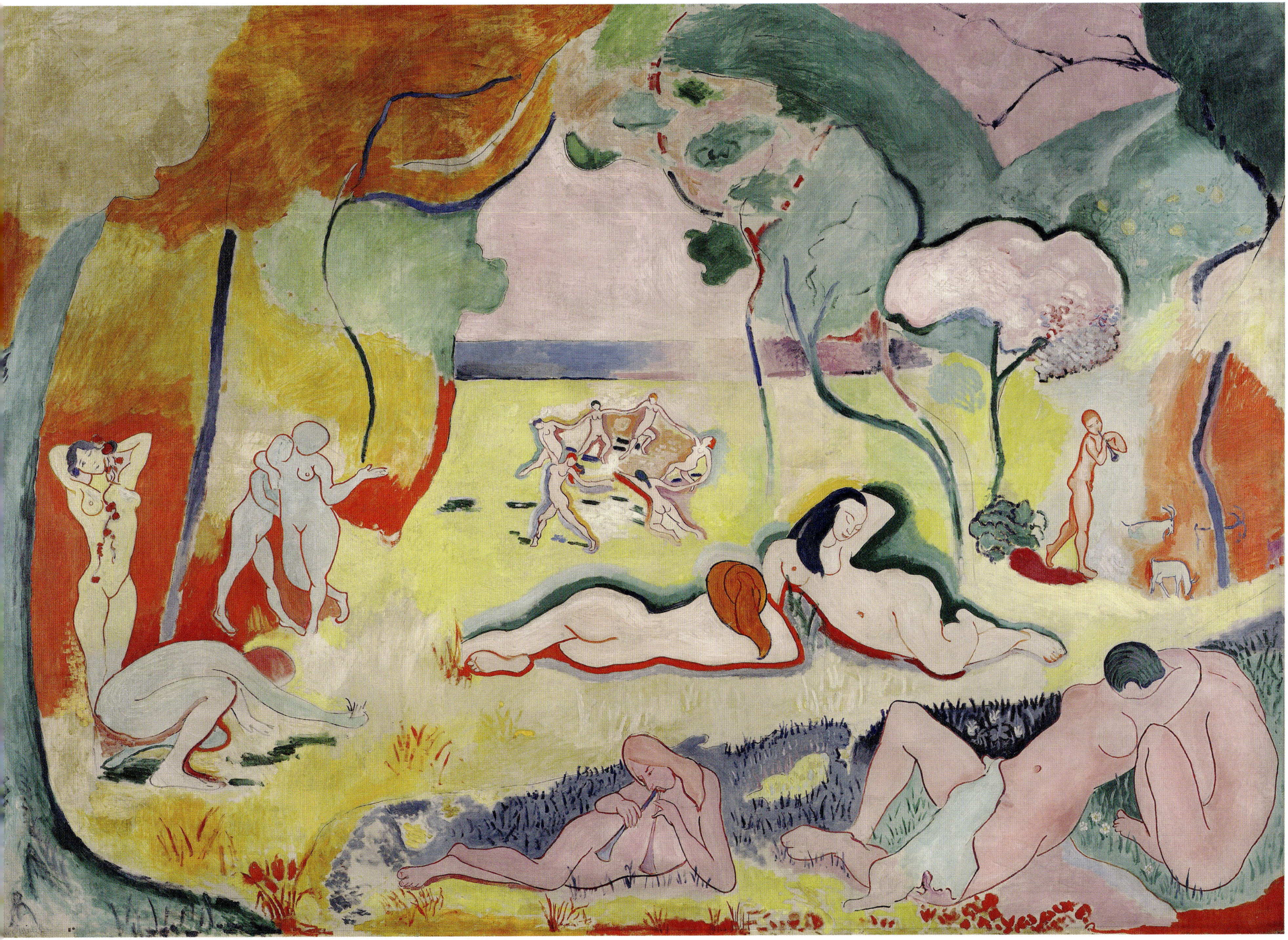

1907

BLUE NUDE (MEMORY OF BISKRA)

Baltimore Museum of Art
Oil on canvas | 92.1 × 140.3cm (36¼ × 55¼in)

Matisse's fascination with African tribal art preceded Picasso's. In spring 1906 the African statuettes in the window of a curio shop on the rue de Rennes caught his attention. He observed that in contrast with European sculpture, with its emphasis on description, 'in African statues the medium dictated the form, while the shapes and proportions were invented.'[35] One day he purchased a statuette (see p. 11) and brought it over to the residence of Leo and Gertrude Stein on the rue de Fleurus, where he showed it to Picasso.

Matisse was soon infusing an African influence into his own sculpture, first with standing figures. Then in Collioure, in early 1907, he began to model in clay *Reclining Nude I*, a female nude in a European pose but with the bulbous breasts and exaggerated buttocks of an African statuette. While work was in progress, disaster struck: the supporting tray flipped over, and the shaped clay was crushed on the floor. Before resuming work on the sculpture, he took out a large canvas and painted *Blue Nude,* a nearly life-size version of the same subject.

Matisse provided a tropical setting and gave the painting a subtitle, *Memory of Biskra*, an oasis in Algeria, which he had visited the previous spring. The figure reclines in an anatomically impossible pose, its upper portion displayed frontally, while the lower limbs are twisted as if in profile. In transforming his sculpture into a painting, Matisse made use of his understanding of Cézanne's techniques, evident in the blue tonality of the figure with its hatched brushstrokes and the tangibility of the space around it. The curves of the figure reverberate with arcs of vegetative growth in the surrounding landscape.

Blue Nude was soon purchased by Leo and Gertrude Stein, whose home Matisse and Picasso both frequented. Matisse's fusion of Cézannian and African art seems to have had an immediate effect on the younger artist, at work on *Demoiselles d'Avignon* (1907, The Museum of Modern Art, New York) that spring. Perhaps the most direct evidence of this influence was Picasso's preparatory painting *Nude with Drapery* (p. 12), in which the pose of uplifted arm and twisted torso echoes that of Matisse's *Blue Nude.*

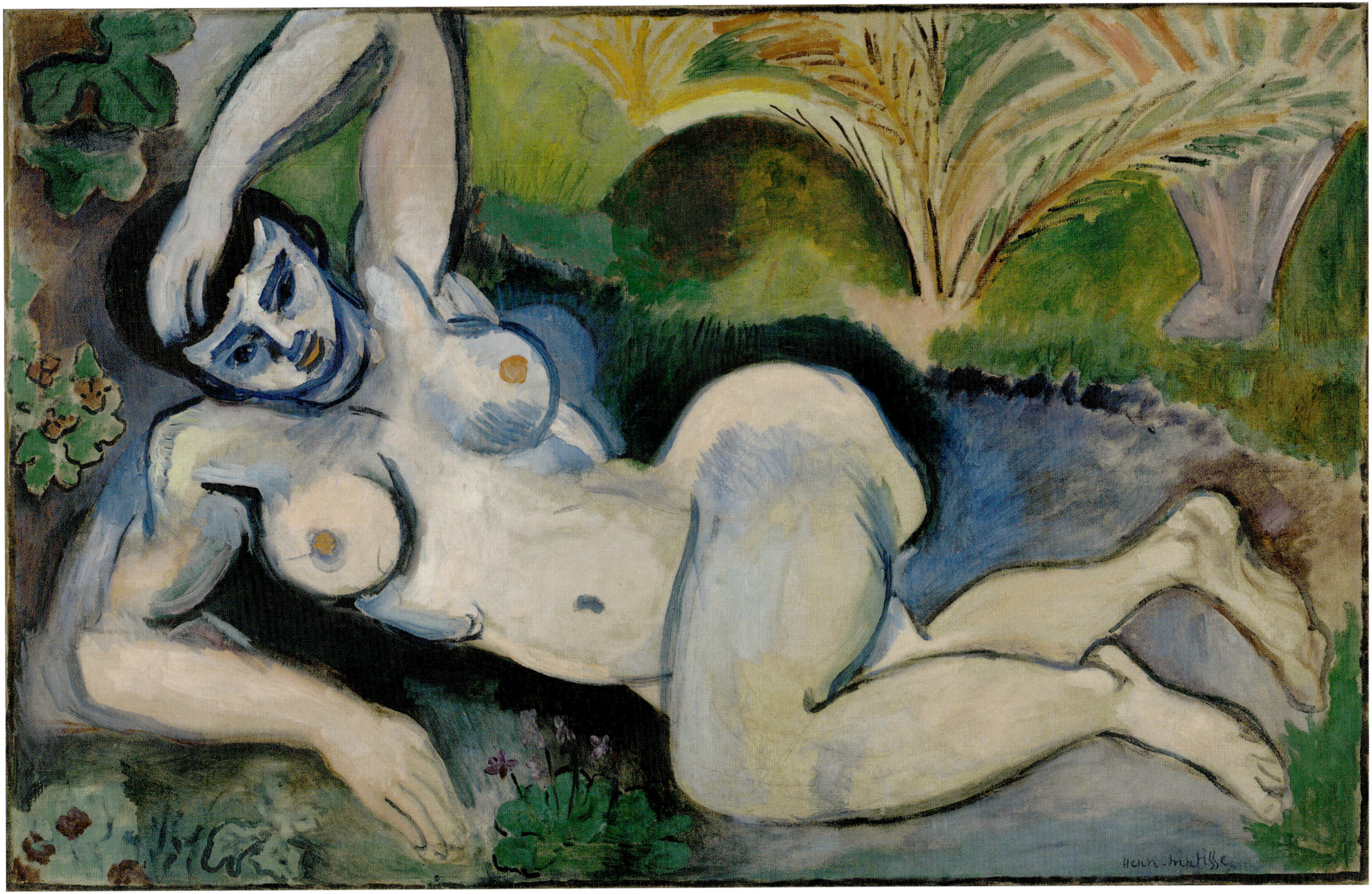
Henri-Matisse

1907

RED MADRAS HEADDRESS

Barnes Foundation, Philadelphia
Oil on canvas | 100 × 81cm (39⅜ × 31⅞in)

Red Madras Headdress, a portrait of Matisse's wife Amélie, marks a shift from the loose brushwork and modelled space of Fauvism toward the flat, decorative style that would characterize his work from 1907 to 1913. This new style was first apparent in the more naïvely rendered *Young Sailor II* of 1906 (p. 49).

The Fauve portraits of Amélie, *Woman with a Hat* (p. 45) and *Madame Matisse: The Green Line* (p. 47) were jarring in their colour juxtapositions and in the aggressiveness of the sitter's gaze; here colours are more harmonious, and while Amélie's gaze meets our own, the result is engaging rather than confrontational. A contrapuntal effect is created by the serpentine rhythms of the limbs and contrasting decorative patterns of the hat, dress, and collar, belt and cuffs. The subtly textured turquoise background, lighter on the left than the right, is nearly flat. The flesh tones are subtly modelled in green, with pink highlights of the cheeks. The luminous red of the headdress, patterned in orange swirls, is echoed by the vermilion leaf and flower patterns of the dress and the orange arm of the chair. The turquoise background is harmoniously echoed by the dark blue of the dress.

Red Madras Headdress was exhibited at the 1907 Salon d'Automne in Paris, and later at two major international exhibitions: the 1912 Second Post-Impressionist Exhibition at the Grafton Galleries, London, and the 1913 Armory Show in New York, Chicago and Boston. The Armory Show was the greater American public's first exposure to Cubism and to the art of Matisse. The work that captured the most attention was Marcel Duchamp's Cubist painting, *Nude Descending a Staircase* (see p. 17); its near abstraction, together with the implied indecency of its subject matter (nudes were traditionally stationary, and one descending a staircase could imply a burlesque house or brothel) rendered it the *succès de scandale* of the exhibition. A close rival in notoriety was Matisse's *Red Madras Headdress*, which was reproduced and lampooned in the press with comparable frequency. For example, it appeared under the following headlines: 'Art Extremists, in Broadsides of Lurid Color, Invade New York and Capture an Armory', *New York Herald*; and 'Art Show Open to Freaks', *Chicago Tribune*. The *New York American* published a caricature of the painting under the title: '"Portrait of a Lady" by Gyp the Futurist'.[36] The critic Frank Jewett Mather, writing in *The Independent*, lambasted the work, citing its 'childish symbolism' and 'fairly appalling ugliness'.[37]

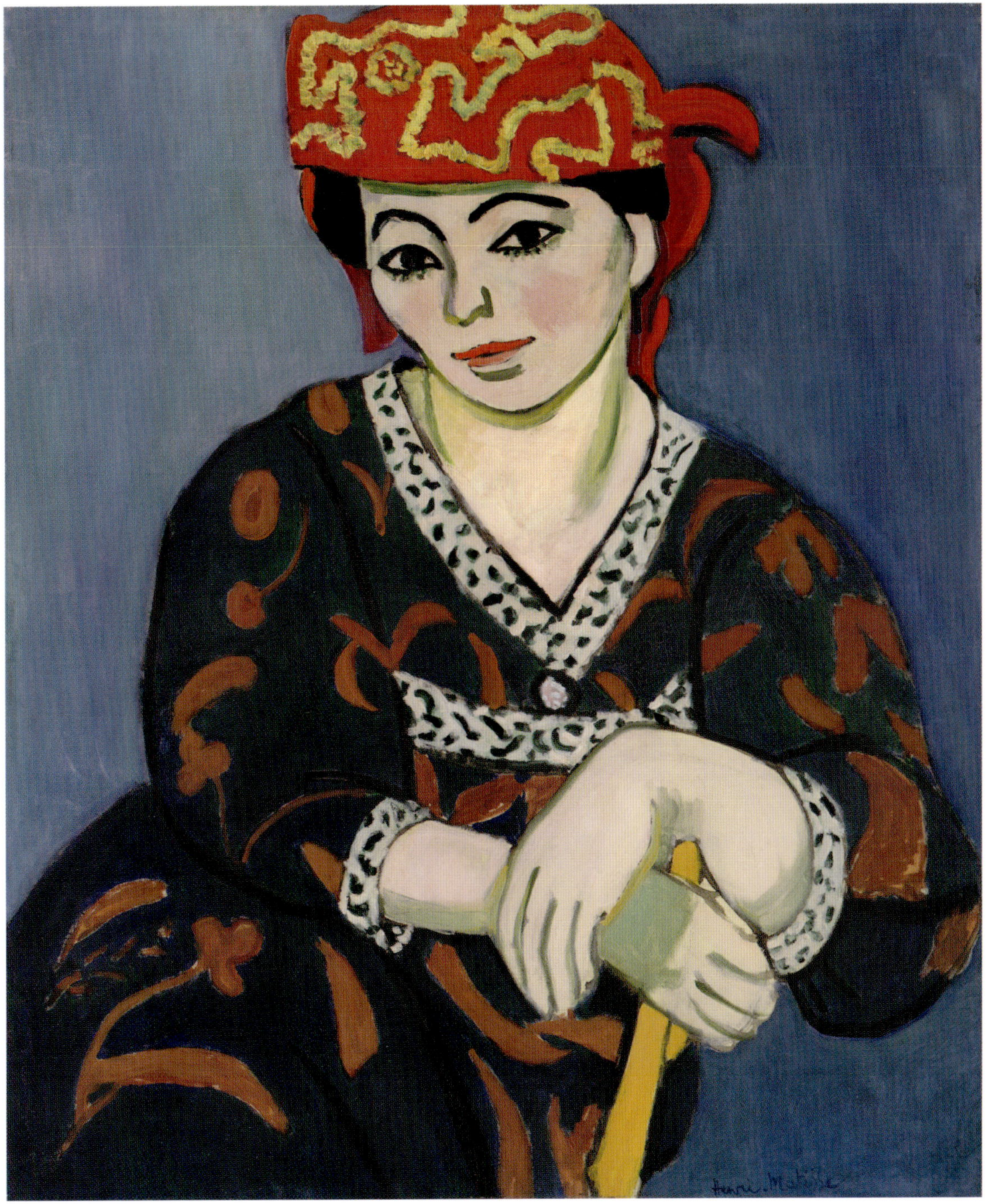

1907–08 LE LUXE II

Statens Museum for Kunst, Copenhagen
Distemper on canvas | 209.5 × 138cm (82½ × 54¾in)

In summer 1907 Matisse travelled to Italy and viewed for the first time Trecento and Quattrocento fresco paintings *in situ*. He visited Leo and Gertrude Stein at their rented villa in Fiesole, where a fellow guest, the young American painter Walter Pach, observed Matisse's infectious enthusiasm: 'He had been seeing the Giottos in Padua and was in awe of their simple grandeur. He ran down to Arezzo for a day and returned with enough admiration for the perfect art of Piero della Francesca to last a lifetime.'[38]

When he came back to Collioure later that summer, Matisse created the work now known as *Le Luxe I*, which was exhibited at the 1907 Salon d'Automne as *Le Luxe* (*esquisse*). Back in Paris, he produced *Le Luxe II*, completing it in late 1907 or early 1908. Whereas *Le Luxe I* is sketchily rendered, *Le Luxe II* is painted in his new flat, decorative style.

The subject matter of the *Le Luxe* paintings, like that of *Luxe, calme et volupté* and *Le Bonheur de vivre* (pp. 41 and 53), is a Golden Age. The three bathers are derived from the four figures on the left in *Bonheur de vivre*. The squatting figure picking flowers, reversed, now dries the standing bather's feet; the two figures behind them are condensed into a single striding bather presenting a bouquet. The narrative, like the title, is evocative rather than explicit. In *Notes of a Painter* (1908), Matisse would write: 'A work of art must carry within itself its complete significance and impose that upon the beholder even before he recognizes the subject matter.' He demonstrated this principle by citing the Giotto frescoes at Padua: 'When I see [them] I do not trouble myself to recognize which scene of the life of Christ I have before me, but I immediately understand the sentiment which emerges from it, for it is in the lines, the composition, the color.'[39]

The series is Matisse's first painting with over-life-size figures. The artist re-created the composition of the first version of *Le Luxe* by means of a full-size charcoal sketch known as a cartoon (now at the Centre Pompidou, Paris), following the practice of fresco painters. Whereas the first version is rendered in oil paint, the second version employs distemper, a water-soluble medium that produces a matte effect comparable to that of fresco painting. With *Le Luxe II*, Matisse, employing spare, luminous colour, three elegant nudes and a simplified composition, has created a powerful, monumental work.

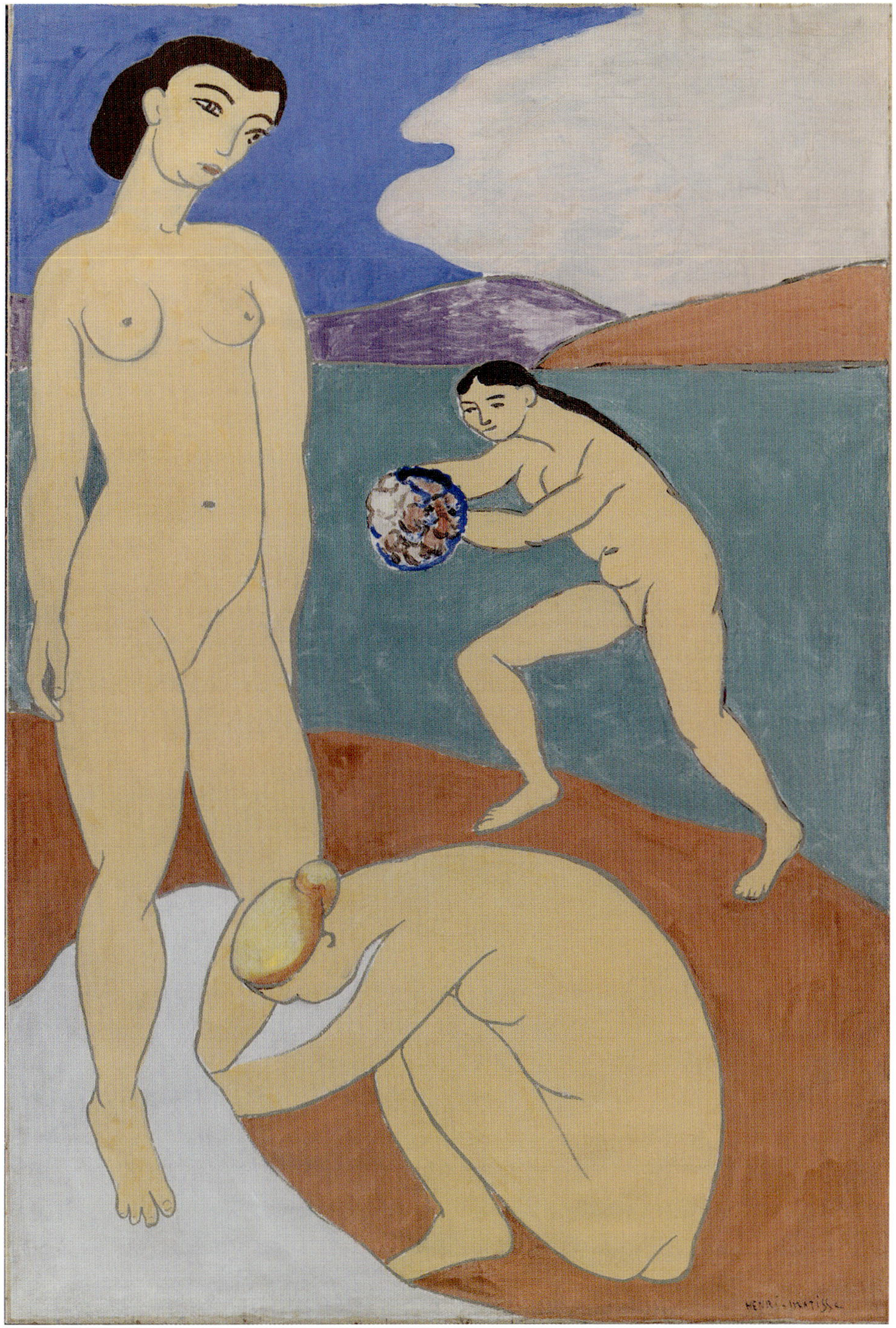

1908

BATHERS WITH A TURTLE

Saint Louis Art Museum
Oil on canvas | 181.6 × 221cm (71½ × 87in)

In autumn 1907 Matisse visited Picasso's studio, where he saw *Les Demoiselles d'Avignon* (1907, The Museum of Modern Art, New York) and related works, including *Nude with Drapery* (p. 12). Picasso's recent works were, in part, responses to Matisse's *Blue Nude* (p. 55). Both artists, in very different ways, sought to synthesize the stylistic innovations of Cézanne with the formal principles of African tribal art.

With *Bathers with a Turtle*, a large, nearly square painting, comparable in size and format to the *Demoiselles*, Matisse continues his dialogue with Picasso. Like Cézanne's *Three Bathers* (p. 9) in his own collection, *Bathers with a Turtle* employs a pyramidal composition of three sculpturally rendered female nudes in a landscape of muted green and blue tonalities. Matisse's bathers, like Cézanne's (and unlike the women in Picasso's painting) focus their gazes downward, rather than outward towards the viewer. The central bather's pose resembles that of the African statuette (p. 11) purchased by Matisse and shown to Picasso in 1906; her arms, like those of the statuette, are bent at the elbow, with her hands placed on her mouth.

In common with *Le Luxe II* (p. 59), *Bathers with a Turtle* presents three nudes in an indeterminate landscape apart from the world of the present. The pose of the figure on the left resembles that of the crouching bather of *Le Luxe* who dries the standing bather's feet; her pose is still closer to that of the figure on the left, picking flowers, in *Le Bonheur de vivre* (p. 53). Matisse had been fluctuating between structural Cézannian compositions and a new flat, decorative style; here he seems to split the difference, with sculptural figures set against an abstract landscape of muted bands of green and blue colour. We are no longer in the Arcadia of *Le Luxe*; this is a primeval setting, one suggested by the cave paintings on the right in *Le Bonheur de vivre*. The features of the central bather in *Bathers with a Turtle* resemble those of a Palaeolithic cave-dweller. All three bathers focus their attention on the turtle, one of the most ancient of reptiles. It is as if the bathers are contemplating their own pasts – and ours.

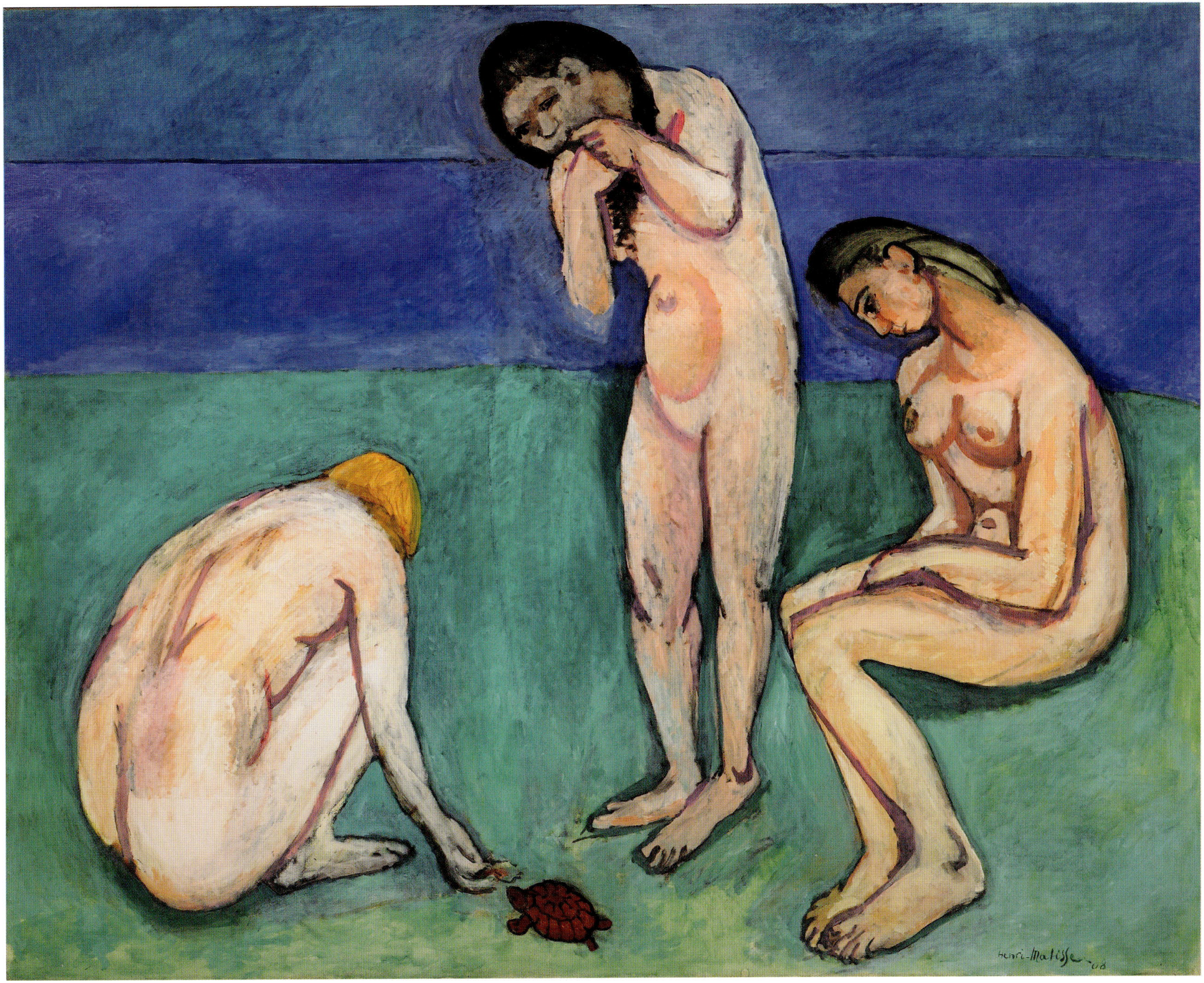
Henri-Matisse 08

1908

HARMONY IN RED

The State Hermitage Museum, St Petersburg
Oil on canvas | 180.5 × 221cm (70⅘ × 86⅗in)

In early 1908 Matisse opened his own school, the Académie Matisse, in the Montparnasse section of Paris, on the site of an abandoned convent, where he also maintained his studio. That spring the school found larger quarters in the Hôtel Biron, an eighteenth-century mansion, which had formerly housed another convent, located in a 7-hectare (17-acre) park in Montparnasse. Matisse moved his family living quarters, as well as his school and studio, to the Hôtel Biron and its surrounding buildings. The vista that Matisse now viewed from his studio window immediately affected his painting. Established at his new quarters, he undertook *Harmony in Red*, an interior juxtaposed with a picture window of a blooming lawn and foliage.

Harmony in Red is an adaptation of an earlier painting, *The Dinner Table* of 1896–7 (p. 33), transformed into a new, decorative style. Like the earlier work, it features a maidservant on the right, clearing the table at the conclusion of a meal, with an open window and a vacant chair on the left. Whereas *The Dinner Table* is rendered in traditional perspective, with the viewer peering down at the diagonally receding table, *Harmony in Red* is a frontal composition rendered without perspectival depth. The blossoming exterior of the window view is echoed by the arabesques and floral patterns of the wallpaper and tablecloth, which, along with the unifying red of background and foreground, create a flattened, yet dynamic, effect. An inspiration for this style was the art of Vincent van Gogh, in such works as *La Berceuse* (1889), a series of portraits in which Mme Roulin, the postman's wife, is surrounded by floral and arabesque patterns that seem to emanate from her, embodying fertility and growth.

That Matisse would look back to *The Dinner Table*, his own work of the previous decade, and adapt it to his new decorative style, suggests the emotional effect that the uprooting from his previous quarters on the quai Saint-Michel took on him. Caroline Joblaud, his companion prior to his marriage to Amélie Payayre – and the mother of his daughter Marguerite – was the model for the maidservant of *The Dinner Table*. In re-creating her in *Harmony in Red*, he revisits her memory. The empty chair, now brought to the foreground, suggests the artist's absence from his remembered past.

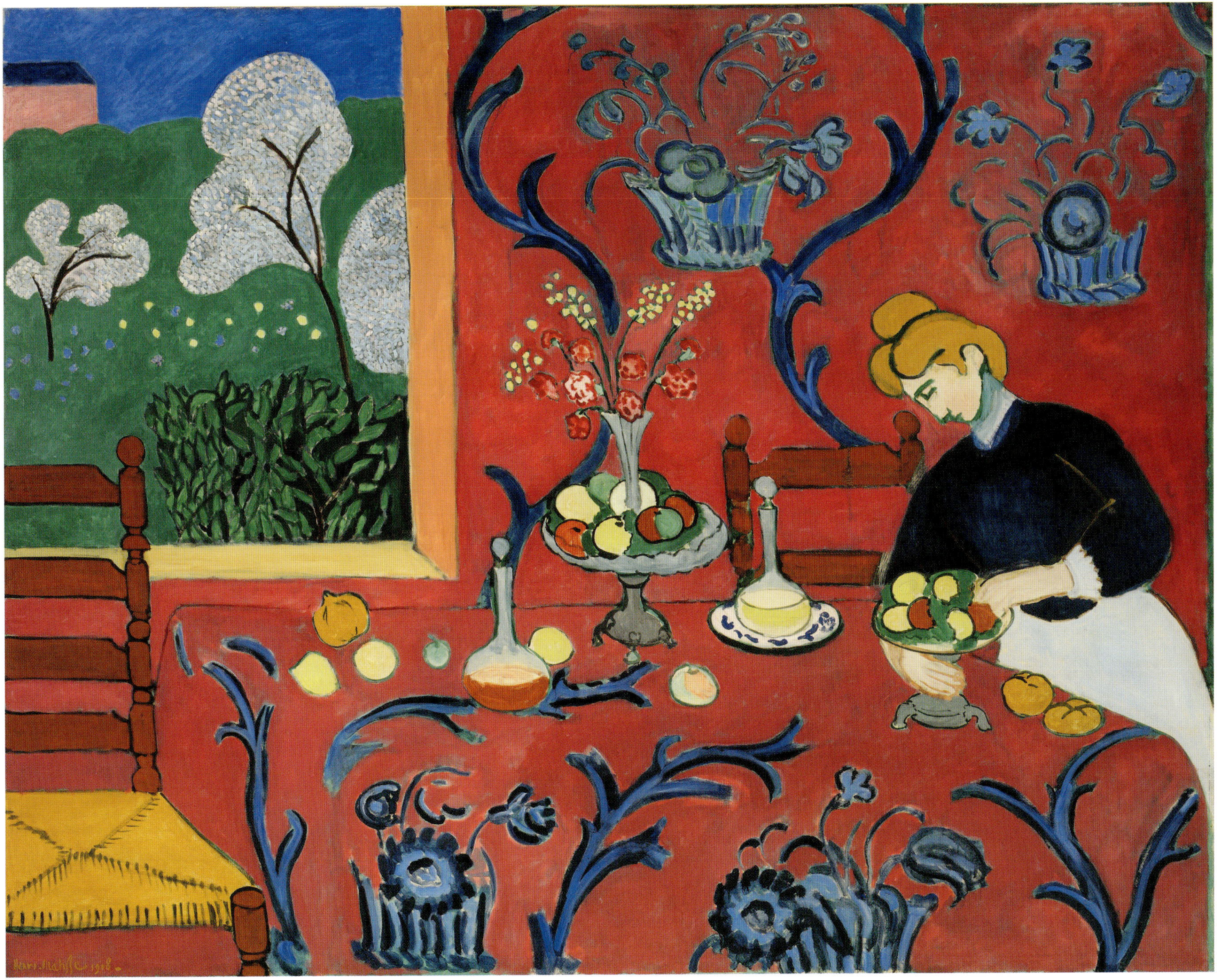

1909

DANCE I

The Museum of Modern Art, New York
Oil on canvas | 259.7 × 390.1cm (102¼ × 153½in)

The Russian merchant Sergei Shchukin was a collector of Matisse's work, beginning in 1906; among the paintings decorating the walls of his mansion in Moscow were *Harmony in Red* of 1908 (p. 63). In early 1909 Shchukin discussed with the artist the possibility of a large decorative panel above the staircase. On the basis of these discussions Matisse painted a preliminary work, *Dance I*. The merchant was sufficiently pleased that he commissioned a second version for his home.

Dance I continues the style of *Le Luxe II* (p. 59), with light-toned, unmodelled figures set against a background of flat fields of colour. Its setting, like that of *Bathers with a Turtle* (p. 61), is unspecified as to time and place. The effect is universalizing; this ring of five nude female dancers becomes stand-in for all of humanity and for the human condition. It is Matisse's largest painting to date and the most reductive in colour, now reduced to black hair and contours, pink flesh, a green hill and blue sky.

The ring of dancers originally appeared in the centre background of *Le Bonheur de vivre* (p. 53). The inspiration was the folk dances of Catalan fisherman in Collioure. The two figures on the left in the earlier painting have been replaced by a single figure, so that the ring of six is now a ring of five. The rounded oblong dance formation has become an arabesque, playing off against the curvature of the hill and accommodating the rectilinear pictorial field. The outstretched arms in the foreground, with hands that do not meet, evoke the creation of Adam on Michelangelo's Sistine Chapel ceiling, underscoring the universalizing theme of the painting.

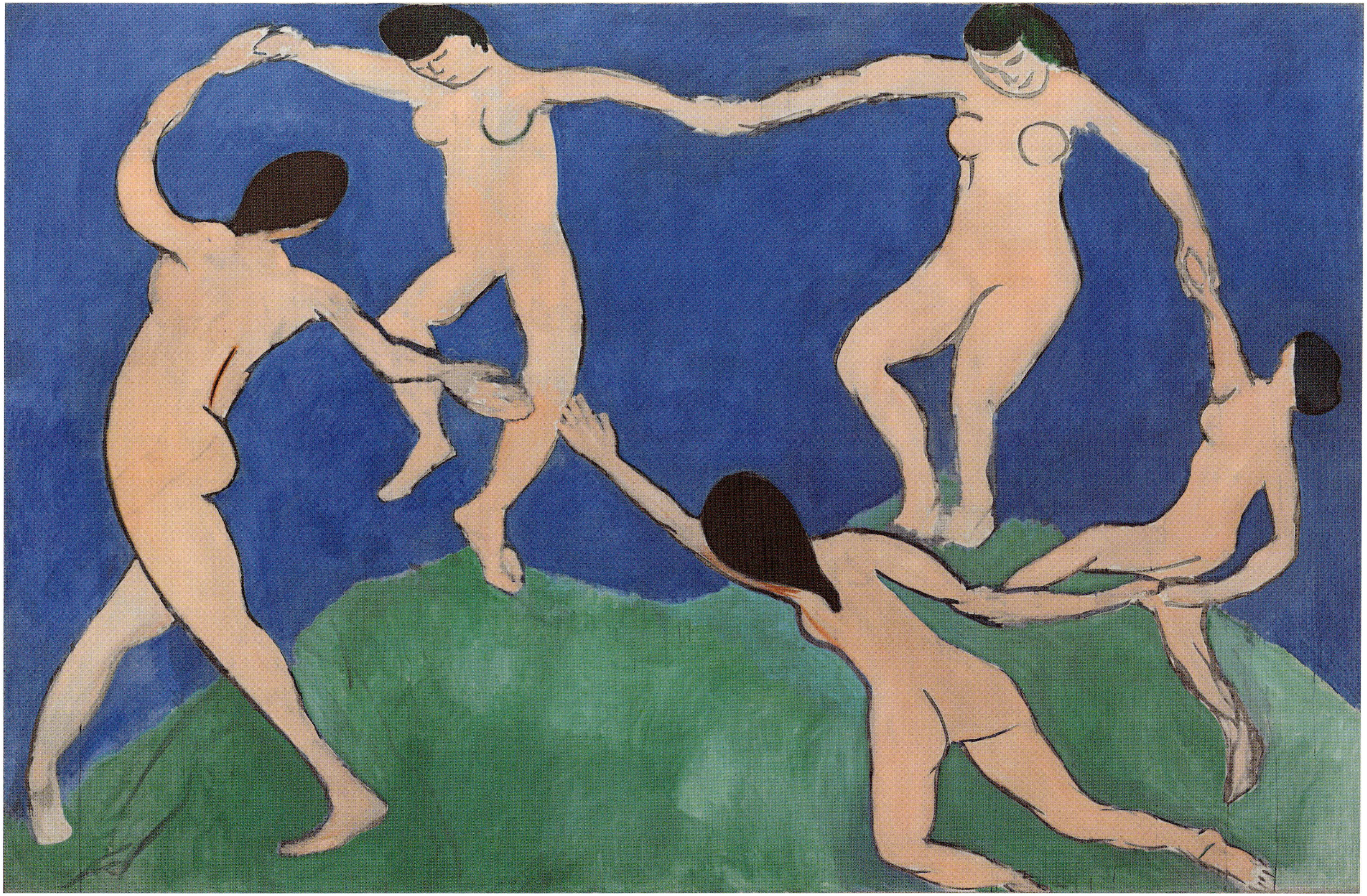

1909 STILL LIFE WITH 'DANCE'

The State Hermitage Museum, St Petersburg
Oil on canvas | 89.5 × 117.5cm (35 × 46⅓in)

In early 1909 Matisse's patron Sergei Shchukin commissioned the artist to create the large decorative panels for his Moscow residence which would eventually be realized as *Dance II* and *Music* (pp. 71 and 68). At this juncture Matisse painted the small but dynamic studio interior *Still Life with 'Dance*'.

In this painting three rectangles interact, each turned at a different angle. The horizontal tabletop points to the vertical *Dance* panel, which is turned away from the viewer; by contrast, a large canvas to the right, its back facing the viewer, is parallel to the picture plane.

Matisse employs compositional devices comparable to those of *Harmony in Red* (p. 63). The tabletop pulsates with energy: loose fruit, a plate of fruit, and two vases of flowers are placed on the tablecloth, which is decorated with a floral and arabesque pattern. Whereas *Harmony in Red* juxtaposes a fruit and flower-laden table with a landscape viewed through a window, the laden table is here contrasted with the painting within a painting, *Dance I*: like a window, the *Dance* panel acts as a passageway from an interior to an exterior world.

The two vases with flowers visually interact with the dance panel. The smaller dark vase on the left holds yellow flowers whose circular arrangement echoes that of the ring of dancers. An oblong box at the table's edge points to the rectilinearity of the upper right of the composition. At the centre an Algerian vase holds dark blooming flowers that appear to merge with the coiffure of the dancer with outstretched arm. A magenta napkin in the foreground rhymes visually with the green hill of the *Dance* panel. The swirling energy of the dancers and the contrapuntal energy of the fruit and flower-laden table are contrasted by the stationary grid of the canvas on the right.

Still Life with 'Dance' is Matisse's earliest instance of placing one of his own previous works within a painting. This device serves an autobiographical function: each of Matisse's works is a moment in his life as an artist. In early 1909 he faced the formidable task of creating a second decorative panel that would be a worthy counterpart of the *Dance*. Art historian Stephanie D'Alessandro has speculated that Matisse 'may have envisioned' this studio interior 'as a proud proclamation of the hard work underway'.[40]

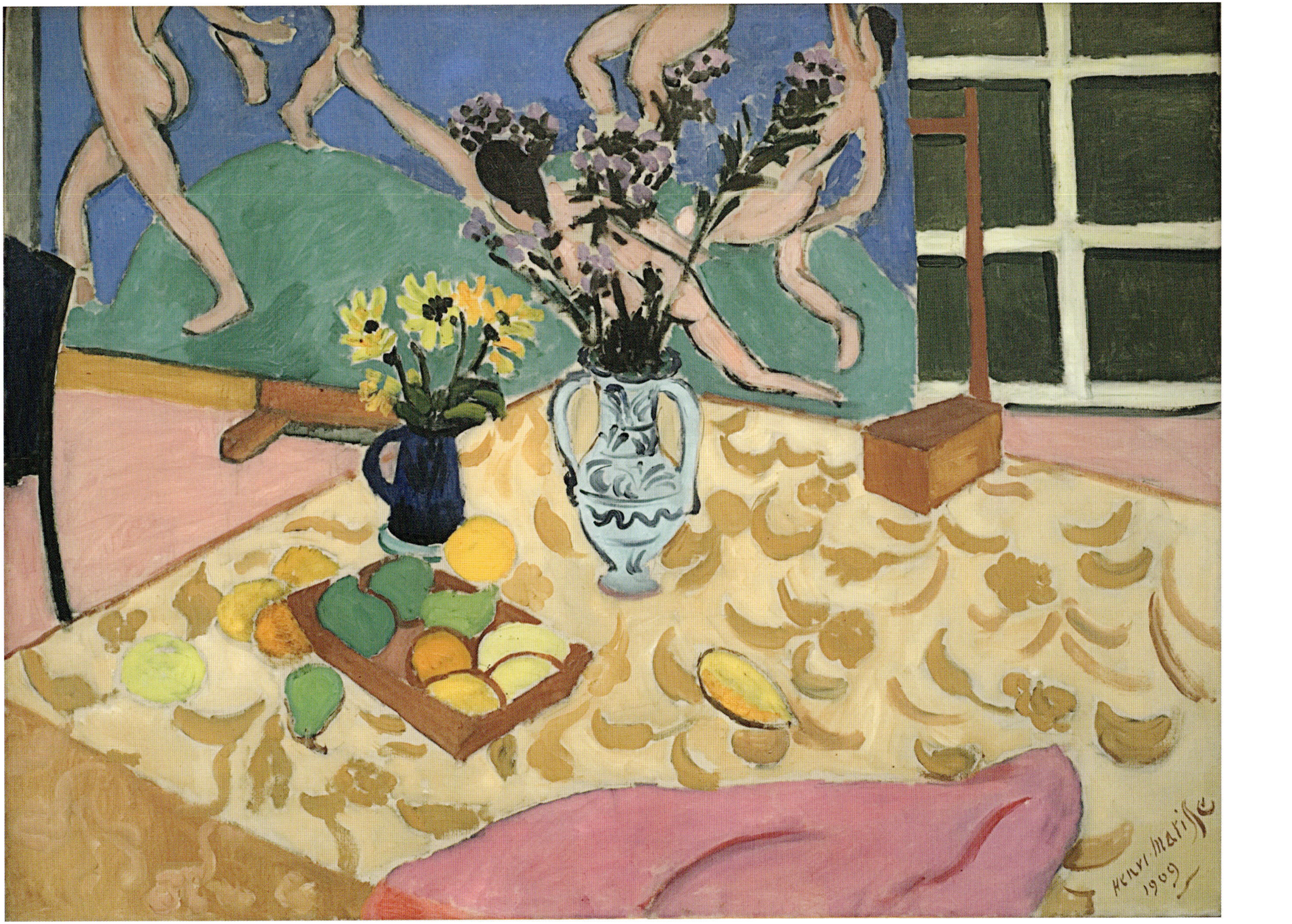
Henri-Matisse
1909

1910 MUSIC

The State Hermitage Museum, St Petersburg
Oil on canvas | 260 × 389cm (102⅓ × 153in)

With *Dance II* (p. 71), *Music* was one of two mural-sized panels commissioned by Serge Shchukin for his palatial home in Moscow. *Dance I* (p. 65) – the prototype for *Dance II* – had been painted in one or two days, as witnessed by Matisse's pupil Hans Purrmann. The artist discovered, however, that devising a panel representing music was far more arduous. The reason is evident: whereas a dance can be presented by description, music can be depicted only by analogy. Matisse's works in progress for *Music*, as compared to the final version, had far more narrative content and included details later eliminated as extraneous, including flowers, a dog, and figures in profile and three-quarter view. After much trial and error, he arrived at a spare, elegant, ingenious and convincing solution.

As a counterpart to the five female dancers of *Dance I* and *II*, Matisse presents five stationary, frontal male figures. Their placement on a hill, unspecified as to time and place, rises and falls like musical notes on a page. The violinist on the left suggests a G clef; he is followed by a piper and three singers. The ensemble evokes an interval in a piece of chamber music.

Matisse, himself a dedicated violinist, had a lifelong interest in the relationship between music and visual art. In a letter to Alexander Romm (1934) he would write of the colour scheme for *Music*: 'I had decided to put colors on flat and without shading. I knew that my musical harmony was represented by a green and a blue (representing the relation of the green pines to the blue sky of the Côte d'Azur) completed by a tone for the flesh of the figures.'[41] In a statement to Tériade (1929), he referred to this flesh tone as a 'violent vermilion'.[42] For the essay 'The Role and Modalities of Colour' (1945) he wrote: 'Colors have a beauty of their own which must be preserved, as one strives to preserve pure tones in music … What counts most with color are relationships … When one composes with it, like a musician with his harmonies, it is simply a question of emphasizing the contrasts.'[43]

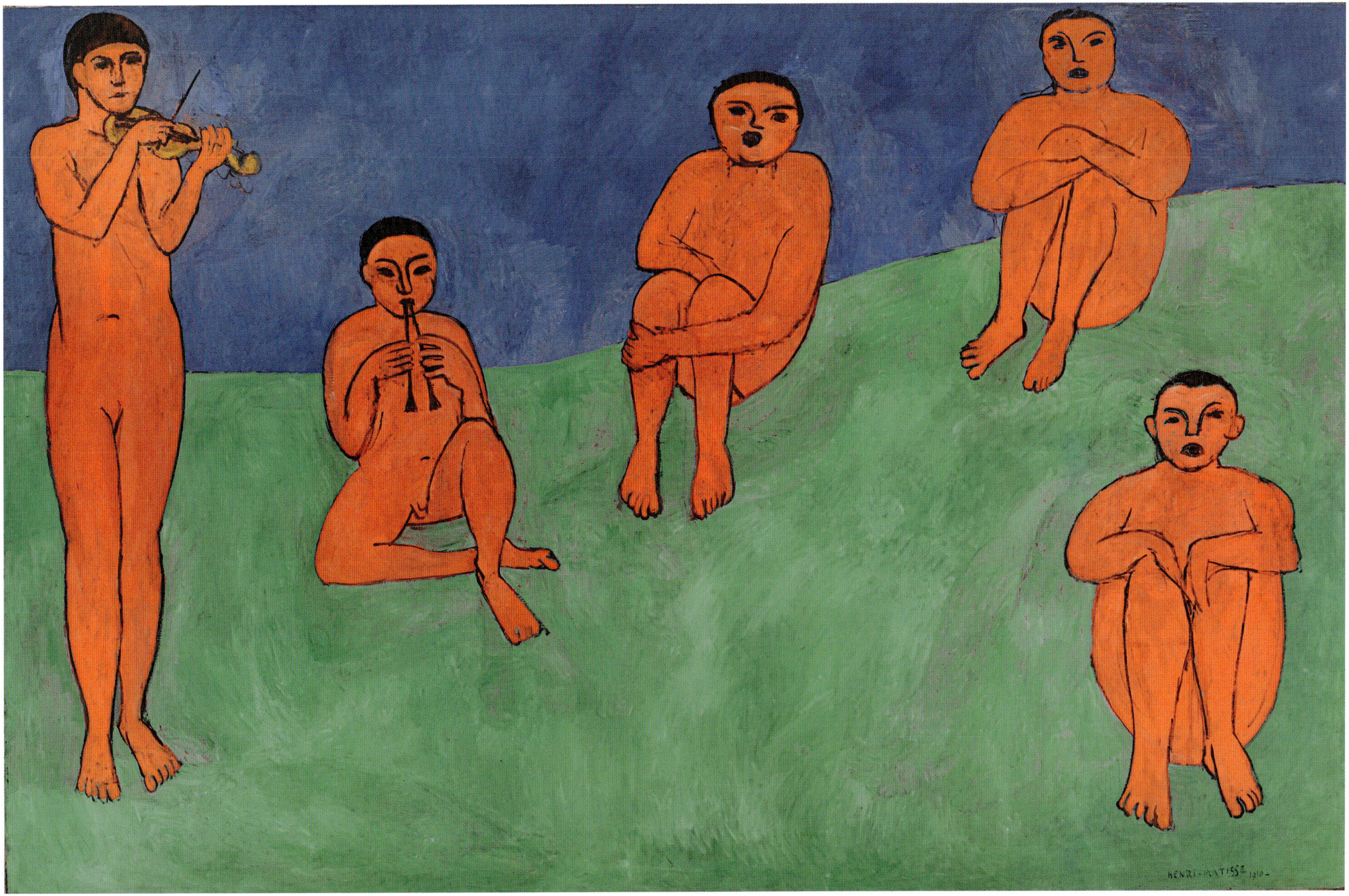
HENRI-MATISSE 1910

1910

DANCE II

The State Hermitage Museum, St Petersburg
Oil on canvas | 260 × 391cm (102½ × 154in)

Dance II, like *Dance I* (p. 65), presents a ring of five nude female figures dancing on a green hill before a blue sky. The overall effect, however, has been transformed. The principal vehicles of this transformation are drawing and colour. The figures of *Dance II* have more interior modelling – especially the dancer second from the left – and as a consequence are more three-dimensional and expressive. (This polarity of flat versus sculptural was present in reverse in *Le Luxe I* and *Le Luxe* II [p. 59], in which the preliminary version contained sculptural figures, the final version flat figures.) The green and blue expanses are now more intense, while the light pink of the dancers' bodies has become a deep red – Matisse would later call it a 'violent vermilion' – equal in intensity to the colours of hill and sky.[44] The interval in the foreground where two hands nearly meet, suggesting Michelangelo's *Creation of Adam,* now seems to transfer a spark of energy to the dancer behind it. The composition of *Dance I* is centrifugal, with energy that flows towards the centre; *Dance II*'s composition is centripetal, propelling outwards. Whereas *Dance I* is an Apollonian vision, characterized by reason, order and control, *Dance II* is a Dionysian vision of passion, spontaneity and frenzy.

Dance II and *Music* (p. 69) were intended to be displayed side by side at Sergei Shchukin's mansion in Moscow (as they are currently exhibited at the Hermitage Museum in St Petersburg). Matisse worked on the two panels alternately and employed the same colour scheme for each. The male figures of *Music*, while they are identical in colour to the female dancers, are flat, frontal, still and calm. The paired panels thus preserve the polarity of Dionysian versus Apollonian that emerged in the transformation from *Dance I* to *Dance II.*

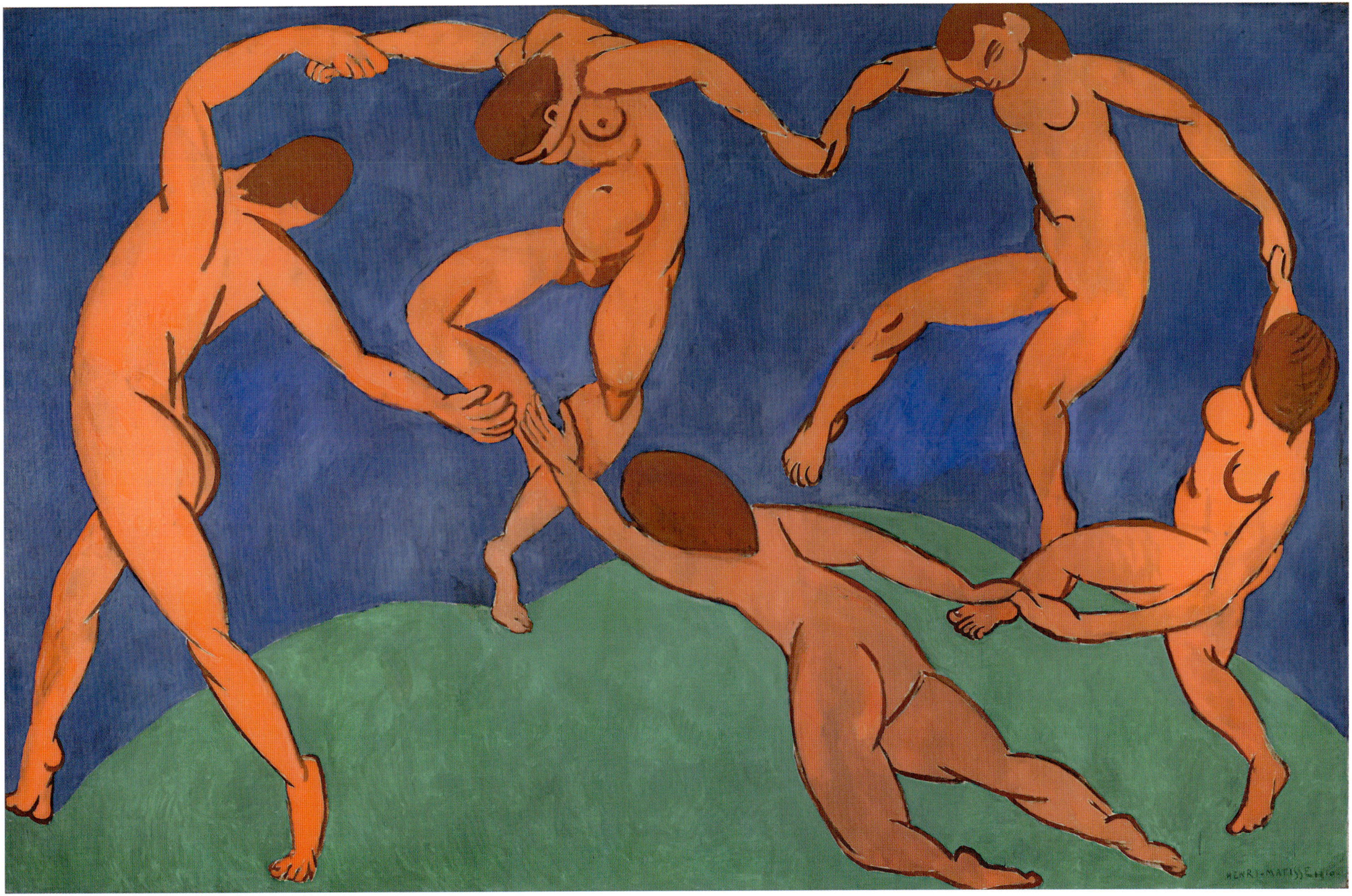
HENRI-MATISSE 1910

1911 THE PINK STUDIO

The Pushkin State Museum of Fine Arts, Moscow
Oil on canvas | 182 × 222cm (71⅔ × 87⅖ in)

The Pink Studio depicts the interior of Matisse's studio in Issy-les-Moulineaux; a glimpse of its exterior is visible through the window in *The Conversation* (p. 85). A visitor described the studio as a 'good-size square structure … painted white, within and without,' which 'had immense windows (both in the roof and at the side), thus giving a sense of out of doors'.[45]

The overall pink of the interior, warmer and more intense on the floor than on the wall, suggests the light of early morning. The composition's flatness is only somewhat undermined by the perspectival rendering of the patterned orange rug on the left and the vermilion table to the right, which are viewed from different perspectives, the rug from below and the table from above. A turquoise-coloured floral-patterned screen in the centre echoes the rug; draped over it is a deep-blue coverlet vigorously decorated with pink plant forms. In front of the screen, dead centre in the composition, is a green vase perched on a vermilion stool, which in turn echoes the table on the right and the cropped, large vase to the left. The window grid above offers a view of the garden outside, with its living tree and plant forms. The segmented, interactive quality of the composition reveals the influence of Persian miniatures, which had deeply impressed Matisse at an exhibition of Islamic art the previous year in Munich.

Set against the wall are Matisse's own artworks, some still in progress, on which he had been working since 1906, presenting a segment of a visual autobiography of his life as an artist. These include the bronze *Decorative Figure* (1908), *Purple Cyclamen* (1911–12, Private Collection), *Le Luxe II* (p. 59), *The Girl with Green Eyes* (1908, San Francisco Museum of Modern Art), *Young Sailor II* (p. 49), *Nude with a White Scarf* (1909, Statens Museum for Kunst), a study for the relief *Back I* (1909), and, on the far right, *Dance I* (p. 65); just to the right of the screen is a plaster cast of the *Mars Borghese* from the Louvre. What dominates the composition, however, is the ensemble in the centre, of simulated plant forms leading skyward into a window view of real plant forms, a metaphor of creativity and growth.

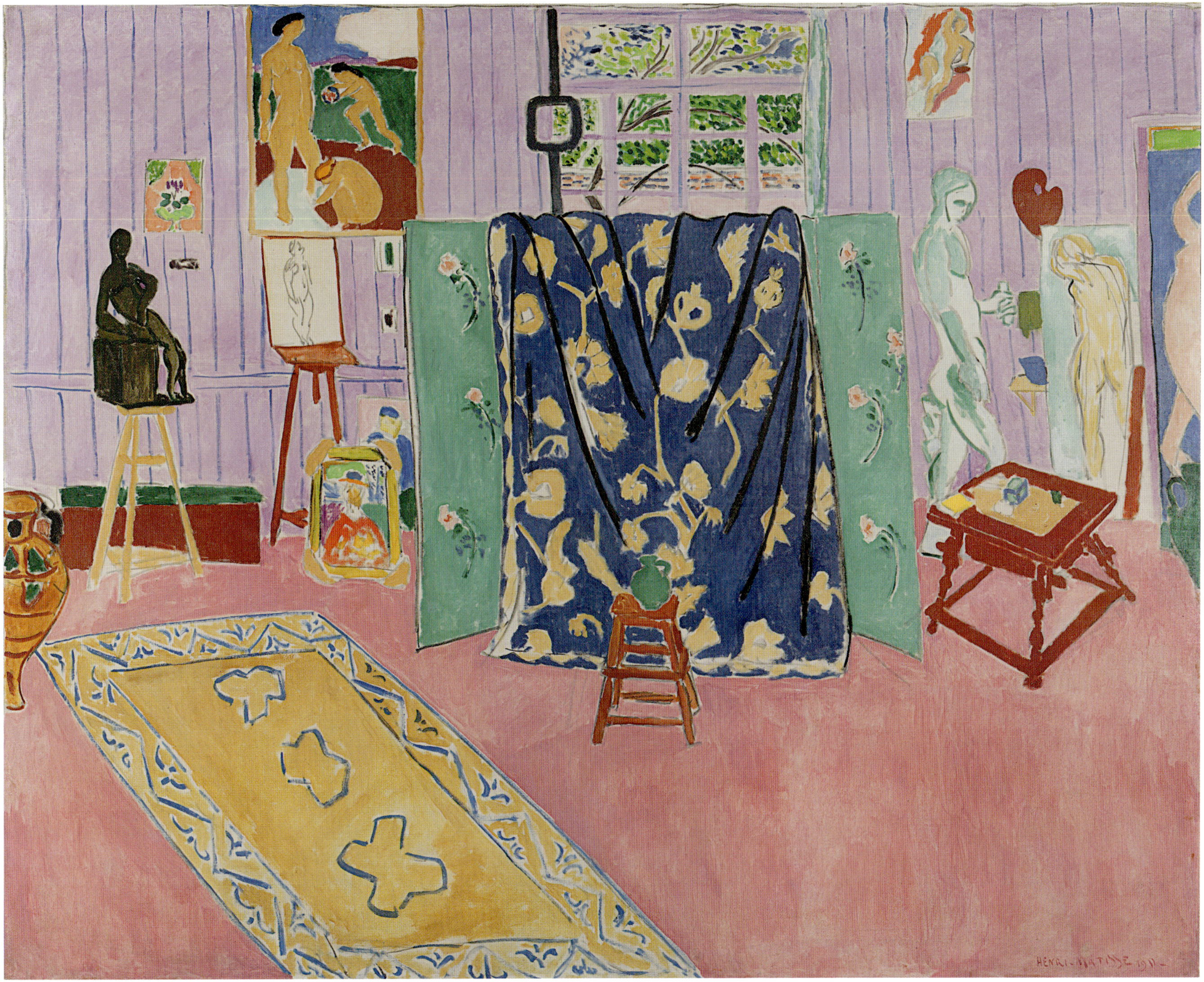

1911 THE PAINTER'S FAMILY

The State Hermitage Museum, St Petersburg
Oil on canvas | 143 × 194cm (56¼ × 76⅜in)

In spring 1911, soon after completing *The Pink Studio* (p. 73) Matisse painted this interior of the family quarters of his home in Issy-les-Moulineaux. As in that work, the composition is constructed around a central square in the centre – here the fireplace – with the head of his son Jean marking a central point. This group portrait is the domestic counterpart of the previous painting's inventory of recent artworks. To the upper left, the artist's wife Amélie, aged 39, seated on a couch, is sewing; their sons Pierre and Jean, aged 11 and 12, are playing checkers; standing in the foreground and holding an indeterminate yellow card is their daughter Marguerite, shortly to turn 17. The family members' facial features are undifferentiated, and there is little or no interaction between them; the boys regard the checkerboard, rather than each other. The brilliant red of their attire and the black of Marguerite's dress command the viewer's attention, whereas Amélie's ochre and yellow-patterned dress nearly becomes part of the background design; the white fabric that she clutches echoes Marguerite's collar and sleeves. Presiding over the group is a stand-in for the artist: his bronze sculpture *The Serf* (1900–04) is perched on the mantle.

By contrast with this taciturn group, the room's surface patterns – the bold designs of the Persian carpet, the miniature floral and geometric patterns on the two couches, the wallpaper, Amélie's dress, and even the mantelpiece and fireplace – interact with garrulous energy. As in *The Pink Studio*, the painting shows the influence of Persian miniatures, such as those Matisse had viewed at the Munich Islamic art exhibition of the previous year. The figures are arranged in a syncopated rhythm, as are the vases on the mantel, which are shown in contrasting scale. The painting has the effect of a variegated textile; the one exception is the checkerboard and its support, depicted in a three-dimensional perspective that only draws attention to the flatness of the rest of the composition. Like the carpet beneath it, the checkerboard is viewed from above, while remaining elements of the room, including family members, are seen at eye level.

The Painter's Family has intriguing visual parallels with a work of Cézanne's early 'dark' period, *Girl at the Piano (Overture to Tannhäuser)* (p. 15): a young woman in profile plays piano, while an older woman attends to sewing – they are the artist's sister and mother. Wall, floor, and an armchair in the foreground have contrasting patterns of arabesques, stripes and floral designs, rhythmically playing off against each other. Though shown at differing angles, the poses of Amélie Matisse and of Mme Cézanne – each seated on a coach, sewing – are nearly identical. Matisse had ample opportunity to see the Cézanne painting, both at the gallery of picture dealer Ambroise Vollard and at the Moscow home of collector Ivan Morosov.

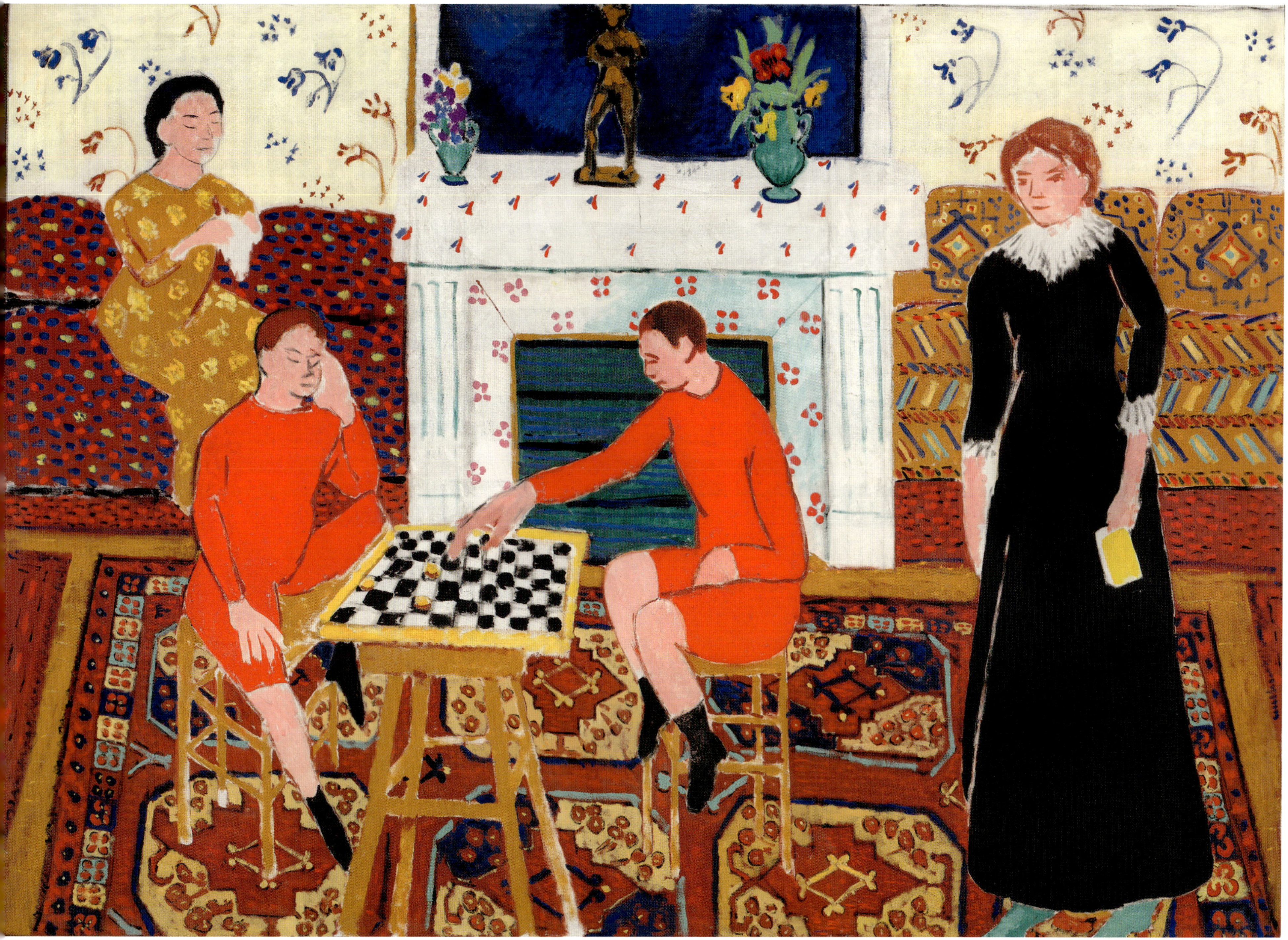

1911

INTERIOR WITH AUBERGINES

Musée de Grenoble
Distemper on canvas | 212 × 246cm (83½ × 97in)

Interior with Aubergines, painted in summer 1911, depicts Matisse's studio on the ground floor of the family's villa in Collioure. Unlike his two other studio interiors of the same year, *The Pink Studio* and *The Red Studio* (pp. 73 and 79), none of his own artworks is present. The only visible works of art are an *écorché* (flayed figure) on the table and an Art Deco statuette on the mantel in the upper left which mimics its pose. A series of rectangles dominates the composition: in the centre is a green screen decorated with light blue arabesques; glued to its right surface is a fragment of ochre wallpaper. Just above the screen is a doorway, including a grid-like hanging; on the upper wall to the left is an empty frame, and to the right is a window view with shapes and colours that echo the interior. The table and its objects – aubergines, *écorché*, fruit and vase set before the screen of contrapuntal floral and plant forms and resting on a red tablecloth with yellow arabesques – is a picture within a picture, as if it were a still life that the artist had arranged to paint. Indeed, such a still life exists, the sketch-like oil painting *Still Life with Aubergines* (1911, The Museum of Modern Art, New York).

The room, with the exception of the oblique mirror and fireplace, is parallel to the picture plane and nearly flat. A blue floral pattern, making virtually no concessions to foreshortening (two exceptions being the four petals on the lower left, just below the fireplace, and the two petals on the wall behind the screen), unifies the composition. So energetic are the floral and plant forms of the room – including the three aubergines which virtually dance on the table – that the Collioure countryside, as seen through the window on the right, seems inert by comparison. John Elderfield has suggested that in this work, Matisse was 'transposing the effect of landscape to an interior setting'.[46]

With its rectilinear segments and its choreography of patterns, this painting is the apotheosis of the influence of Persian miniatures on Matisse's work. Moreover, it anticipates the effects of Cubist collage, and of Synthetic Cubism – collage effects transposed into painting – which emerged the following year. Since Georges Braque visited Matisse in Collioure in summer 1911, and Picasso would soon view the painting at the home of Sarah and Michael Stein, it is likely that *Interior with Aubergines* had a direct influence on Synthetic Cubism.

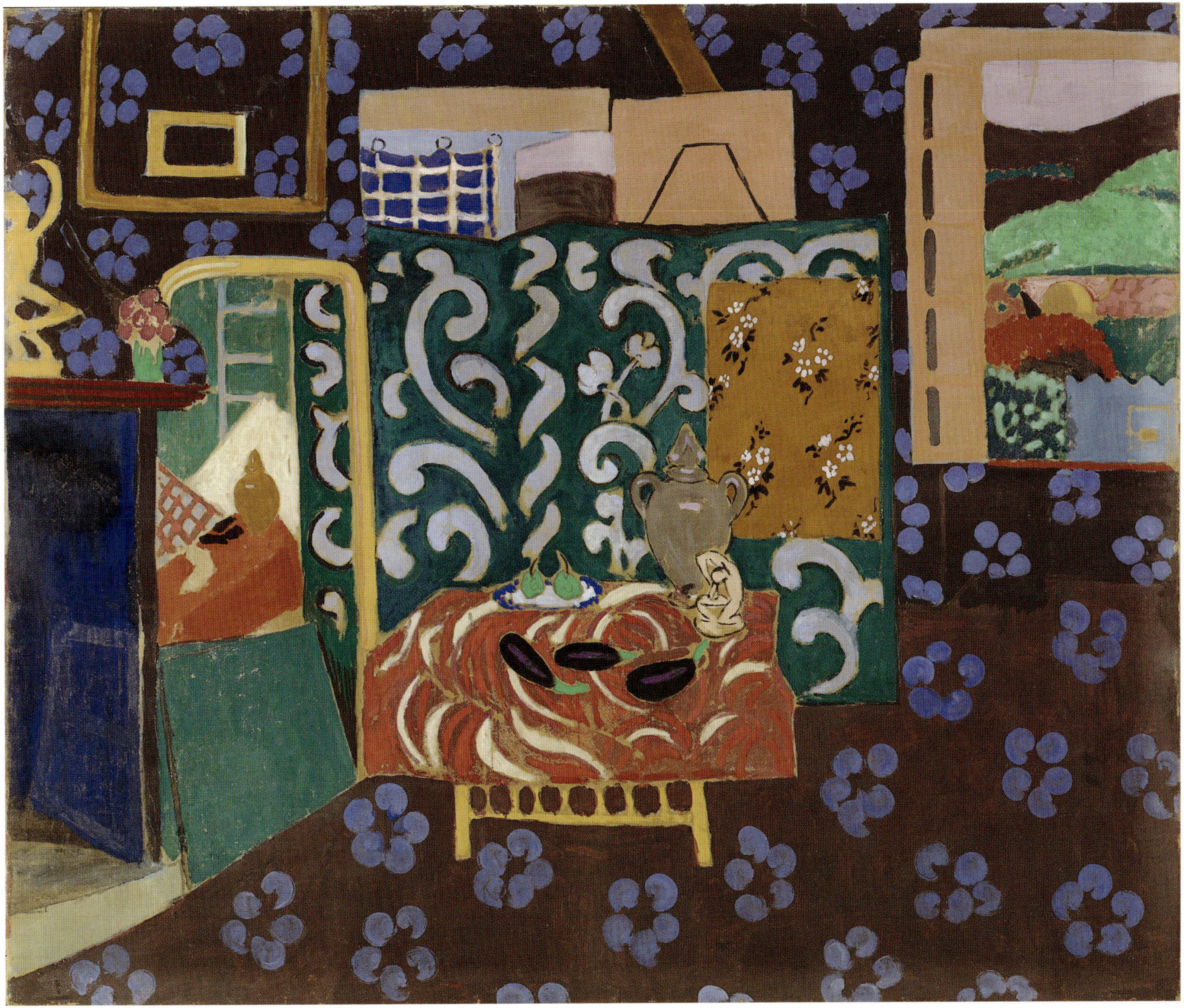

1911

THE RED STUDIO

The Museum of Modern Art, New York
Oil on canvas | 181 × 219cm (71¼ × 86¼in)

Like *The Pink Studio* (p. 73), *The Red Studio* depicts Matisse's studio in Issy-les-Moulineaux. The view shown is to the left of that presented in the earlier painting; in the upper right in *The Red Studio* are *Le Luxe II* (p. 59) and the bronze *Decorative Figure* (1908), works shown in the upper left in *The Pink Studio.* Despite this continuity of views, *The Red Studio* seems to belong to a different world, due to the field of deep red that encompasses the entire canvas. This world seems to be illuminated not by natural light, but by the artist's imagination.

Upon the red field, orthogonals of the walls and floor, and contours of less important objects, are drawn by means of fine lines formed by the absence of red pigment, in which the pale underpainting of the canvas shows through; as a consequence, objects are seen as if in silhouette. These less important objects comprise most of the furniture: a table and chair in the foreground, a chest of drawers and two sculpture stands by the rear wall. A hierarchy is established, in which significant objects are fully painted in; these objects include, but are not limited to, Matisse's own artworks. In both *The Pink Studio* and *Interior with Aubergines* (p. 77) a large rectangle played a prominent place in the centre of the composition; here, an understated grandfather clock plays this role. The clock is in silhouette except for its face, and significantly, it is without hands – suggesting that time has been frozen.

Like *The Pink Studio*, *The Red Studio* contains a partial inventory of Matisse's artistic production since 1906, but due to the subjective character of this work, it reads more emphatically as spiritual autobiography. These works include: *Large Nude* (1911, now destroyed), *Nude with White Scarf* (1909, Statens Museum for Kunst, Copenhagen), *Young Sailor II* (p. 49), *Purple Cyclamen* (1911–12, Private Collection), *Nymph and Satyr* (1909, The State Hermitage Museum, St Petersburg), and *Le Luxe II* (p. 59); on the sculpture stands are the *Decorative Figure* and *Jeannette IV* (1911). On the table in the foreground is a ceramic plate by the artist, which is paired with a second ceramic plate, on a table on the far right; also on the table, in semi-silhouette, is a small sculpture, *Upright Nude with Arched Back* (1904), which has a counterpart in a vase on the floor, also in semi-silhouette, to the upper right. A box of pencils, with two pencils ready for use, is set in the foreground; also prominently placed is a yellow reclining chair which faces *Large Nude* – indications of the making and contemplating of art. A pale blue window on the far left is opaque. The only living and growing thing in the room is the nasturtium plant, spilling out from its vase. *The Red Studio* is a laboratory of creation and growth, as much an emanation of the artist's mind as a place in the physical world.

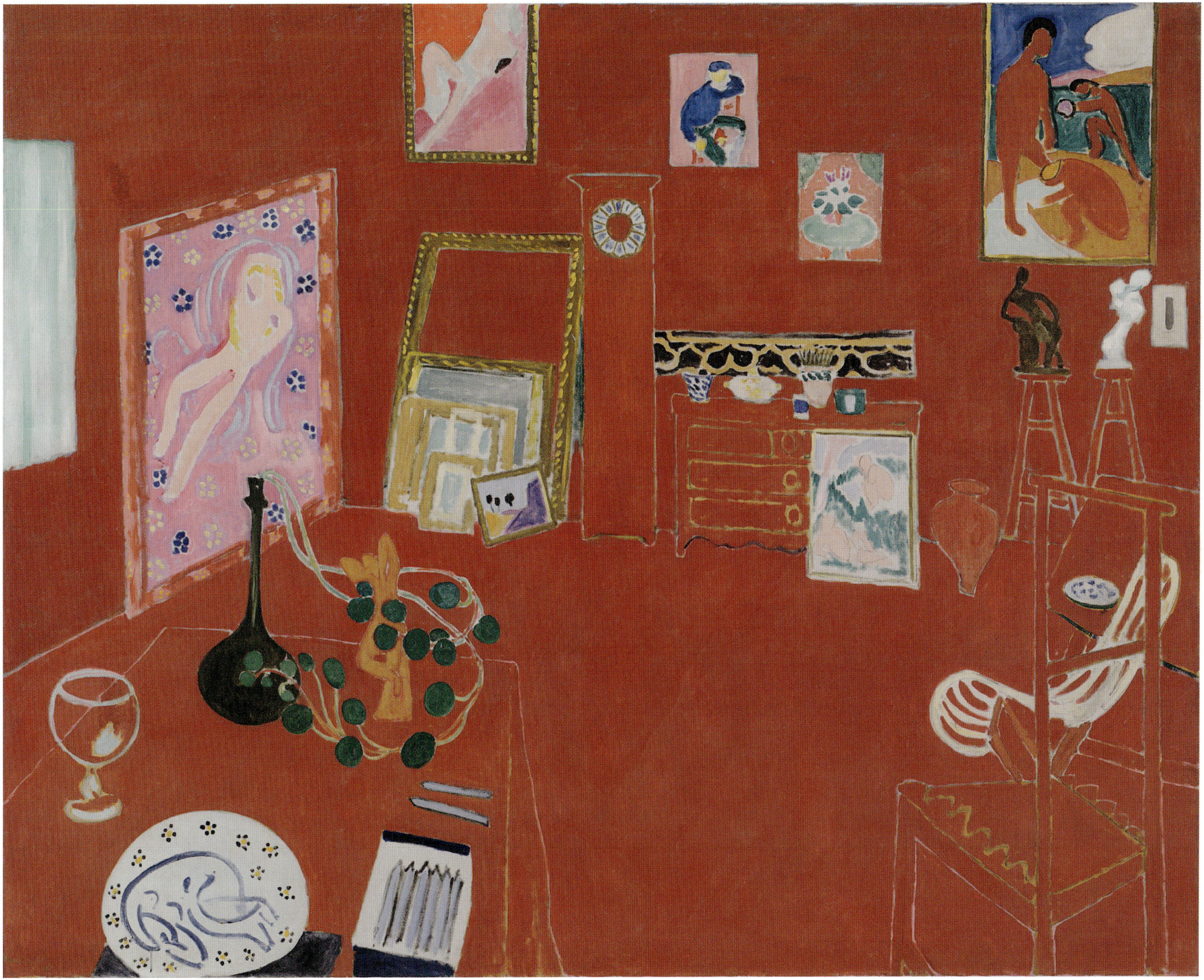

1912

GOLDFISH

The Pushkin State Museum of Fine Arts, Moscow
Oil on canvas | 140 × 98cm (55 × 38⅝in)

In the course of a two-month visit to Morocco in early 1912, Matisse saw bowls of goldfish being used as objects of contemplation. Upon his return to France, he installed in his studio a bowl of goldfish, which in ensuing years would make frequent appearances in his still lifes and interiors.

Goldfish was painted in the greenhouse of Matisse's garden at Issy. A cylindrical bowl containing four goldfish, resting on a circular table and adjacent to a wicker chair of which only a portion is visible, is seen from multiple points of view: the bowl and table legs are seen frontally, while the table top is viewed from above. Moreover, the fishbowl and tabletop are viewed in close-up, whereas the legs are seen as if from a distance.

The composition is a symphony of lines, shapes and complementary colours. The top of the bowl, the water line, the base of the bowl, the tabletop and the circular bracing of the legs make up five concentric circles (or ellipses). Four fish in brilliant red – Anglophones should bear in mind that 'goldfish' in French is *poisson rouge*, 'red fish' – which are seen a second time as reflections in the surface of the water, are surrounded by green and yellow plants whose colours are reflected in the fishbowl. The violet of the tabletop is echoed in the background to the upper left and in the crimson hues of the flowers, while the circular leaf forms to the upper left and lower right reflect the circular forms of the bowl and table. Finally, the shapes of the green wickerwork and of the leaves adjacent to the fishbowl are counterparts to the shapes of the red fish.

The four fish display a degree of motion that is rarely seen in a still life. They are looked at, and they look back at the viewer. Matisse, who was red-headed and red-bearded and who viewed the world through thick eyeglasses, identified with the *poissons rouges*, and used them as stand-ins for himself in his paintings. His friend, the painter Jean Puy, later compared him to a 'goldfish who intensely exults in the iridescence of colors and forms through the dematerializing globe of his bowl.'[47]

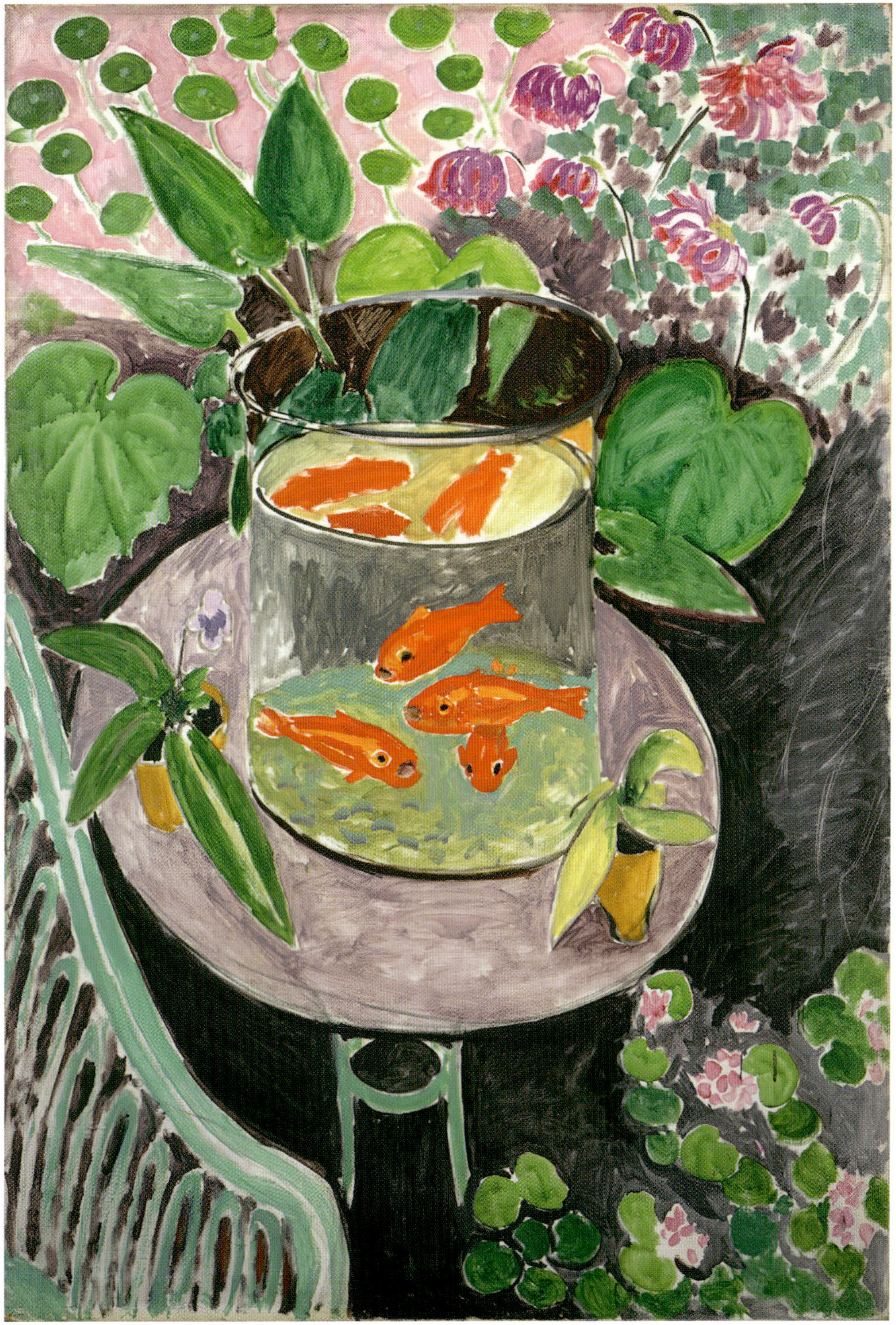

1912 GOLDFISH AND SCULPTURE

The Museum of Modern Art, New York
Oil on canvas | 116.2 x 100.5cm (46 x 39⅝in)

Matisse's painting *Goldfish and Sculpture* is a light-filled interior with a monumental still-life arrangement in the foreground. The still life comprises a cylindrical bowl containing three goldfish, a ceramic plate and vase with flowers, and a terracotta sculpture, the artist's *Reclining Nude I* (1907). Above them in the background, a yellow ochre door opens to reveal a garden view divided by a diagonal shadow that echoes the sea-green colour of the fishbowl and vase. On the right in the background are a table and shelf, trappings of the mundane world of the studio.

Compositional devices employed in *The Red Studio* (p. 79) appear again here: the ground is painted in a single colour, in this case, a translucent celestial blue which allows the white of the canvas to show through, imbuing the painting with a watercolour quality. In addition, forms are described with outlines, made by either the white of the canvas or by thin lines of black paint. Finally, as in *The Red Studio*, the forms are drawn with foreshortening, implying a three-dimensionality that is contradicted by their absence of modelling.

Each of the three foreground figures, in differing ways, combines features of the animate and the inanimate. The ambiguous life-form of the reclining figure – is she woman or statue? – is emphasized by the terracotta colour, which is close to flesh tones. The flowers in the vase seem to crown her coiffure like a wreath, evoking the Arcadian realm of *Le Bonheur de vivre* (p. 53), where she first appeared. The goldfish have been deputized as the conscious presence of the artist. Unlike the woman, they have visible eyes; while one fish regards the spectator, the other two regard her. The interaction of these three foreground figures is a demonstration of the power of art to transform the mundane into the cosmic.

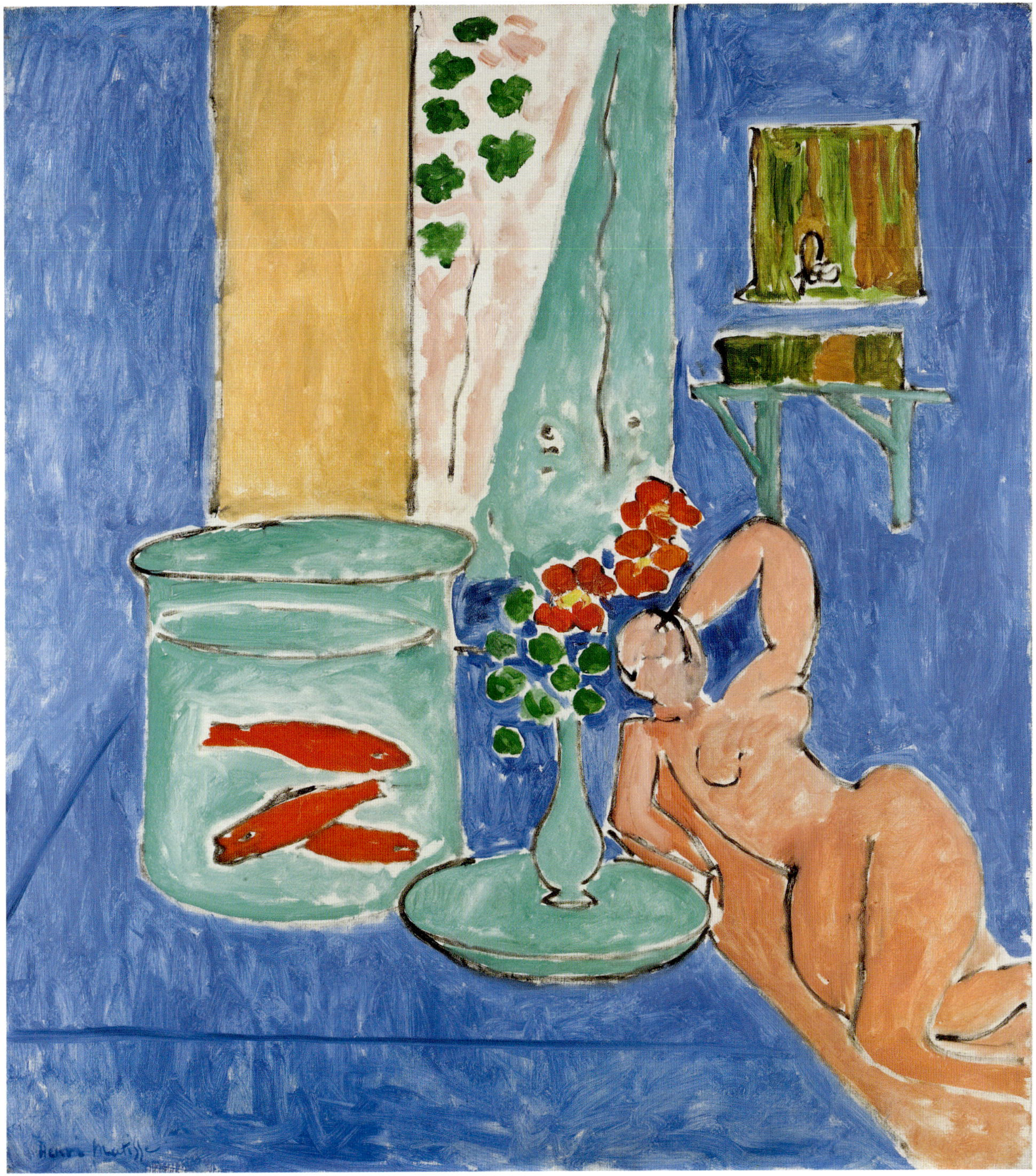

1908–12 THE CONVERSATION

The State Hermitage Museum, St Petersburg
Oil on canvas | 177 × 217cm (69⅝ × 85⅜in)

The Conversation, like *Harmony in Red* (p. 63), is an interior dominated by a single colour featuring a domestic scene juxtaposed with a picture window. The window, in the centre, presents the view from the living room of the Matisses' house in Issy-les-Moulineaux, a suburb of Paris, to which the family had moved in autumn 1909. The window reveals a tree, lawn, flowerbeds, and, at the top, a segment of the exterior of Matisse's studio, bathed in pink morning light.

Facing each other, in profile, are the standing figure of the artist and the seated figure of his wife Amélie, he in white-striped light-blue pyjamas, she in a black bathrobe with a shawl collar that echoes the green of the lawn and foliage. The title *Conversation* seems to be ironic: as their eyes meet, they appear to stare at each other in silence.

Pictorial depth is minimized; absent are the orthogonal lines of Renaissance perspective. The blue ground of the interior dominates the composition; it is echoed by the blue of the exterior flower beds and studio building. The blue of Amélie Matisse's chair flattens it and adheres it to the picture plane. The positioning of the two figures was altered while the work was in progress, and the artist has allowed not all pentimenti to show through.

The painting is a study of contrasts: the straight lines of the man and the curves of the woman; the cool blues and black of the room and the warm reds, brown and green of the garden; the stillness of the man and woman and the dynamism of the flowerbeds. The window railing, composed of contrasting curved and parallel lines, spells out the word '*NON*' ('no'), reading in both directions, reinforcing the standoff of the two figures.

As Matisse scholar Jack Flam has observed, *The Conversation* has a prototype: *The Stele of Hammurabi* (p. 16) from ancient Mesopotamia, which Matisse had seen at the Louvre.[48] Hammurabi, King of Babylon and author of the law code carved in cuneiform below, stands before the seated Shamash, the sun god whose shoulders erupt in flames. By analogy, it would appear that Amélie is posed to issue orders; Henri, however, is not compliant: hands in pockets, he faces her down.

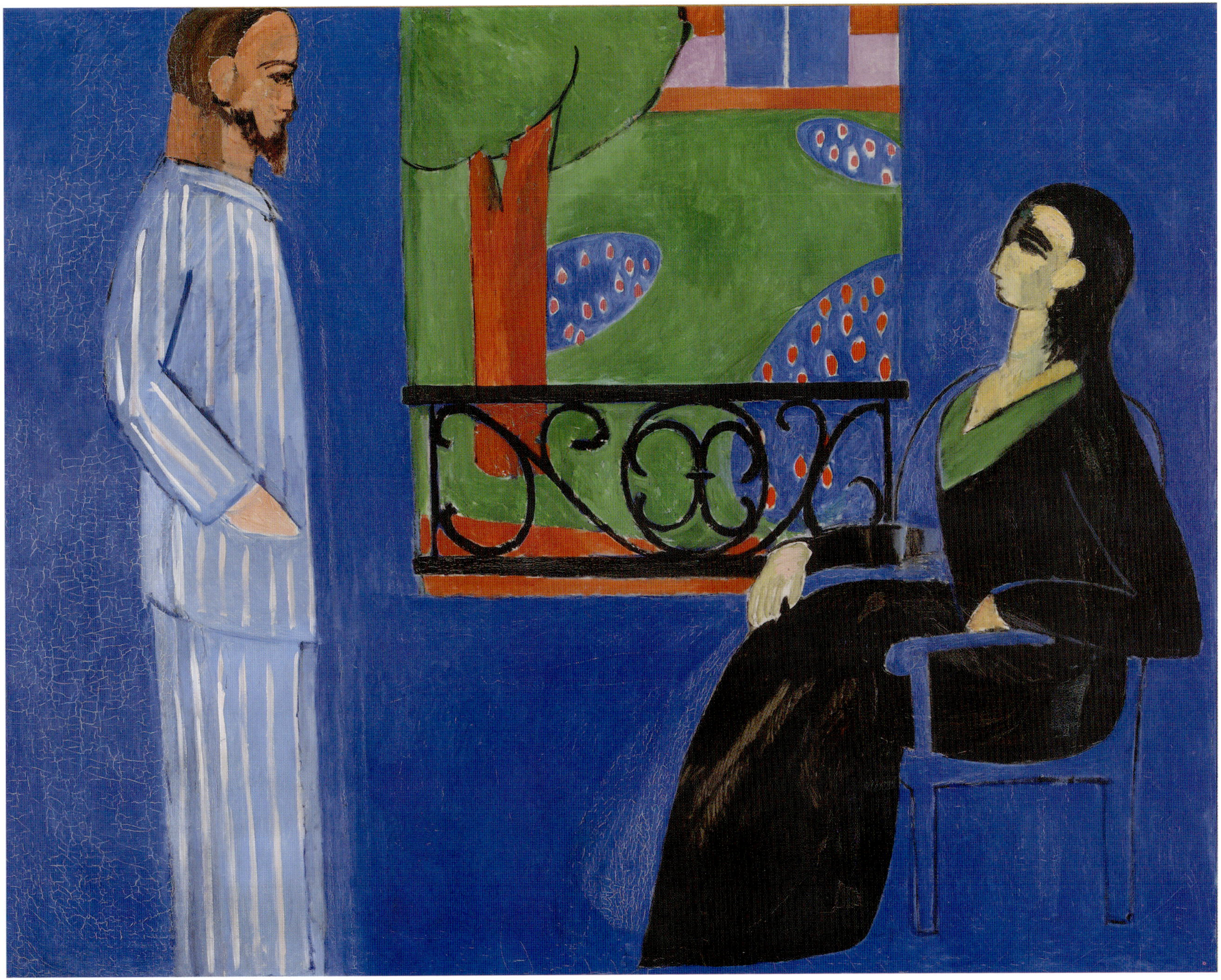

1912

SEATED RIFFIAN

Barnes Foundation, Philadelphia
Oil on canvas | 200.3 × 160.7cm (78⅞ × 63¼in)

In November 1912 Matisse wrote from Morocco to his daughter Marguerite that he had begun 'a portrait of a Riffian, a type of mountain dweller, magnificent and wild as a jackal.'[49] This portrait, *Standing Riffian* (1912, The State Hermitage Museum, St Petersburg) was the first and smaller of two paintings of this model. *Seated Riffian* is, perhaps appropriately, over life-size; as Alfred Barr has noted, 'if the figure stood up he would be over ten feet high.'[50] The Riffians, members of the Berber ethnic group and named after the Rif mountains in Morocco, are inhabitants of northern Africa and southern Spain. A travel writer of the era described their reputation as 'fierce-looking dwellers of the mountains' noted for 'their pride of bearing and by their imperious tones and gestures, as well as by their distinctive dress…The Rifs are eternal rebels, they bow to no authority, and are restrained by no laws.'[51]

The Riffian is seated as if enthroned as a ruler. His face and torso are frontal, while his lower limbs are turned at a 45-degree angle from the viewer, projecting casual self-assurance, notwithstanding his imperial pose. He occupies a well-defined space, supported by a simple ochre block, before an orange and green curtain set against a yellow wall; behind him, to the upper left, is a window revealing a blue sky but no other signs of nature. The luminous magenta of the floor is intensified by its juxtaposition with the green complementaries of the curtain stripes and of the Riffian's shirt and cloak. Beneath his body is an ochre block, the colour reappearing in the strap across his chest and of his cap. The brilliantly coloured jewels on his cloak are a shimmering counterpoint to the overall stability of the composition.

The painting as a whole is rendered in a flat, decorative style. The exception is the Riffian's face, with its bold patches of green and ochre, which evoke the background and his attire, a return to a technique first seen in *Woman with a Hat* (p. 45). It is as if Matisse has summoned up his Fauve style to convey the fierce reputation of his subject.

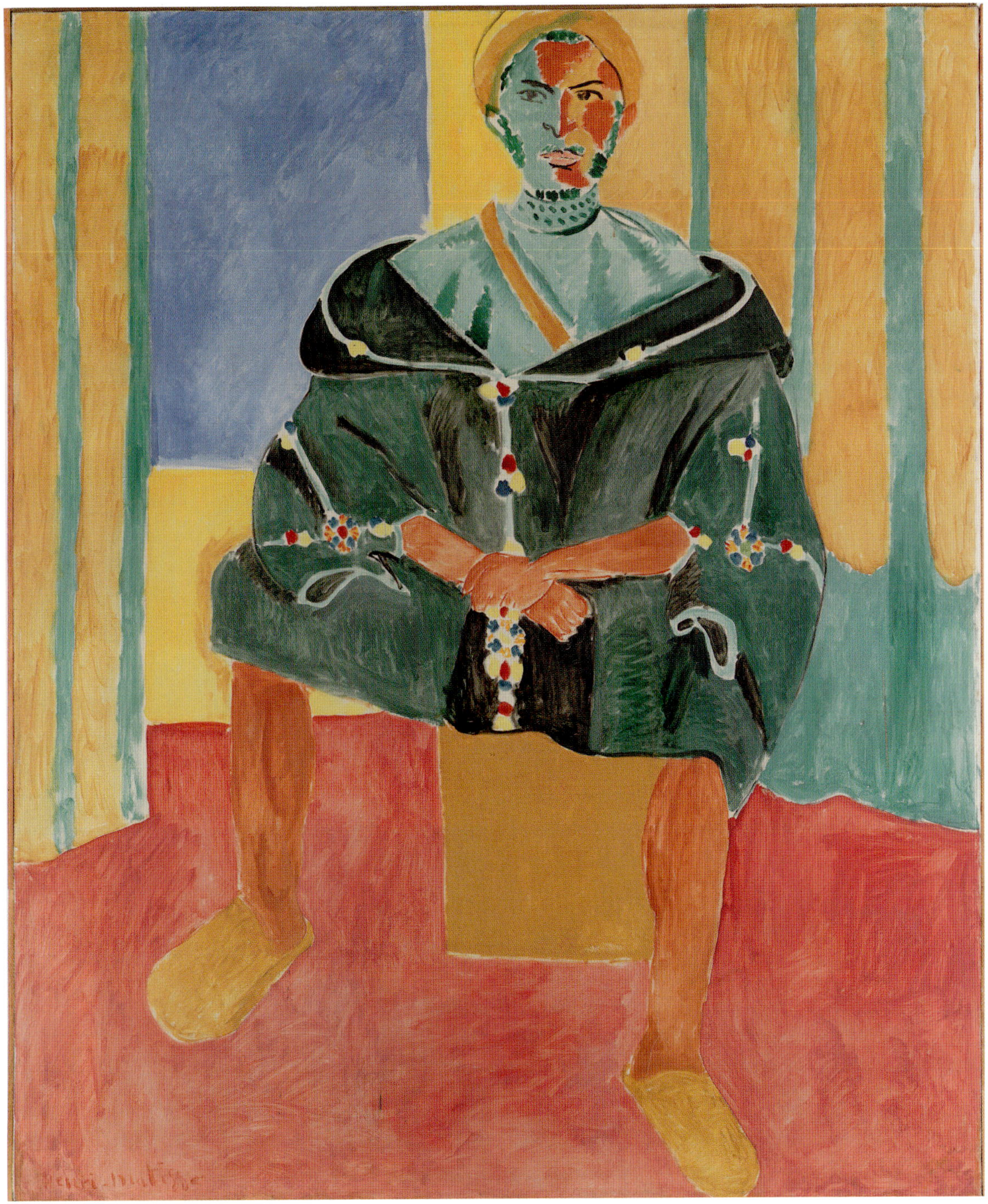

1912–13 ENTRANCE TO THE CASBAH

The Pushkin State Museum of Fine Arts, Moscow
Oil on canvas | 116 × 80cm (45⅝ × 31½in)

Matisse made two visits to Tangier, Morocco, from January to April 1912 and from October 1912 to February 1913. Inspired by the intensity of the sunlight, the lushness of the vegetation, the severity of the architecture, and the exotic dress and appearance of the populace, he completed 23 paintings during his sojourns there. Upon his return, an exhibition of the Moroccan paintings was held at the Bernheim-Jeune Gallery, Paris. On 19 April, the last day of the exhibition, he sent a letter on which he included an ink sketch to the Russian collector Ivan Morosov: 'The three paintings in question … should be hung together in a particular order – that is, that the view from the window should be on the left, the Casbah gate on the right, and the terrace in the middle, as the sketch indicates.'[51] In addition to *Entrance to the Casbah,* the three (now known as *The Moroccan Triptych*) include *Landscape Viewed from a Window* and *On the Terrace* (both 1912–13, The Pushkin State Museum of Fine Arts, Moscow).

Entrance to the Casbah depicts a lookout gate that cuts through the wall of the Casbah, the oldest and highest part of the city, where the sultan maintained a fortified palace. The gate is a passageway from the citadel to the rest of old Tangier. The viewer is placed just inside the Casbah, looking out at the old city, and beyond it to the European quarter (where Matisse temporarily resided). Thus the gate performs a role comparable to that of a window that links an interior to a view of a landscape.

The pictorial field is divided into geometric shapes, dominated by the horseshoe arch, a characteristic of Islamic architecture. The colour combinations generate a vivid luminosity. Light is evoked by the juxtaposition of the predominant blue and the white stucco (which is permeated by the blue ground behind it); the stucco colour is repeated in the patch of sky seen through the gate, and again by the pinkish-white disk on the floor and by segments of this white on the walls. Yet more potent is the magenta light of the floor and its complementary, the bright green inside the doorway. In this work, sunlight and architecture are dominant. The transparent, spectral seated figure at the gate blends into the wall, barely registering a presence.

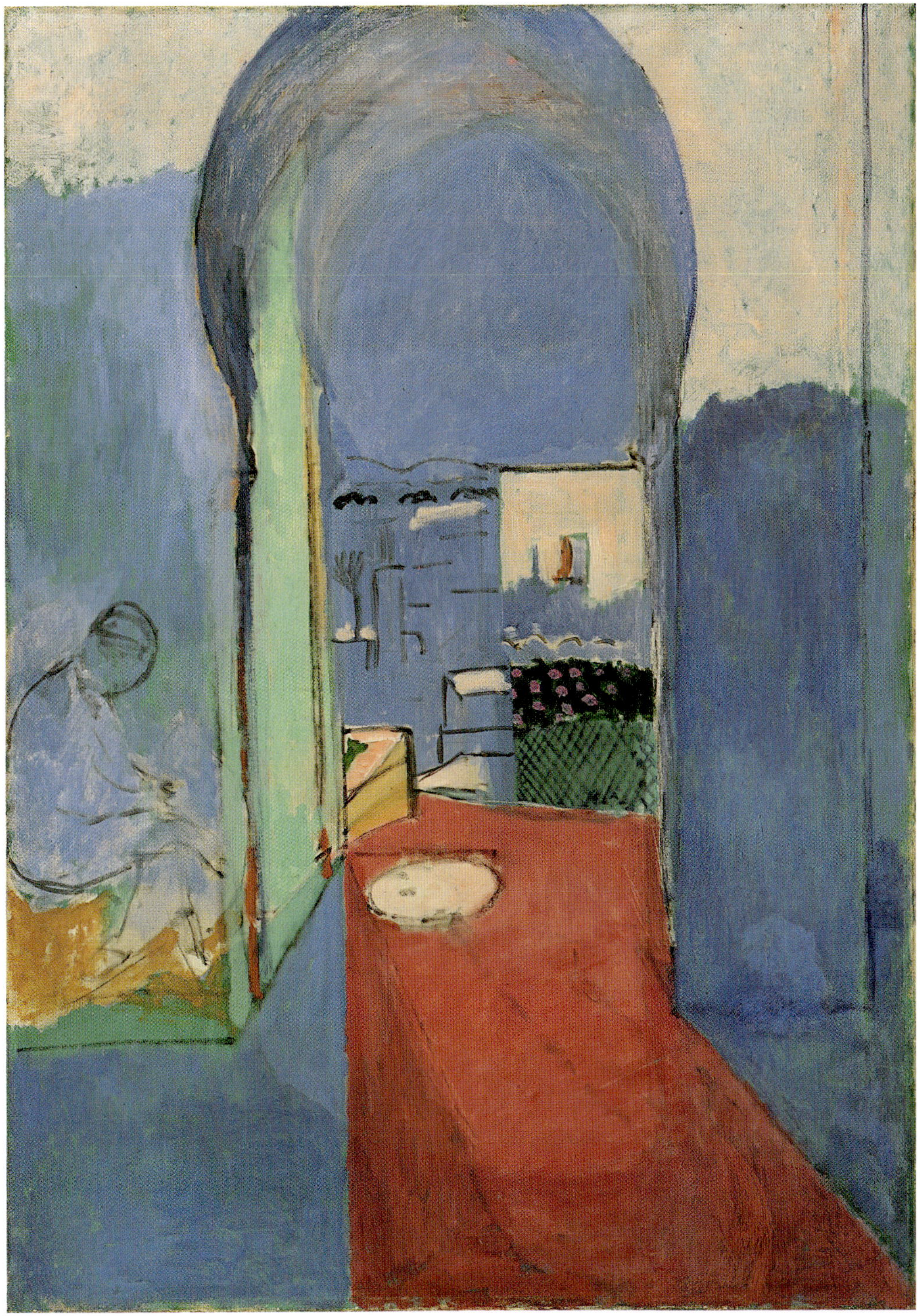

1913

PORTRAIT OF MADAME MATISSE

The State Hermitage Museum, St Petersburg
Oil on canvas | 146 × 97.7cm (57⅞ × 36¼in)

Matisse spent the summer of 1913 at his home in Issy, where he produced relatively few works, due to his preoccupation with a single painting: this portrait of his wife Amélie, which he laboured over for more than a hundred sittings. Evidence of multiple reworkings is visible on the surface of the canvas, where paint has been scraped and reapplied, and where alterations in the position and scale of the figure and chair are visible. The portrait began as a naturalistic work and evolved into a more abstract rendering. The figure expanded in scale as it grew more abstract.

This painting is a response by Matisse to the challenge of Cubism. With its linearity, fragmentation of form, shallow relief space and colouristic restraint, it reveals the influence of Picasso and Braque, c.1911, and it shares the verticality of Cubist portraits of that period. Amélie is depicted in subdued tonalities of blue, green and black, seated on a blue chair that repeats the blue of her blouse, against a flat, textured blue background. The exception is the radiant complementary orange scarf that drapes her arms and shoulder.

Amélie, elegantly attired, sits gracefully in the chair, her legs crossed, her head tilted. Yet her facial expression is unreadable. Her eyeballs have been blacked out and her face is mask-like; she seems a spectral presence. The mask that Matisse chose to replace his wife's facial features resembles the Fang mask from Gabon, Central Africa, that once belonged to Matisse's Fauve colleagues, Vlaminck and then Derain (p. 19). Amélie was delighted when the painting was in its early stages and it bore a close resemblance to her, yet she is said to have wept when she saw the final result.[52] Indeed, it is hard not to read this painting, like *The Conversation* (p. 85), as an indication of strains in their marriage.

The portrait was Matisse's sole entry in the Salon d'Automne of 1913. It was glowingly reviewed by the poet and critic Guillaume Apollinaire, the champion of Cubism whose book *The Cubist Painters* had appeared in March. Apollinaire claimed that it 'would seem to inaugurate a new stage in Matisse's art' and declared, 'If there is a masterpiece on view at the Salon d'Automne, it is this and nothing else.'[53]

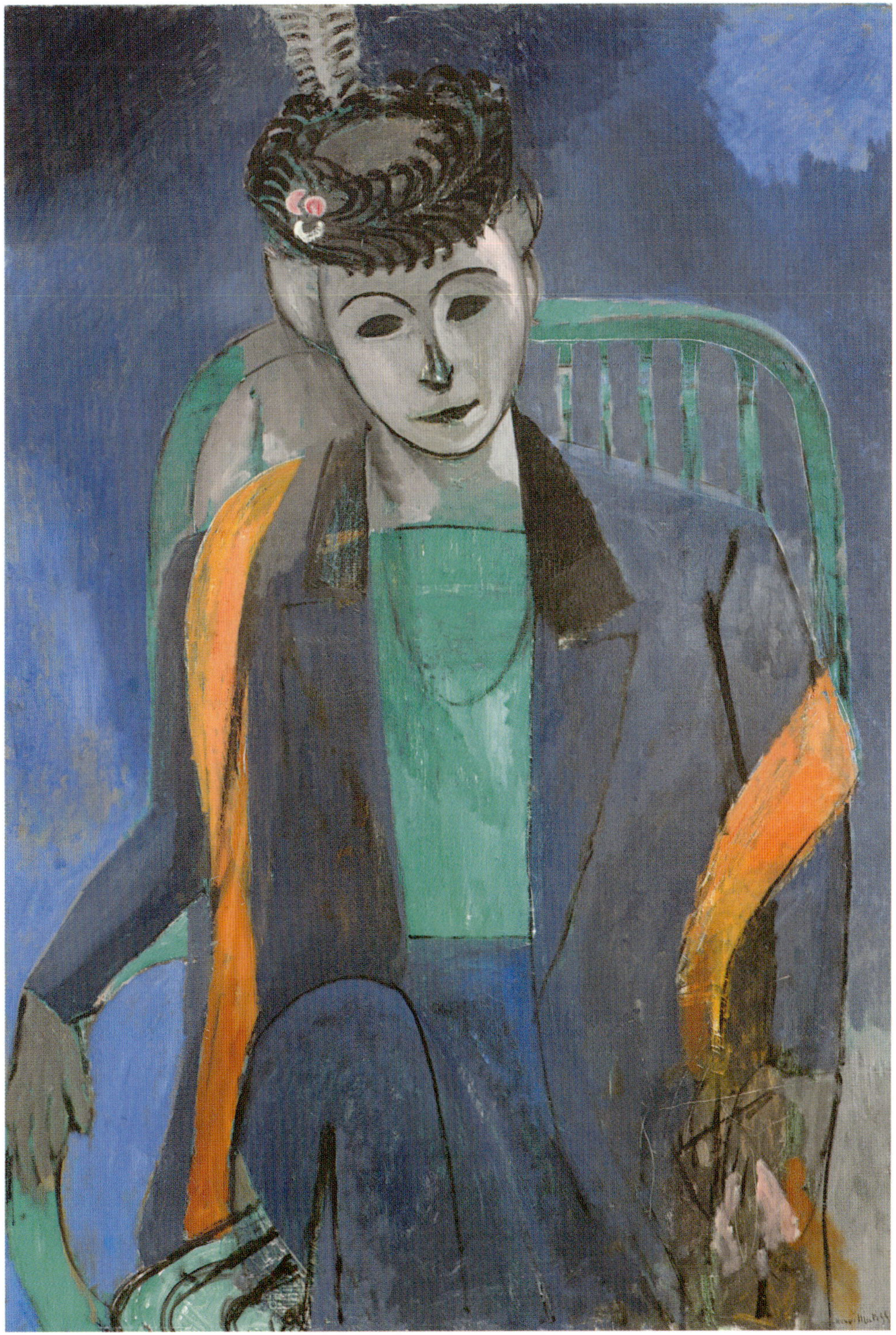

1914 VIEW OF NOTRE-DAME

The Museum of Modern Art, New York
Oil on canvas | 147.3 × 94.3cm (58 × 37⅛ in)

In spring 1914 Matisse painted two versions of the view of Notre-Dame Cathedral from the window of his studio on quai Saint-Michel. The first version was in a sketchy, descriptive style, with the transparency of a watercolour (p. 21). The second was austere, geometric, and nearly abstract, on a field of pale blue. In 1908 Matisse had explained to the interviewer Charles Caffin the process of simplification by which he would transform 'what exists' into an image that is '*organisé*'.[54] This process is made visible, not only in the pairing of the two versions of *View of Notre-Dame*, but within the second version itself. As John Elderfield has observed, pentimenti beneath the blue field indicate that the painting was originally closer in appearance to the view from Matisse's window.[55] Buildings and the far quai of the Seine to the left have been deleted, and the cathedral has been enlarged and moved higher in the painting.

View of Notre-Dame is closer to pure abstraction than any of Matisse's previous paintings. The banks of the Seine and the Petit Pont that spans it are indicated by a few horizontal, vertical and diagonal lines, and by one arcing curve, in black. The foliage is distilled to one oval green patch, which seems to cast a shadow, in the lower right of the cathedral. The Petit Pont is schematically indicated in the centre by two horizontals, an arc and a vertical. There is no indication of the bank of the Île de la Cité, as the needs of the composition led the artist to carry the longer, main diagonal of the picture from the patch of green along a path that actually falls in the middle of the river. The rectangle that frames the composition corresponds to the studio window, while the space of the view presented is compressed into one plane. The painting is vigorously brushed, its surface enlivened by bold scumbling and its drawing dominated by powerful black architectonic lines. The tops of the towers and the left of the façade have been shaded by scratching the wet paint with the wooden end of the brush, a device that would be employed later that same year for the Futurist force lines of *Portrait of Yvonne Landsberg* (p. 95).

Like Matisse's cut-outs, created four decades later (*Memory of Oceania*, *The Swimming Pool* and *The Snail,* pp. 129, 131–3, and 135), *View of Notre-Dame* influenced abstract painters of the 1960s. It was not exhibited publicly until its appearance in Matisse's first posthumous retrospective, held in Los Angeles in 1966, where it would serve as an inspiration for such artists as Richard Diebenkorn and Robert Motherwell.

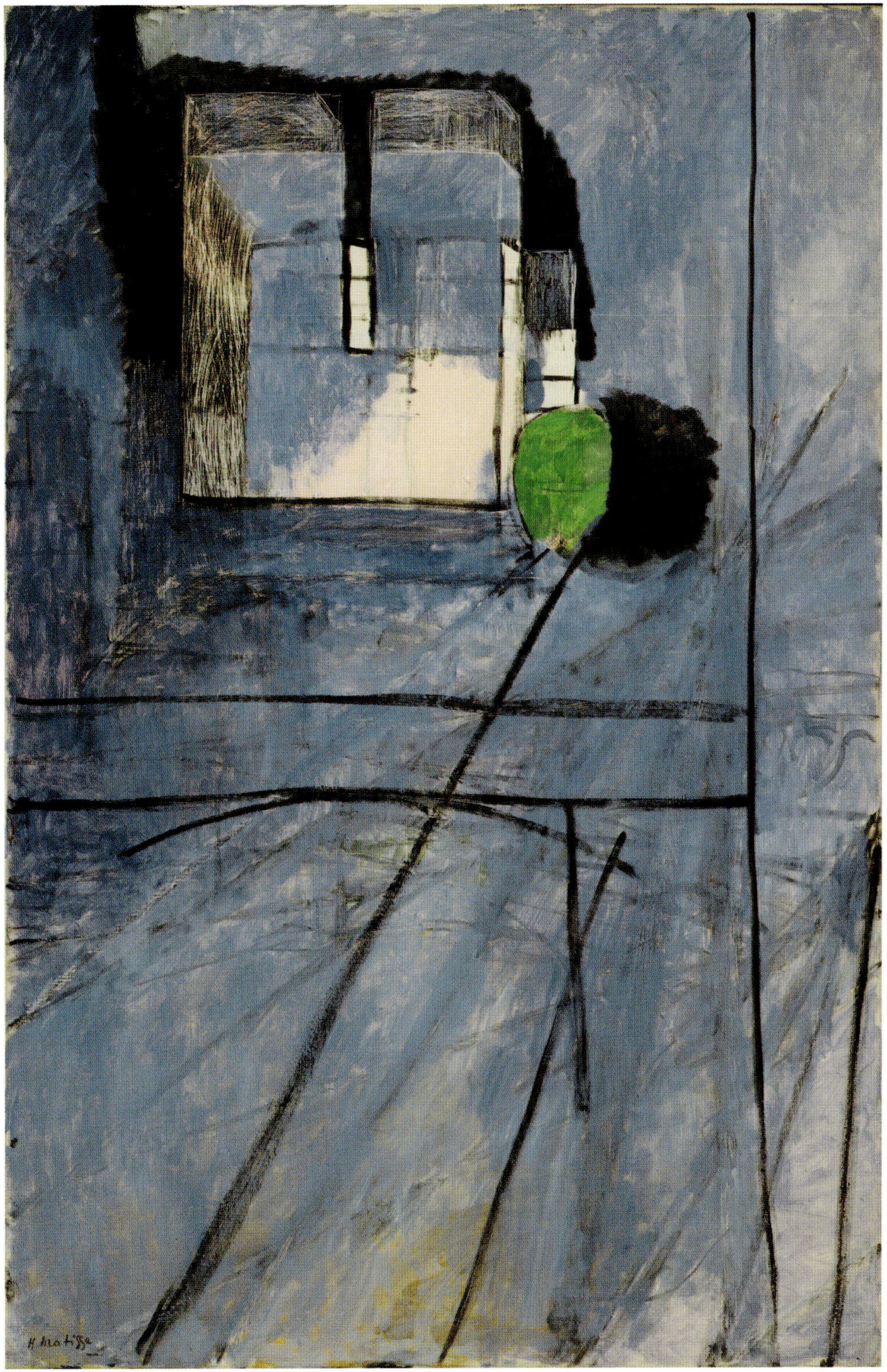

1914

PORTRAIT OF YVONNE LANDSBERG

Philadelphia Museum of Art
Oil on canvas | 147.3 × 97.5cm (58 × 38⅜in)

In spring 1914, the Landsberg family, wealthy Brazilians living in Paris, commissioned Matisse to do a portrait drawing of their daughter Yvonne, a beautiful but shy and ungainly young woman, aged 19. The family were pleased with the result, and Matisse, intrigued with his subject, proposed that he do an oil portrait, with the understanding that the family would not be obliged to purchase the final work.

In the course of the posing sessions – all of which were chaperoned by Yvonne's older brother Albert 'Bertie' Landsberg, an aesthete on the periphery of Matisse's circle – the painting grew increasingly abstract. 'At each sitting,' Bertie later recalled, 'the painting became *less* physically but – possibly – *more* spiritually like my sister.'[56] To a greater degree than the artist's portrait of his wife of the previous year (p. 91), which followed a similar protocol of increasing abstraction with multiple sittings (and with which it shared a mask-like countenance), the Landsberg portrait reveals the influence of Picasso's Analytic Cubism. The linear, textured figure is seated in a shallow relief space against an abstract ground. Paint is thinly applied and then scraped away, in nearly monochrome greys, blues and black, with a tiny blush of red in the face. Force lines, which were scraped into the canvas at the final posing session, reverberate from the curves of Yvonne's shoulders. These force lines, which emanate from her but of which she is unaware, resemble hearts or blooming flowers; they seem to signify her emerging sexuality. This device is similar to those employed by the Italian Futurists, many of whom were represented by Matisse's own Bernheim-Jeune Gallery in Paris.

The Landsbergs declined to purchase the radically abstract portrait. By August, Europe was at war, and it was not to be a propitious time for the European art market. The portrait would be among the fourteen paintings included in Matisse's comprehensive solo exhibition at the Montross Gallery, New York, which opened in January 1915. A year after the close of the exhibition, in March 1916, it was bought by the American collector Walter Conrad Arensberg. Although it would be his sole painting by Matisse, it would be a keystone of his collection. Arensberg, a friend and patron of Marcel Duchamp, purchased the Landsberg portrait in part to compensate for his failure to acquire Duchamp's *Nude Descending a Staircase* (p. 17) at the time of the Armory Show of 1913 (he would buy it later, in 1919). The two paintings are similar in size and format, and share a dynamic vitality that marks the influence of Futurism.

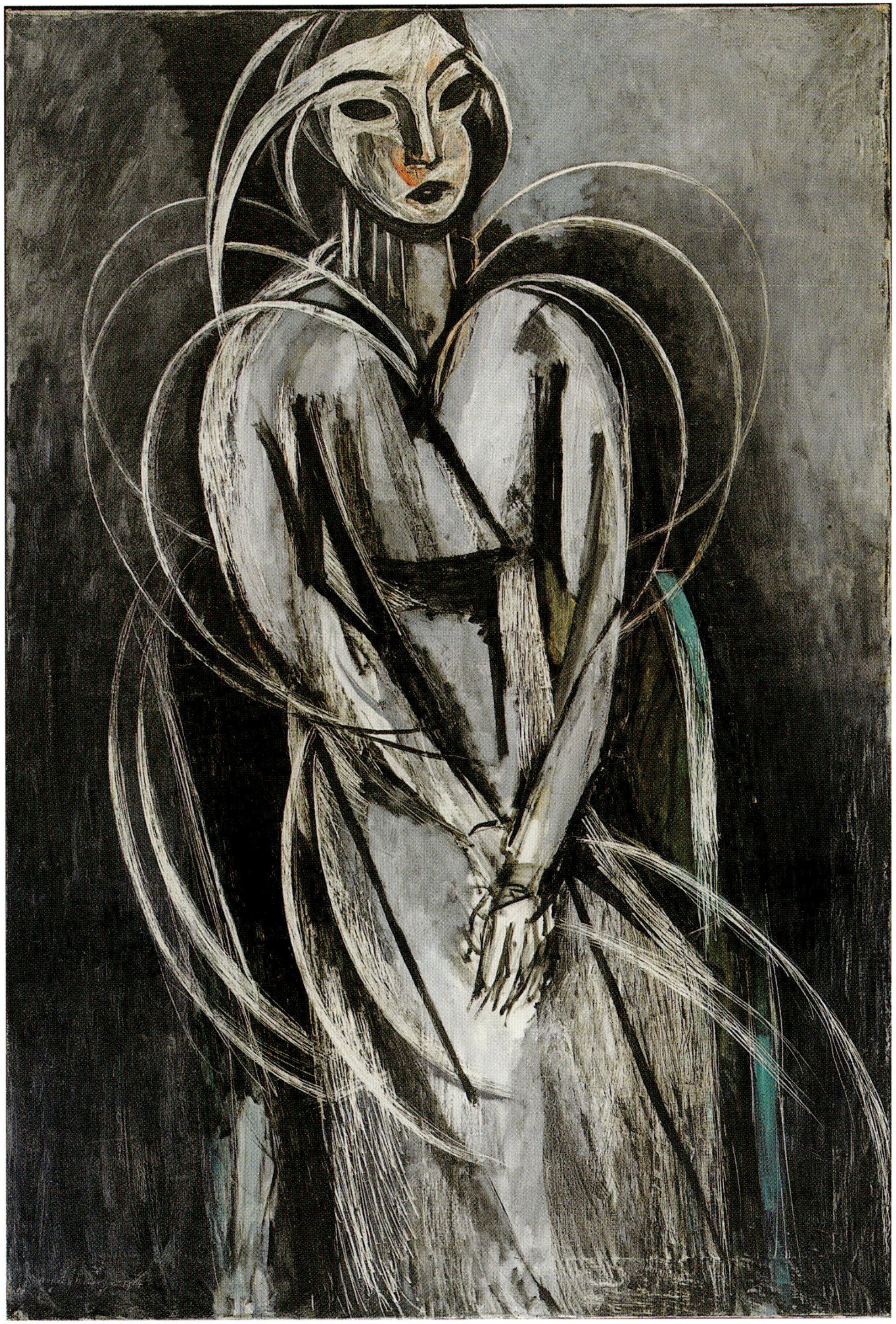

1914 FRENCH WINDOW AT COLLIOURE

Centre Pompidou, Paris
Oil on canvas | 116.5 × 89cm (45⅞ × 35in)

September to October 1914, when *French Window at Collioure* was painted, was a time of anxiety for Henri Matisse. War had broken out in August, and his mother and brother, who lived in the north of France on the Belgian frontier, were behind enemy lines. His house in Issy had been temporarily requisitioned by the French army. Many of his friends and colleagues were now in the armed services; he had tried to enlist, but at the age of 44, he had been rejected as he was too old. He was joined in Collioure by Albert Marquet, his old friend from their days in Moreau's studio, and by the Cubist painter Juan Gris. Matisse was grappling with Cubism, and he and Gris were having spirited aesthetic discussions. 'We argue so heatedly about painting that Marquet can hardly sit still for boredom,' Gris wrote to his dealer, Daniel-Henry Kahnweiler.[57]

French Window at Collioure is unusual in Matisse's oeuvre, not just in its near-abstraction, but in the sombre mood that it conveys. (A 'French window' – in French, *porte-fenêtre*, a window which is also a door – is one which rises from floor level.) The painting consists of four vertical bands of blue, black, grey and green, and one horizontal band of dark grey. The blue band on the left, with four horizontal lines which suggest windowpanes, represents a fully open panel, while the grey panel on the right is partially open; the adjacent green band represents a wall. The centre – the largest section of the painting – is a void. The work makes a striking contrast with the joyous sunlit Fauve painting *Open Window, Collioure* of 1905 (p. 43). Applying Matisse's own dictum of the function of a window – 'a passageway between the exterior and the interior' – the painting suggests a future that was a perilous unknown.

Like *View of Notre-Dame* (p. 93), Matisse's previous venture into near abstraction painted the same year, *French Window at Collioure* was exhibited for the first time at his 1966 retrospective, which opened in Los Angeles and subsequently travelled to Chicago and Boston. Reviewing the exhibition for *Artforum*, Nancy Marmer lauded Matisse for his relevance to the hard-edge and Colour Field painters of the 1960s, citing *French Window at Collioure* as 'a striking anticipation of [Barnett] Newman done in 1914'.[58]

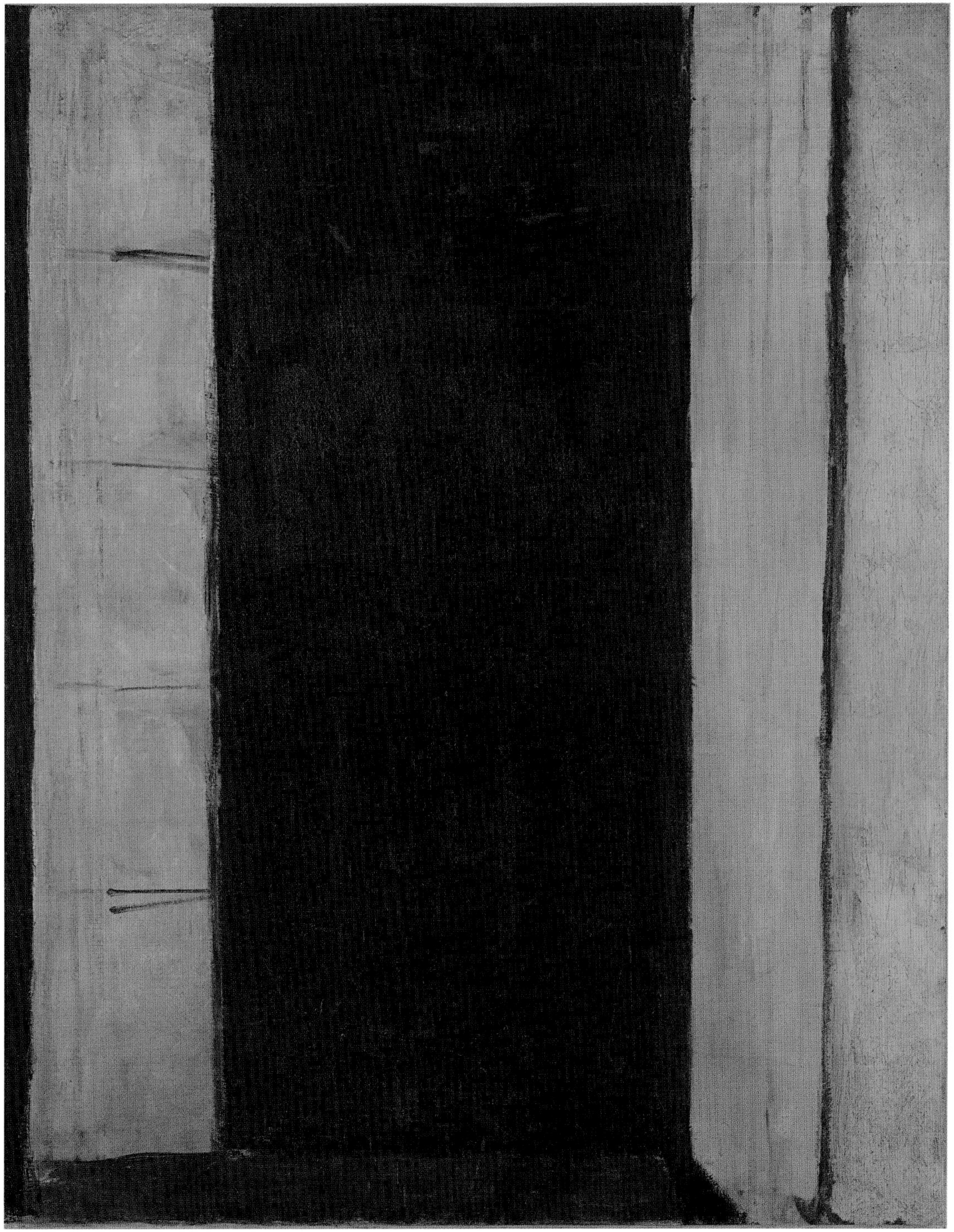

1914–15 GOLDFISH AND PALETTE

The Museum of Modern Art, New York
Oil on canvas | 146.5 × 112.4cm (57¾ × 44¼in)

'I've done a picture,' Matisse wrote to his friend Charles Camoin in December 1914. 'It's my goldfish picture, which I am redoing with a figure holding a palette and studying (harmony brown-red).'[59] The note is written on a postcard of Albrecht Dürer's engraving *St Jerome at His Study* (1514), which features the saint at his desk, intensely focused on his work; a halo of light frames his head, and to the left are windows separated by the vertical band of a shadowed wall. The note includes Matisse's sketch of a seated man in three-quarter profile, studying a bowl of goldfish on the table before him.

The 'goldfish picture' which Matisse informed Camoin he was redoing was *Interior with Goldfish* (1914, Centre Pompidou, Paris), a realistic view of the interior of his Paris studio, with a bowl of goldfish on a table in front of a window; there is no human figure in the painting.

It is evident from the surface of *Goldfish and Palette* that by the time the painting was completed in spring 1915, it had undergone considerable reworking. The 'figure holding a palette and studying' to which Matisse alluded in his postcard is apparent only in the scumbled white rectangular palette, with a thumb poking through, which has no clear means of support. (Matisse derived the motif of palette and poking thumb from Cézanne's *Self Portrait with Palette* [1886–7, Bührle Foundation, Zürich].) In addition to the palette and thumb, translucent triangular and rectilinear forms above and below the palette, in black, white, grey and pink, allude to an anthropomorphic seated presence to the right. The artist's consciousness is also reflected in the most vivid presence in the room, the vermilion *poissons rouges*, surrounded by a halo of luminous white in their cylindrical bowl, and resting on the transparent rectangle of a tabletop, which is tilted towards the viewer and set against a vertical band of black shadow. The window is indicated by curvilinear black railings set against a field of blue. The painting as a whole, with its near abstraction, grid-like structure, shallow relief space and subdued colour, is Matisse's personal and complex adaptation of the Cubism of Picasso, Braque and Juan Gris.

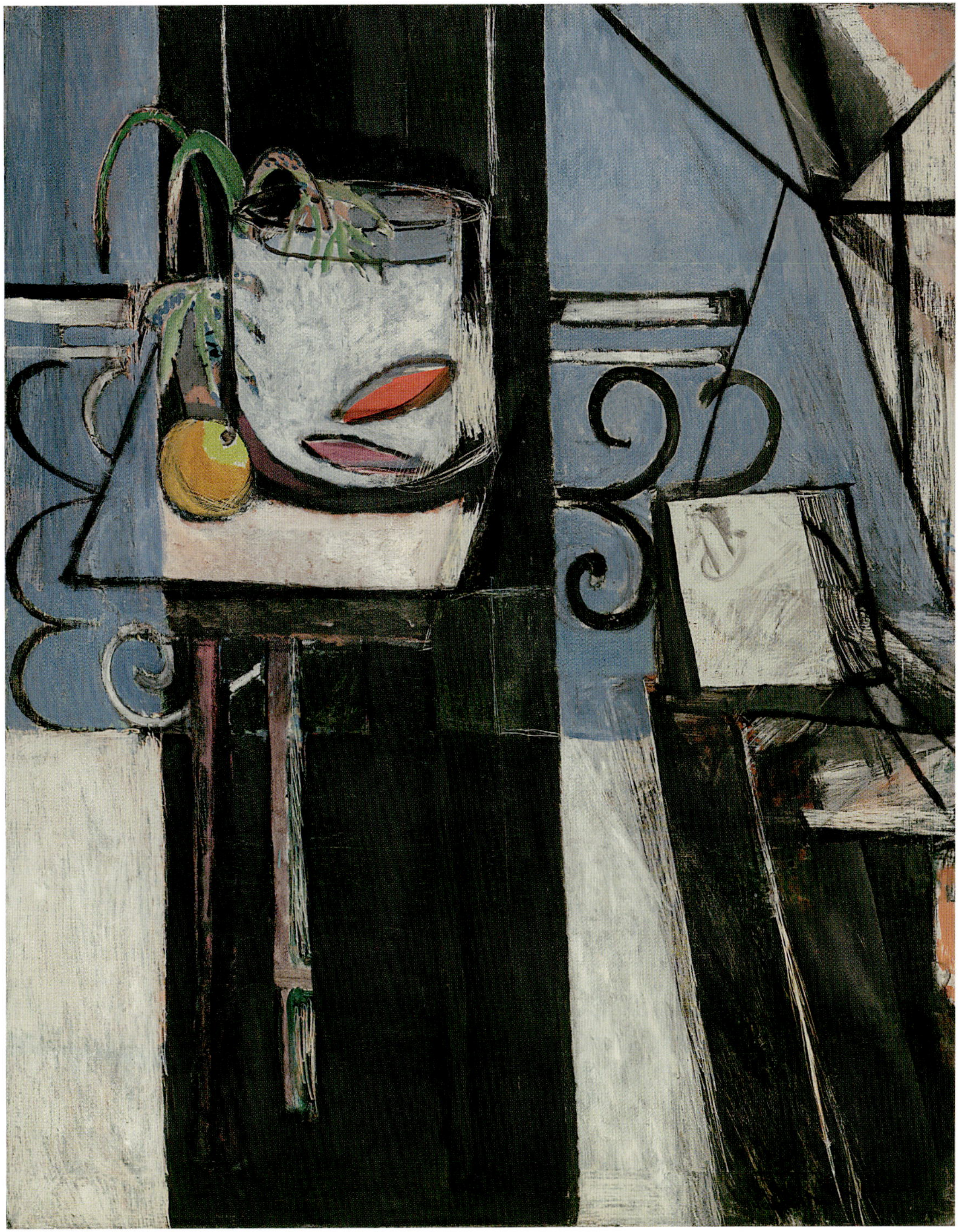

1915–16 THE MOROCCANS

The Museum of Modern Art, New York
Oil on canvas | 181.3 x 279.4cm (71⅜ x 110in)

In late 1915, nearly three years after his return from his second and final Moroccan sojourn, Matisse informed his friend Charles Camoin that he had just begun a canvas of mural-like proportions: 'It's a memory of Morocco.'[60] His current artistic style – geometric, restrained in colour, nearly abstract, and informed by Cubism – was well-suited to this purpose, which was to convey images based on subjective experience rather than direct observation.

Matisse was greatly affected by three aspects of Morocco: its nature, its architecture and its people. The painting consists of three sections. To the lower left, four ochre-coloured melons, with massive green leaves, are displayed at a marketplace. At the upper left is a balcony with a trellised roof; a pot of four striped, circular flowers rests on the ledge; in the background is the dome of a mosque. To the right, in the most abstract section of the painting and the most difficult to read, are human figures: a seated Moroccan in the foreground, back turned to the viewer; the large form to his left appears to be his raised arm; the circular and oval forms above his head seem to be a seated figure viewed from above and an arched doorway; two angular geometric forms at the upper register may represent figures glimpsed through windows. Alfred Barr likened the three sections to 'three movements within a symphony … or perhaps three choirs of instruments within the orchestra itself.'

Like the human-figure section, that of still life is ambiguous: the melons with their leaves could be read as Moroccans kneeling in prayer. The painting is unified by its geometric forms: the circular melons echo the striped circles of the flowers above and the heads of two Moroccans on the right. There is a reverberation of linear, angular forms throughout: the tiles under the melons; the railing and roof of the balcony; the window grids, and the back of the large seated figure.

Each section has its own colour motif: the ochre and green of the melons; the grey, white and blue of the balcony; the black, white and lavender of the Moroccans. Small touches of colour link the three sections: lavender in the two left ones, blue and ochre on the right. Paradoxically, the powerful sunlight of the Moroccan landscape is conveyed by a field of black. In his essay 'Black is a Colour', written three decades later, Matisse commented on his use of black in this work, maintaining that in *The Moroccans* he used 'a grand black, which is as luminous as the other colors in the painting.'[61]

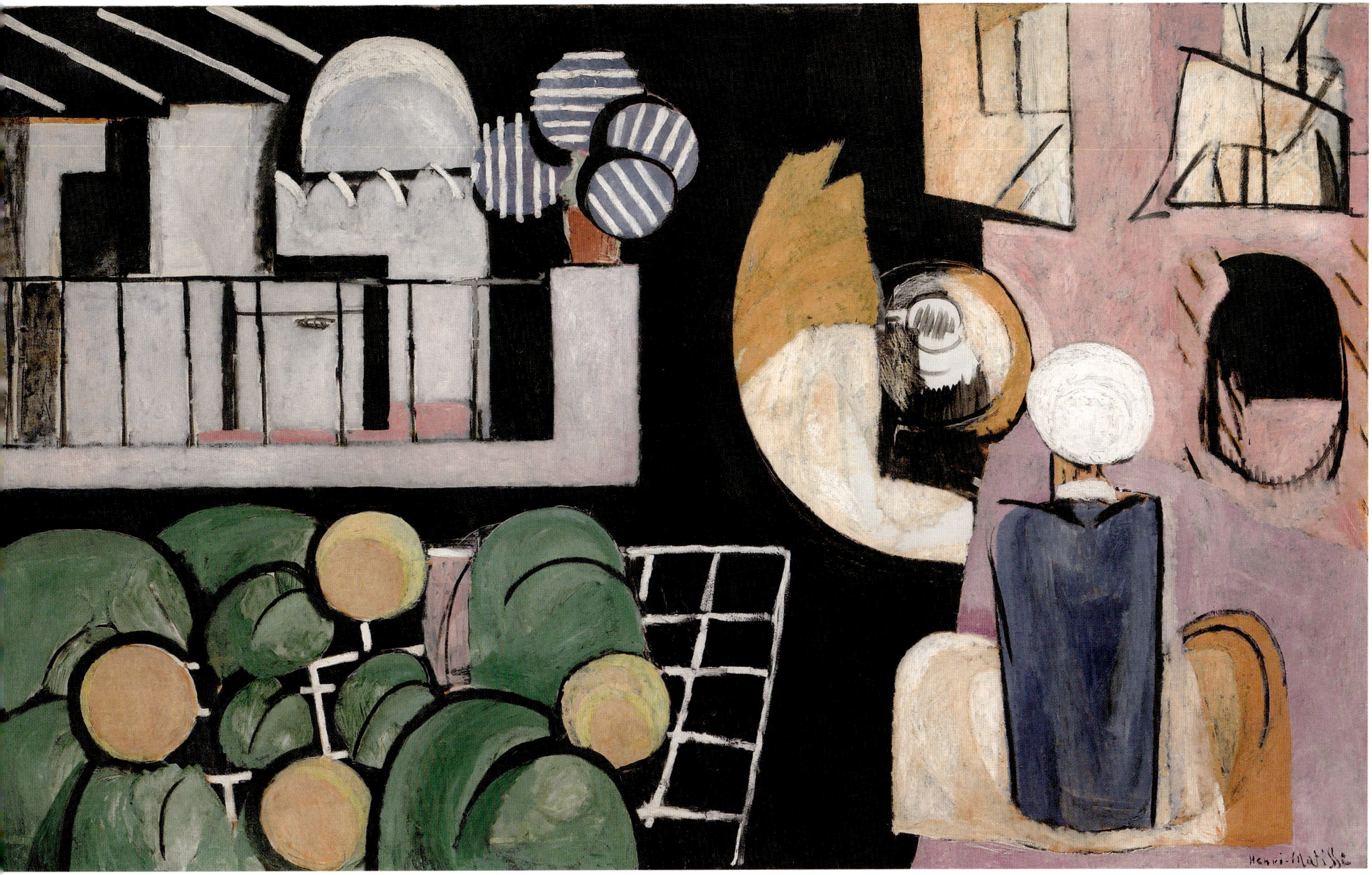

1916

GOURDS

The Museum of Modern Art, New York
Oil on canvas | 65.1 × 80.9cm (25⅝ × 31⅞in)

The years 1913–1917 were a period of vigorous experimentation in Matisse's artistic life, when he was confronting Cubism on his own terms. During the months when *The Moroccans* and *Bathers by a River* (pp. 101 and 107) were works in progress, he was creating portraits and still lifes on a more intimate scale. *Gourds,* the final still life of the series, was an opportunity both to apply techniques he was using in the larger paintings, and to work out problems posed by them.

Gourds and *The Moroccans* employ the same pictorial language. Each work has a background of rich black in the left two-thirds, while the right third is of a muted colour, blue and lavender respectively; each has a void in the centre and curved or circular objects overlapping the shared boundary. *The Moroccans* is composed of three sections: still life, architecture and human figures. In *Gourds,* each of the five still-life objects is a 'section' of the painting, with each object appearing to float in space. There is no overlap, except for the long fruit stem that bends in front of the floating tureen. Only the pitcher and the plate – on which rest two pinecones and four fruits of varying sizes and shapes – are modelled in light and shadow.

Matisse described *Gourds* as 'a composition of objects which do not touch but nonetheless participate in the same intimacy'.[62] He implied that his device of using black to convey luminosity was done experimentally in *Gourds* before it appeared in the larger painting: 'In this work I began to use pure black as a color of light and not as a color of darkness.'[63]

As with much of Matisse's output, the apparent simplicity of the painting is deceptive, for close examination reveals multiple reworkings, among them an evolution from description to semi-abstraction, and a reversal of the black field from right to left. Though small in scale, *Gourds* is a rhythmic, powerful composition of monumental organic form and nuanced colour, like a theme and variation in a chamber quintet.

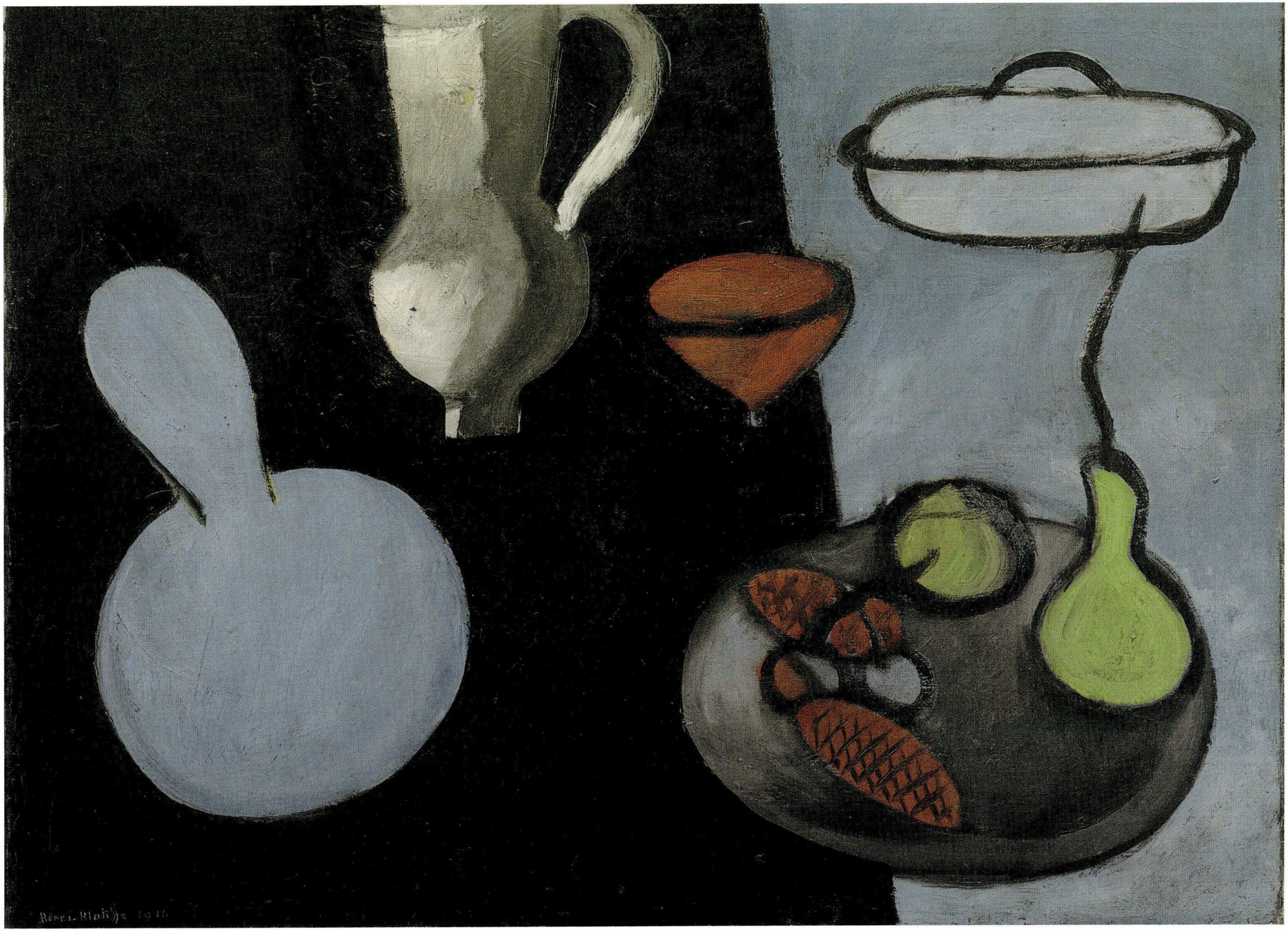

1916

THE PIANO LESSON

The Museum of Modern Art, New York
Oil on canvas | 245.1 × 212.7cm (96½ × 83¾in)

The Piano Lesson is a mural-sized picture, nearly square in format, set in the living room of the Matisse home in Issy. The artist's son Pierre sits at a piano on the right; to the left an open window faces the garden. The painting was created in summer 1916, when Pierre was 16 years old, but as portrayed he appears to be 9 or 10. On either side of him is a work by the artist: to the upper right, the painting *Woman on a High Stool* (1914, The Museum of Modern Art, New York); diagonally across, to the lower left, the bronze sculpture *Decorative Figure* (1908). Resting on the piano lid are a lit candle and, directly in front of Pierre, a metronome.

The room is enveloped by a soft grey field which extends to the exterior viewed through the window. Figures occupy the edges of the field, while a central broad area is composed of interacting geometric shapes: the arabesques of the window grill and the light-blue horizontal of the rail intersect with the green triangle of late-afternoon sunlight cast on the lawn, which in turn is mirrored by the pink trapezoid of the piano lid. A smaller pink triangle seems to be implanted on the boy's forehead as he stares at the pyramidal metronome. He is either entranced by the music or constrained by the lesson, or perhaps a bit of each. The arabesques, as they shift across the visual field from the 'Pleyel' music rack to the window grillwork, evoke the changes in rhythm or pitch of a line of music.

Pierre sits midway between two female personae, one stern and controlling, the other sensual and beguiling. The polarities of warm and cold, free and restrained, are reinforced by the candle and metronome. The view through the window of adjacent green and grey trapezoids is purely abstract. If a window is a metaphor for the art of painting, interior versus exterior here present another polarity: representation versus abstraction. Pierre can be viewed as a surrogate for the artist. He produces the music, and he is the nexus where the forces in the picture converge: among them sensuality and discipline, emotion and reason, angularity and curvilinearity, flatness and illusion, line and colour.

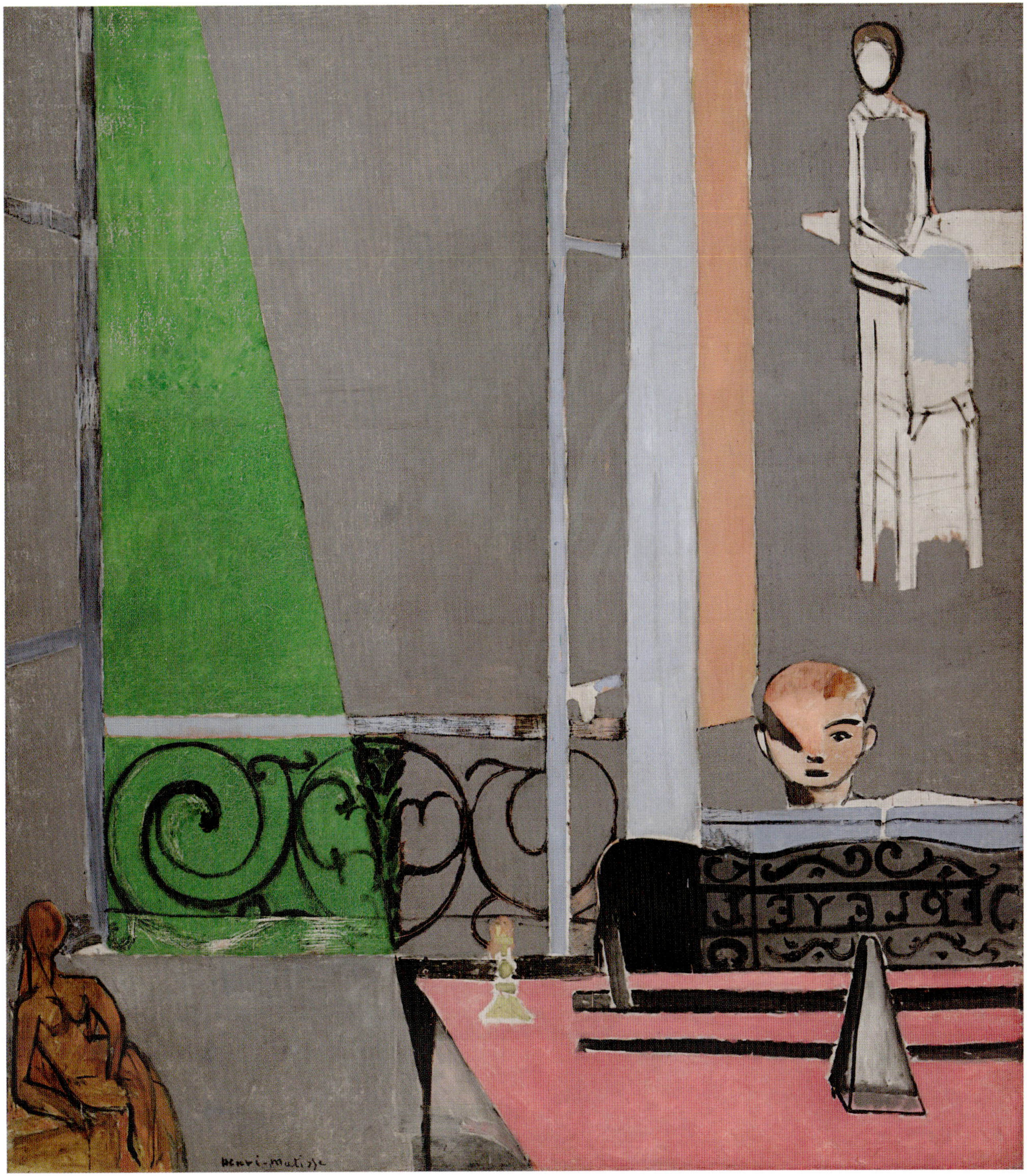
Henri-Matisse

1909–17 BATHERS BY A RIVER

Art Institute of Chicago
Oil on canvas | 260 × 392cm (102½ × 154⅓in)

In 1953 Daniel Catton Rich, director of the Art Institute of Chicago, wrote to Matisse, informing him that the museum had acquired *Bathers by a River.*[64] The artist replied that he considered the painting to be one of the five pivotal works of his career, adding that he would also place *The Moroccans* (p. 101) in that category. *Bathers by a River* is notable for its large size – it has virtually the same dimensions as *Dance I*, *Dance II* and *Music* (pp. 65, 71, and 69) – and for its long gestation period. It was originally conceived as five bathers at a waterfall, related to the Shchukin commission of *Music* and *Dance*. In its present form, largely composed in 1916, it is a pendant to *The Moroccans*. Like the pairing of *Music* and *Dance,* the two works contrast female and male ensembles. It is painted in the style of *The Moroccans,* defined by Alfred Barr as one of 'austere form', 'restrained color', and 'experiment with abstract design', and though not as explicitly, it likewise presents a memory of Morocco.[65]

The palette is restricted to black, white, grey, green and pink. The green and grey tropical foliage to the left evokes Morocco, as does the grey silhouetted snake in the centre, conjuring memories of snake charmers in Tangier. The snake also evokes a primeval world, and is being contemplated by at least one of the figures, like its fellow reptile of *Bathers with a Turtle* (p. 61). None of the women has visible facial features; and the seated figure, though her head is nearly abstract, seems to be veiled. They hover in space, each turned to a different angle; depicted in tones of grey, highlighted in pink, they adhere to the picture plane in geometric, sculptural relief, evocative of the *Back* series of sculptures on which Matisse was working contemporaneously. The background comprises four vertical bands, abstract except for the green band on the left. At the centre is the barrier of white and black bands, both of which seem to emanate light. The figures are syncopated in their poses, their vertical positions in space, and in their rhythmic placement before the background bands. The painting is a diploma picture of what Matisse called his 'methods of modern construction', as *Le Bonheur de vivre* (p. 53) was a manifesto of Fauvism.[66]

The critic Clement Greenberg later recalled how influential *Bathers by a River* was for American painters of the forties and fifties, both in its facture and in its scale: Jackson Pollock and Mark Rothko were among those who were indebted to Matisse for the 'loosening up of the painted surface' which characterized New York School painting. In addition, the influence of Matisse 'was largely responsible … for the specifically "abstract expressionist" version of the big picture; Matisse's huge *Bathers by a River* … hung for a long time in the lobby of the Valentine Gallery, where I myself saw it often enough to feel able to copy it by heart'.[67]

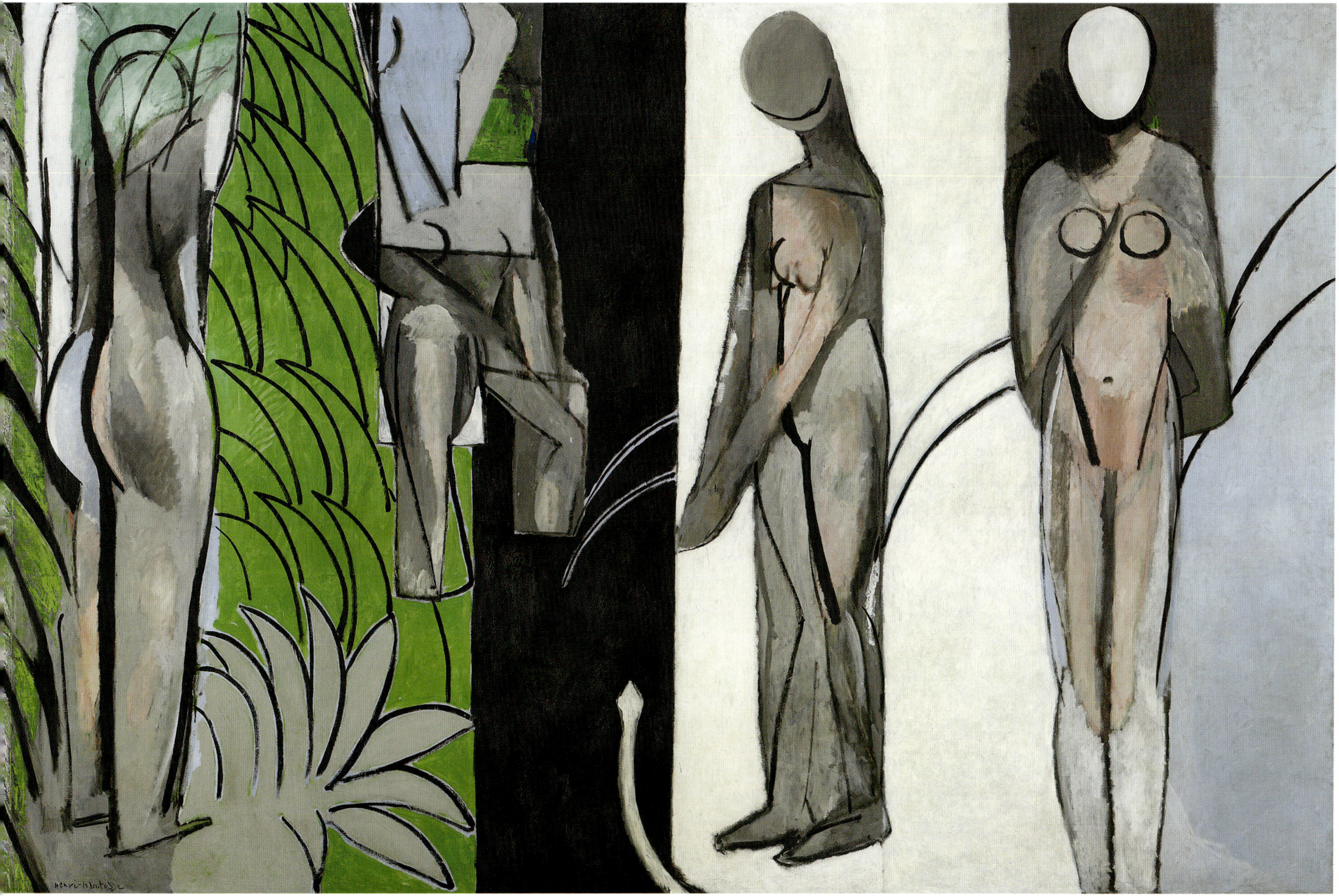

1918–19 INTERIOR WITH A VIOLIN CASE

The Museum of Modern Art, New York
Oil on canvas | 73 × 60cm (28¾ × 23⅝in)

The years immediately following World War I coincide with a change in Matisse's artistic approach: from the architectonic, nearly abstract style of the war years to a return to nature and naturalism. In June 1919 he explained to a visitor at his quai Saint-Michel studio: 'One must always keep one's eye, one's feeling, fresh; one must follow one's instincts. Besides, I am seeking a new synthesis.'[68] At this time Matisse was spending summers in Paris and Issy, but for the greater part of the year he worked out of hotel rooms in Nice on the Côte d'Azur.

Interior with a Violin Case was painted in Matisse's room at the Hôtel Méditerranée, looking out on the Baie des Anges. Its opulent decoration presents a variety of patterns and textures: the arabesques and floral designs of the wallpaper and hanging, the balustrades of the balcony, the folds of the translucent white curtains, the semi-circles of the ceiling moulding, the cross-hatchings and streaks of sunlight on the tiled floor. Years later, in 1941, he would remember the hotel with gleeful nostalgia: 'What lovely Italian-style ceilings! What tiles! … Everything was fake, absurd, terrific, delicious.'[69]

Colour, while pleasingly rendered and syncopated, is not intensified as in, for example, *Harmony in Red* or *The Conversation* (p. 64, p. 85). The artist sacrifices colouristic exaggeration for convincing effects of light. Nor is the composition flattened; space is rendered in convincing three-dimensional perspective. The window does not unite exterior and interior; rather, those boundaries are respected. The viewpoint is elevated, as we look down on the chairs, footrest, table and mirror. The artist, a dedicated violinist, often rendered violins in his interiors as surrogates for himself. Here the open, black-bordered case and the blackened mirror and notebook connote the solitude of this sun-filled room amid a Nice winter. The emphasis on light and the loose, painterly manner suggest that Impressionism is the prototypical style of the work; during the Nice period Renoir supplants Cézanne as Matisse's master.

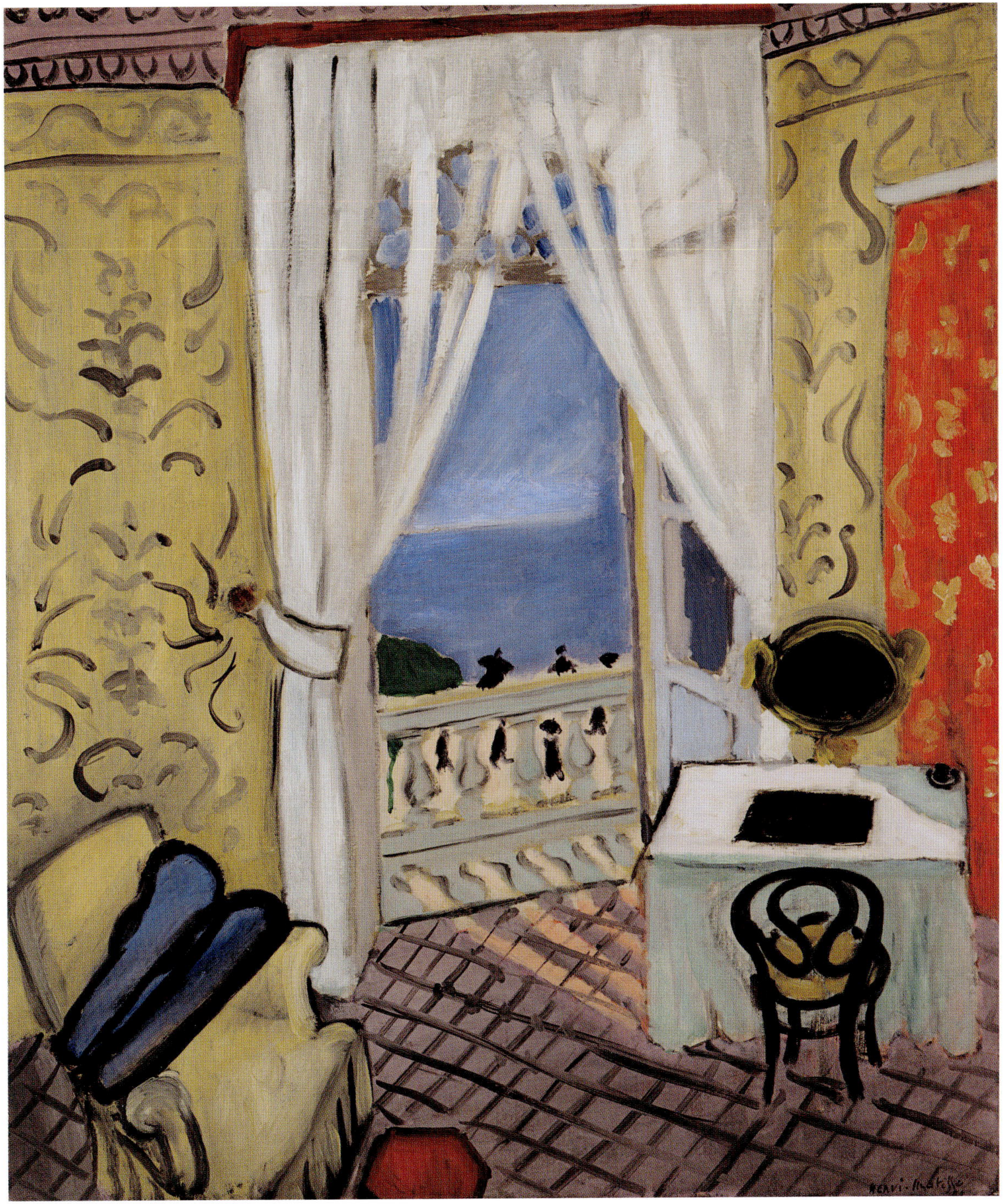

1924 PIANIST AND CHECKER PLAYERS

National Gallery of Art, Washington, DC
Oil on canvas | 73.7 × 92.4cm (29 × 36⅜in)

Pianist and Checker Players, set in the living room of Matisse's apartment in Nice, shows the artist's principal model, Henriette Darricarrère, playing piano at the upper left while, in the foreground, her two brothers focus intently on their checker game. The scene is presented in the artist's naturalistic style of the early Nice period, as seen in *Interior with a Violin Case* (p. 109). While we perceive the space three-dimensionally, we see various parts of the room from different viewpoints: the pianist and the sculpture at eye level, the table, bureau, carpet and tiled floor from above. The prevailing colour scheme is the harmonious interplay of the yellow dress and the reds of wall, tablecloth and floor. Decorative elements of wall and floor interact contrapuntally: the arcs and floral designs of the wallpaper, the astral and vegetal patterns of the Persian rug, the grid of the floor tiles. The arcs on the wall above the piano, and the reverberating patterns of the room, evoke the music that Henriette plays. The absent painter is symbolized by the vacant armchair, the two violins hanging from the cupboard, and, in a bit of understated whimsy, the statue on the bureau, a plaster cast of a Michelangelo *Slave* (1513–16) from the Louvre.

Matisse had painted such a vibrantly patterned domestic scene before, in *The Painter's Family* of 1911 (p. 75), rendered in his flattened decorative style of that year. In Nice, with his family left behind in Issy, he portrays a surrogate family, with Henriette a proxy for his daughter, and her brothers, for his sons. In both paintings a sculpture in the background becomes *his* proxy – here the Michelangelo *Slave*, there the Matisse *Serf* (1900–03).

Pianist and Checker Players – to a greater degree than *The Painter's Family* – bears a resemblance to Cézanne's *Girl at the Piano (Overture to Tannhäuser)* of 1869 (p. 15). In these two paintings, a woman in profile on the left plays a piano, while the rhythmic patterns of the room become visual counterparts of her music.

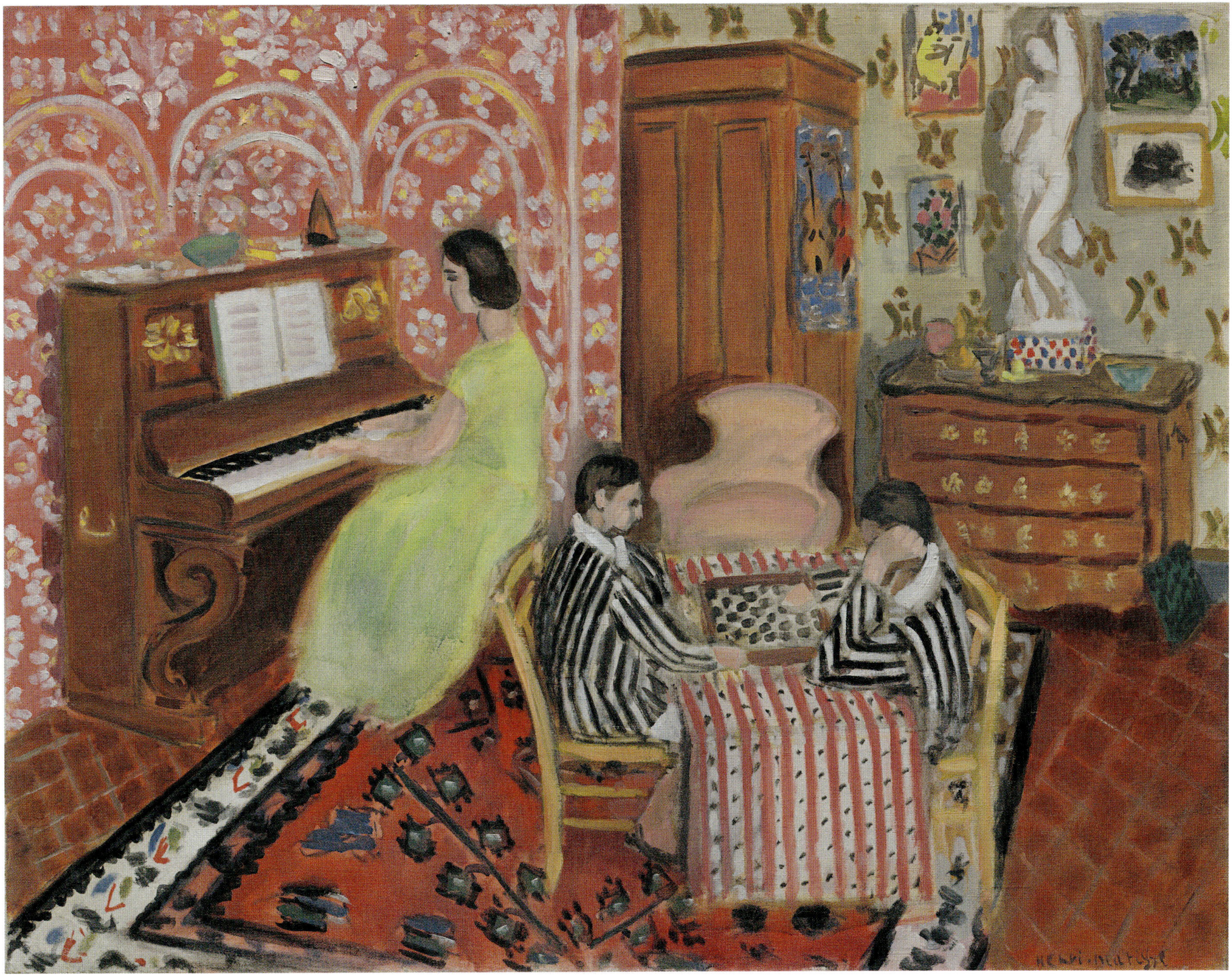

1925–6 DECORATIVE FIGURE ON AN ORNAMENTAL GROUND

Centre Pompidou, Paris
Oil on canvas | 130 × 98cm (51⅛ × 38½in)

When Matisse resumed his life in Nice in autumn 1921, rather than continuing to reside at the Hôtel Méditerranée, he established more permanent roots in the city by renting a flat and studio in an apartment block at 1, place Charles Félix. He equipped the studio with fabrics, mirrors, cushions and screens with which to stage his paintings (see photograph, p. 5). Henriette Darricarrère, his principal model, posed nude and in harem costume for a series of odalisques, a designation going back to the eighteenth century for depictions of a woman, often reclining, in a Near Eastern interior. The culmination of this series, *Decorative Figure on an Ornamental Ground,* was a milestone for the artist, a return to the avant-garde after the naturalism of the earlier Nice period.

An inspiration for this return was the artist's monumental sculpture *Large Seated Nude* (1922–9, p. 23), which he was modelling in clay and continually revising, and for which Henriette was intermittently posing. This sculpture was, in turn, influenced by the figure *Night* from the Medici Tombs of Michelangelo (1519–34, Florence), an artist who greatly interested Matisse at this time. From *Large Seated Nude* he derived the pose of raised knee with the other leg passed under it, the cylindrical neck, the oval head, and the bodily proportions.

The painting's strength derives from the tension between the three-dimensional figure and the two-dimensional decoration of floor and wallpaper. Transitional between figure and background are the leafy plant, the blue and white Chinese flowerpot, the bowl of lemons and the Rococo mirror. Henriette's body is geometrically simplified to an extreme degree: the aforementioned head and neck, ruler-straight back, and the contrasting rounded, massive yet graceful limbs and nearly rectangular torso. The maroon wallpaper contains a repeated motif of two elements: a brown curvilinear frame enclosing a cluster of pink, white and red flowers with green leaves on a blue ground, and independent leaf and flower clusters. The carpeted floor, running diagonally to the wall, has three varying stripes of arabesque, ovoid and floral patterns in red, ochre, blue and black. To the lower right is an anomalous indeterminate object – a flat, upright rectangular shape with one curved side and a painterly floral design that echoes the mirror frame – which may be the back of a brocaded chair. The painting's ultimate success lies in the sculptural presence of Matisse's model Henriette to hold her own against the surrounding riot of pattern and colour.

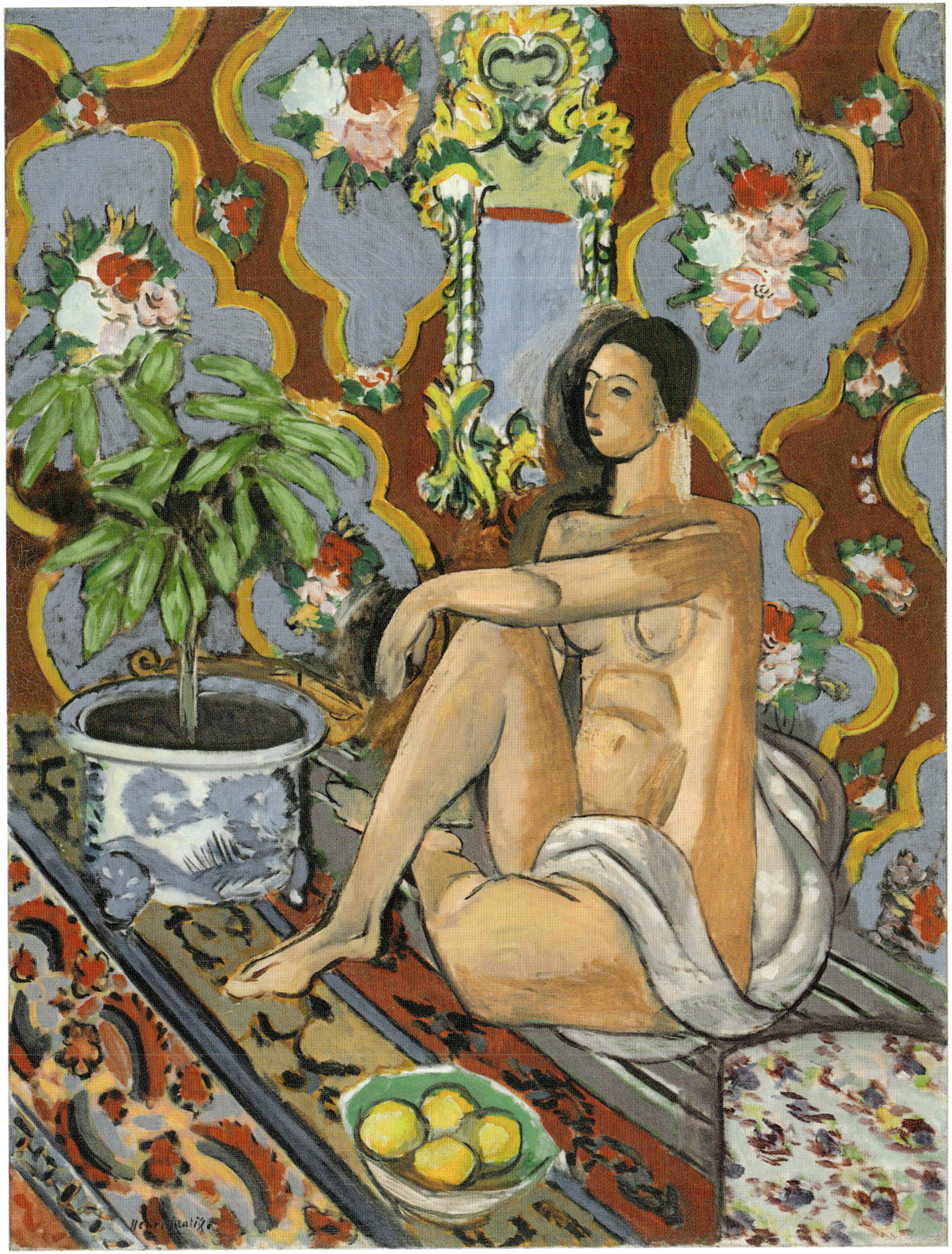

1927

WOMAN WITH A VEIL

The Museum of Modern Art, New York
Oil on canvas | 61.6 × 50.2cm (24¼ × 19¾in)

Woman with a Veil is a portrait of Matisse's primary model of the Nice period, Henriette Darricarrère. She is seated, frontal, and – unlike numerous depictions of her as an odalisque – fully clothed. Her centralized, pyramidal form anchors the composition as, tilting forward, she gazes intently at the viewer and, by implication, at the artist. Her forearm and elbow rest on her knee, forming a vertical axis that supports her ovoid head, like a plinth propping up a sculpture. In contrast to the impassivity of Henriette's features, her garments and the background are dynamic in colour and pattern. Her cloak and skirt, divided into quadrants – red on the left, green and black on the right – are unified by a yellow diamond pattern which, rather than yielding to the folds of cloth, appears as a grid of wet paint strokes on the picture plane. Behind Henriette's seated form are the pink arabesques on pastel blue ground of the wall; on one side, two yellow arcs suggest an armchair; on the other, in diminishing scale, are flat areas of pink, pale green and yellow.

Henriette's pose – seated, chin resting on hand – is traditionally associated with contemplation and melancholy, recalling such prototypes as Dürer's engraving *Melencolia* and Rodin's statue *The Thinker.* The black arcs of her eyebrows and the horizontal contour of her half-veil, together with her patterned costume, evoke, as Matisse scholar John Elderfield has observed, the image of a masked harlequin.[70] Beneath a placid exterior, a mood of tension and sorrow is intensified by the roughness of the facture: the artist has scratched into the picture surface, scraping away paint on the eyes, lips, hand and forearm, as well as a portion of the background to the left.

In *Woman with a Veil* Matisse departed from the sensuous naturalism of the Nice period, returning to the geometric rigour of his works of the years 1913–17. The mask-like face and fragmented planes of the figure recall the *Portrait of Madame Matisse* (p. 91) and the *Portrait of Yvonne Landsberg* (p. 95), sharing the latter's vigorous scratchings of the picture surface. But whereas in the earlier portraits, the faces of the sitters seem remote, even absent, Henriette – though veiled – is emphatically present, as she unflinchingly confronts the viewer.

Woman with a Veil was painted at a time of transition in Matisse's life and work. It was the last picture he would paint of Henriette, soon to leave his employ. For the next several years he would paint few easel pictures, devoting himself mainly to travel, to an illustrated book of the poetry of Mallarmé, and to the Barnes *The Dance* mural (pp. 118–9).

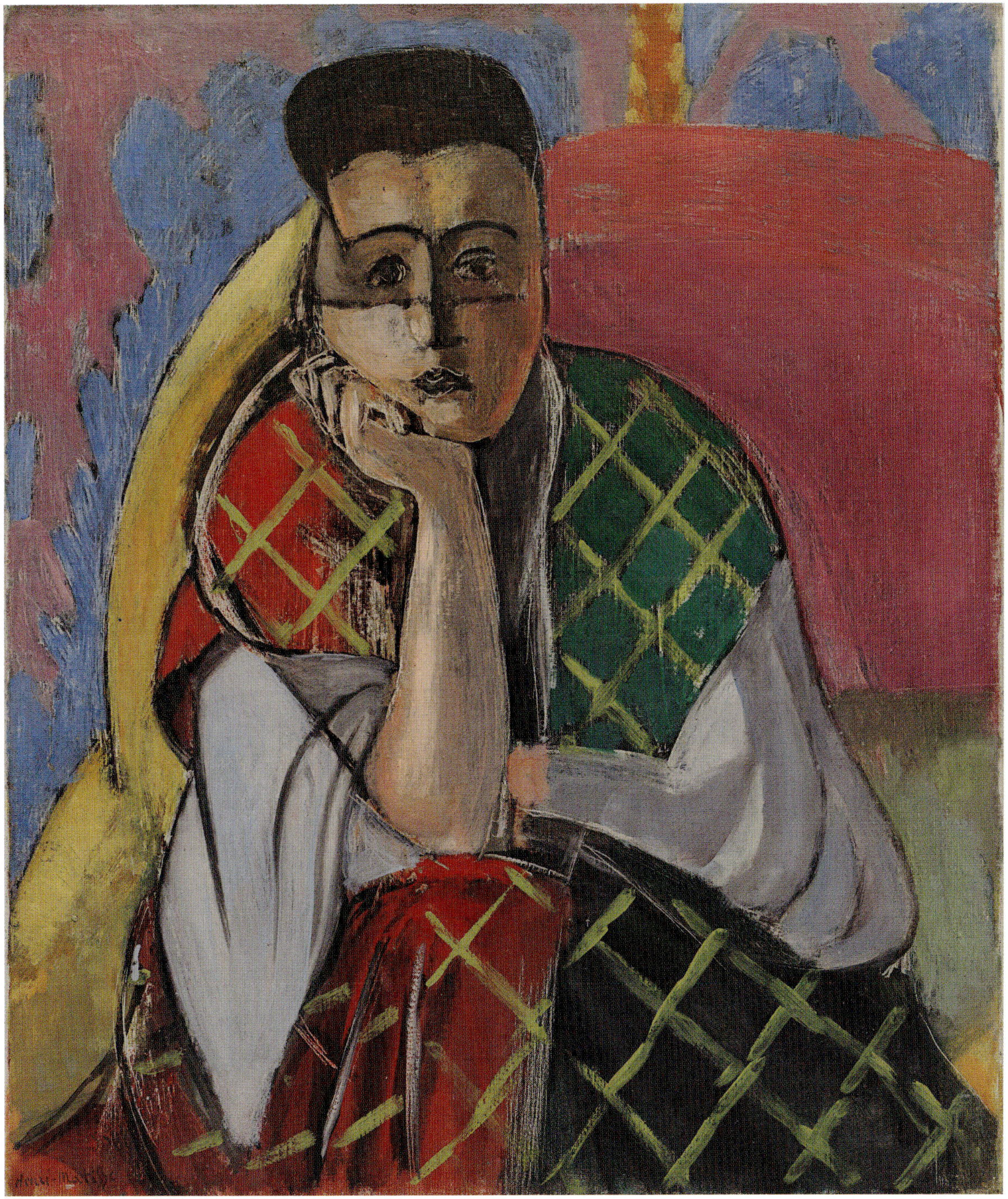

1932–3 THE DANCE (MURAL)

Barnes Foundation, Philadelphia

Oil on canvas | Left: 339.7 × 441.3cm (133¼ × 173¾in), centre: 355.9 × 503.2cm (140⅛ × 198⅛in), right: 338 × 439.4cm (133⅜ × 173in)

In 1930 Matisse travelled to the United States to serve on the jury of the Carnegie International Exhibition in Pittsburgh. After completing his official duties, he was eager to visit the Barnes Foundation. Founded by Dr Albert Barnes, the Foundation was the greatest repository in America of Matisse's work, and was, in addition, rich in Renoir and Cézanne, two artists of importance to him. Then an educational institution rather than a public museum, it was housed in a Renaissance Revival building in Merion, Pennsylvania. Upon their first meeting, Barnes offered Matisse a commission to paint a mural for the lunettes of the main hall, and after some deliberation, Matisse agreed to the project.

Having been given free rein to choose a theme, Matisse chose the dance, the subject of one of two murals he had painted for Sergei Shchukin's house in Moscow (p. 71). The ring of dancers had originally appeared in *Le Bonheur de vivre* (p. 53), which had been in Barnes' collection since 1922. Whereas the Shchukin panel had been completed rather quickly, the task of depicting a group of dancers within the restrictive format of three lunettes would be immeasurably more difficult. Moreover, after working on the project for over a year, when it was near completion Matisse discovered to his horror that he had been employing the wrong dimensions and had to begin again with new canvases. (The original mural, usually designated the first version of *The Dance* mural although it was completed later, is now permanently housed at the Musée d'Art Moderne de la Ville de Paris.)

Matisse developed a technique of composing the mural with cut pieces of coloured paper; in the final stage, he removed the papers and applied paint in their place. This method allowed him to work full scale, while making rapid changes that would have been more difficult with pigment or charcoal alone. Colour is restricted to the grey of the dancers, and bands of black, blue and pink behind them, recalling the black bands in *Bathers by a River* (p. 107). The composition comprises a pair of leaping figures under each of three lunettes, with a reclining figure under each of two pendentives, facing forward and backward, respectively, a reversal of the poses of the two central figures of *Le Bonheur de vivre*. The backs and arms of four figures – one on the left and right, two at the centre – visually rhyme with the curve of the architecture. The dancers do not seem restricted by the architectural framework; where necessary, their bodies are cropped by the borders. To a greater degree than the Shchukin panel, the Barnes mural has a Dionysian spirit, like a quasi-violent tribal dance.

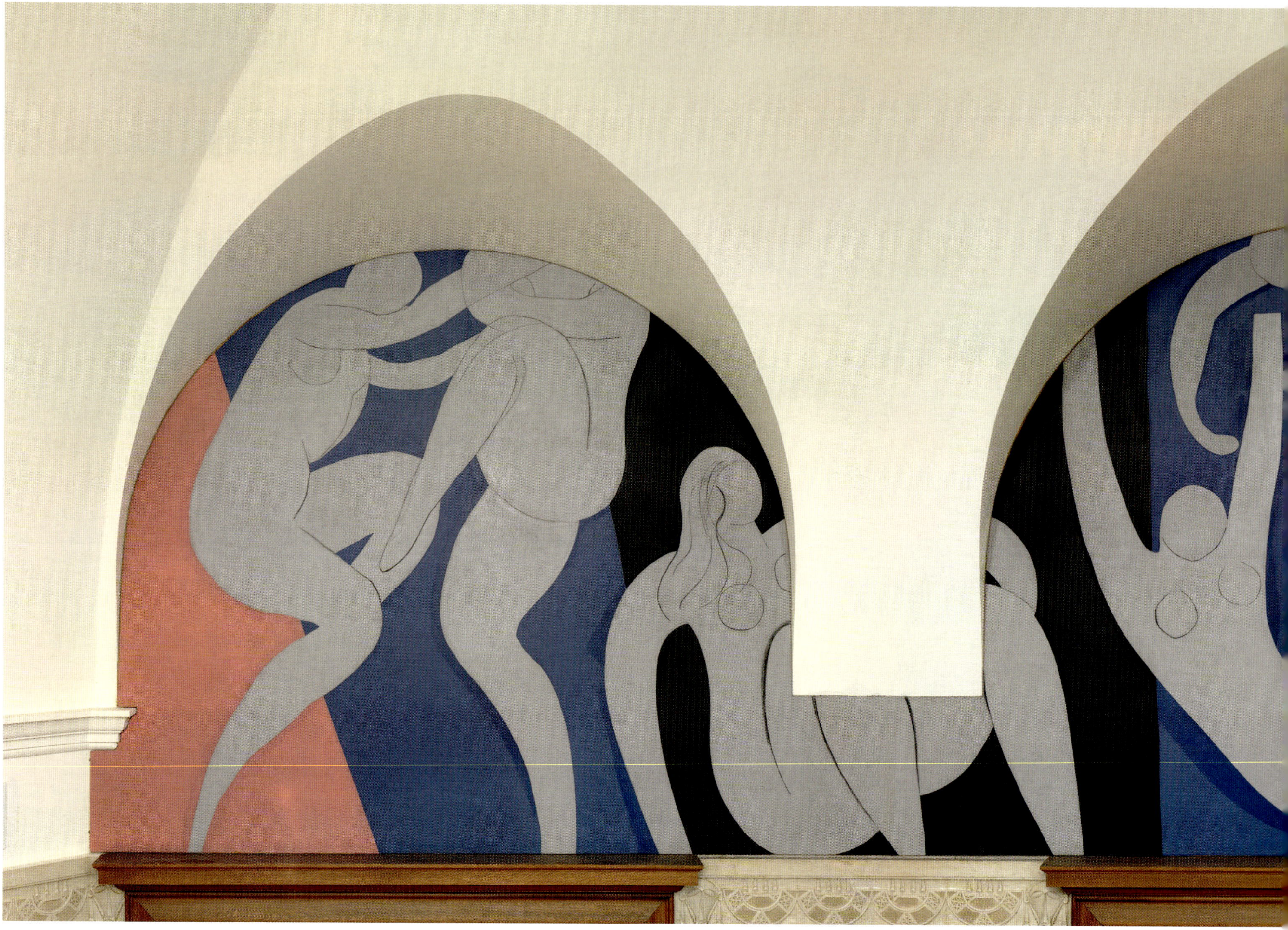

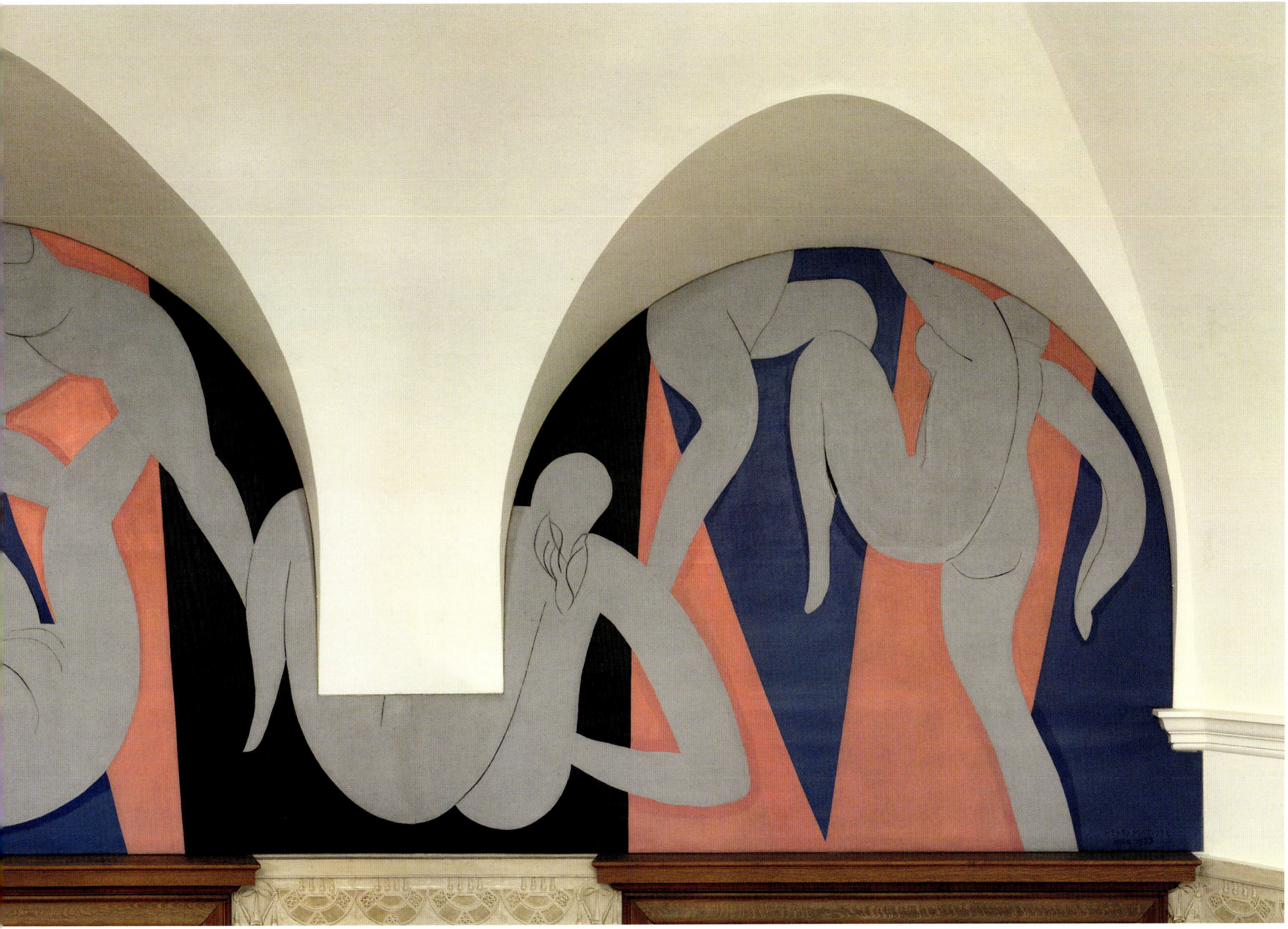

1935 LARGE RECLINING NUDE (THE PINK NUDE)

Baltimore Museum of Art
Oil on canvas | 66.4 × 93.3cm (26⅛ × 36¾in)

While Matisse was at work on the Barnes *Dance* mural (pp. 118–19), he engaged the services of the 22-year-old Russian émigré Lydia Delectorskaya, who would be, for the remainder of his life, an invaluable personal assistant, secretary, model and companion. Following his return to Nice after his installation of the mural, Lydia posed for a series of works, among them *Large Reclining Nude*, better known as *The Pink Nude*. Over a period of six months, from early May to late October, 1935, this painting evolved from naturalism to near abstraction, and from perspectival illusionism to the simplified, flattened style of the mural. The artist documented this transformation in a series of twenty-two photographs, eight of which were published that same year in the revised edition of Roger Fry's book *Henri Matisse*.

The documentary photographs are an aid in deciphering the abstract shapes in the background of the painting, which Matisse called 'plastic signs' for the original objects.[71] Thus the blue and white horizontal L-shape is a chaise longue; the ochre double-spiral is the back of an ornate chair; the flesh-toned circle is a vase, with a bulbous cluster of yellow flowers above it. The horizontal pink and red wall moulding, the white and green gridded wall and the blue and white gridded chaise longue are juxtaposed with the arcs of the chair, vase, flowers and the woman's body. The vase, flowers and spiralled chair seem to emanate from the woman, metaphors of fertility and growth. Like the dancers of the Barnes mural, she is unencumbered by the borders of the pictorial field: her toes, right knee and left foot are cropped by the edges of the picture.

The reclining pose of *The Pink Nude*, with a bent raised arm, had earlier incarnations in Matisse's work – from naturalistic odalisques of the Nice period, going back to the Cézannist, sculptural *Blue Nude* of 1907 (p. 55). Like the *Blue Nude*, she is contorted in an anatomically impossible pose. As her gaze directly meets the viewer's, her flattened form is pressed up against the picture plane, and her left arm forms a triumphal arch encircling her head. Matisse arrived at this resolution with the aid of cut and pasted papers, a method that he had first employed in composing the Barnes mural. With its planes of unmodelled colour, *The Pink Nude* anticipates the cut-out compositions of the subsequent two decades (pp. 129, 131–3 and 135).

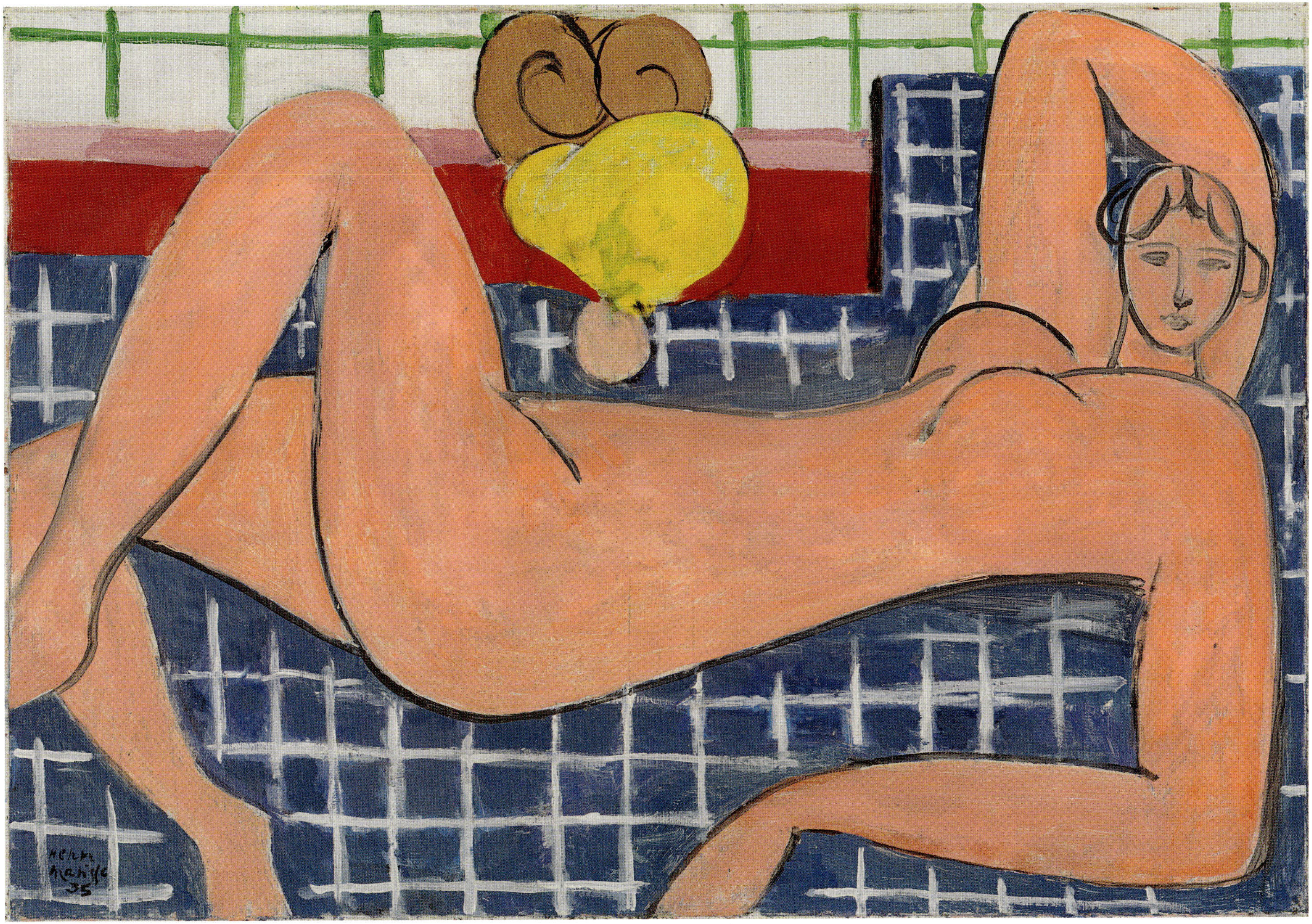
Henri Matisse 35

1940

THE DREAM

Private Collection
Oil on canvas | 81 × 65cm (31⅞ × 25⅝in)

At the time he created *The Dream,* Matisse, at 70, was feeling the burdens of his advancing years, of his legal separation from his wife, and of the war and its impact on his family. In September 1940 he wrote to his son Pierre that he had completed the painting: 'It was a big adventure … When I began it, months ago, *The Dream* was a very realistic picture, with a beautiful dark young woman asleep on my marble table … Now she has turned into an angel…I won't say that this painting made me forget everything else, but at least it brought me some relief.'[72]

The composition, notwithstanding its simplicity of total effect, is a complex interplay of line, shape and surface pattern. From the Romanian painter Theodor Pallady, fellow student of Gustave Moreau, Matisse had acquired a group of Romanian peasant blouses that appeared in a series of paintings and drawings. Here, the sitter's blouse – with the jagged and floral patterns of the sleeves and the wavy lines on the back – interacts with the waves of her hair and the contours of her face, hands, eye and eyebrow. Her arcing right arm, hands, and facial profile spiral counter-clockwise, in counterpoint to the arabesque of the tabletop. The yellow embroidery on her back and the ochre voids adjacent to her profile intensify the violet of the table, the blue underpainting of the blouse and the luminous red ground.

The snail-like spiralling of the composition and the opposition of yellow and violet complementary colours recall Picasso's paintings of Marie-Thérèse Walter, the Spanish artist's companion from 1927 to 1935 and mother of his daughter Maya. See, for example, Picasso's *Woman with Yellow Hair* of 1931 (p. 27); this rendering of the sleeping Marie-Thérèse evokes Matisse in its curvilinearity, its use of black contours and in the unfinished depiction of the hand. This voluptuous young woman, Picasso's junior by twenty-eight years, inspired the most Matissean works of his career. We have seen that in such works as *Portrait of Madame Matisse* of 1913 (p. 91), *Portrait of Yvonne Landsberg* of 1914 (p. 95) and *Goldfish and Palette* of 1914–15 (p. 99), Picasso's Cubism had a strong impact on Matisse. Accordingly, the Matisse-Picasso influence was a two-way street.

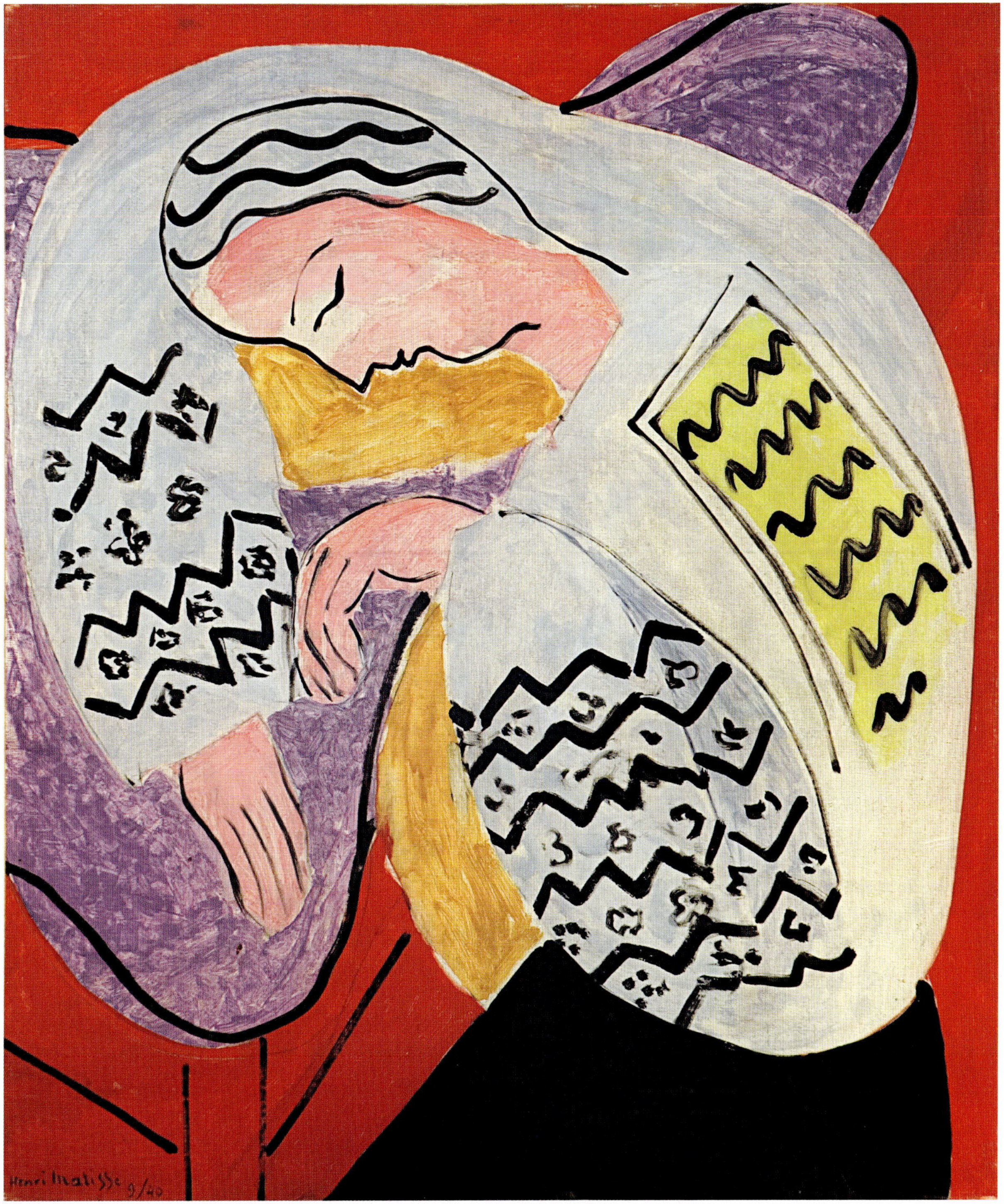

1941 STILL LIFE WITH MAGNOLIA

Centre Pompidou, Paris
Oil on canvas | 74 × 101cm (29⅛ × 39¾in)

Still Life with Magnolia was created over an extended period, from August to December 1941, in an immensely stressful time of Matisse's life. In the previous year his marriage of over forty years to his wife Amélie had ended in legal separation, causing great tensions within the family. Moreover, in 1940 the Germans invaded Paris, and the Vichy regime was installed in unoccupied southern France where the artist lived. Above all, Matisse's physical health had reached a point of crisis; he was diagnosed with duodenal cancer, and intestinal surgery was deemed necessary. While downplaying the severity of the situation to family and friends, he quietly made plans for the distribution of his assets in the event of his death.

Matisse's surgery took place in Lyon in January 1941; he recuperated in Lyon for several months, returning to the Hôtel Régina in Nice-Cimiez in May. Matisse had long regarded his art as a means of restoration to physical and spiritual health, and he was determined to return to work. After painting a series of self-portraits, he began a series of still lifes, culminating in this work.

Still Life with Magnolia is a return to the bold, experimental modernism of his early post-Fauve period. It is painted on a solid, luminous red ground, evoking such works as *Harmony in Red* (1908, p. 63) and *The Red Studio* (1911, p. 79). A series of photographs made by the artist documents the process by which he arrived at the final composition: the elements are gradually simplified and made bolder and more frontal.

The final composition contains six still-life objects. Four of them – a blue-green patterned vase, a violet tin pitcher, a light yellow conch shell, and a blue potted plant – surround the central forms: a tall green vase with green leaves and a single white magnolia, framed by a circular yellow-orange cauldron. The haloed form in the centre surrounded by the four objects in attendance suggests the reliefs of Christ or the Madonna surrounded by saints that Matisse had often seen on the portals of Romanesque churches.

The work's overall effect of radiance and joy seems to have given comfort to the artist. He told an interviewer: 'For several years, it has been my favourite painting … I think I put into it all of my power.'[73]

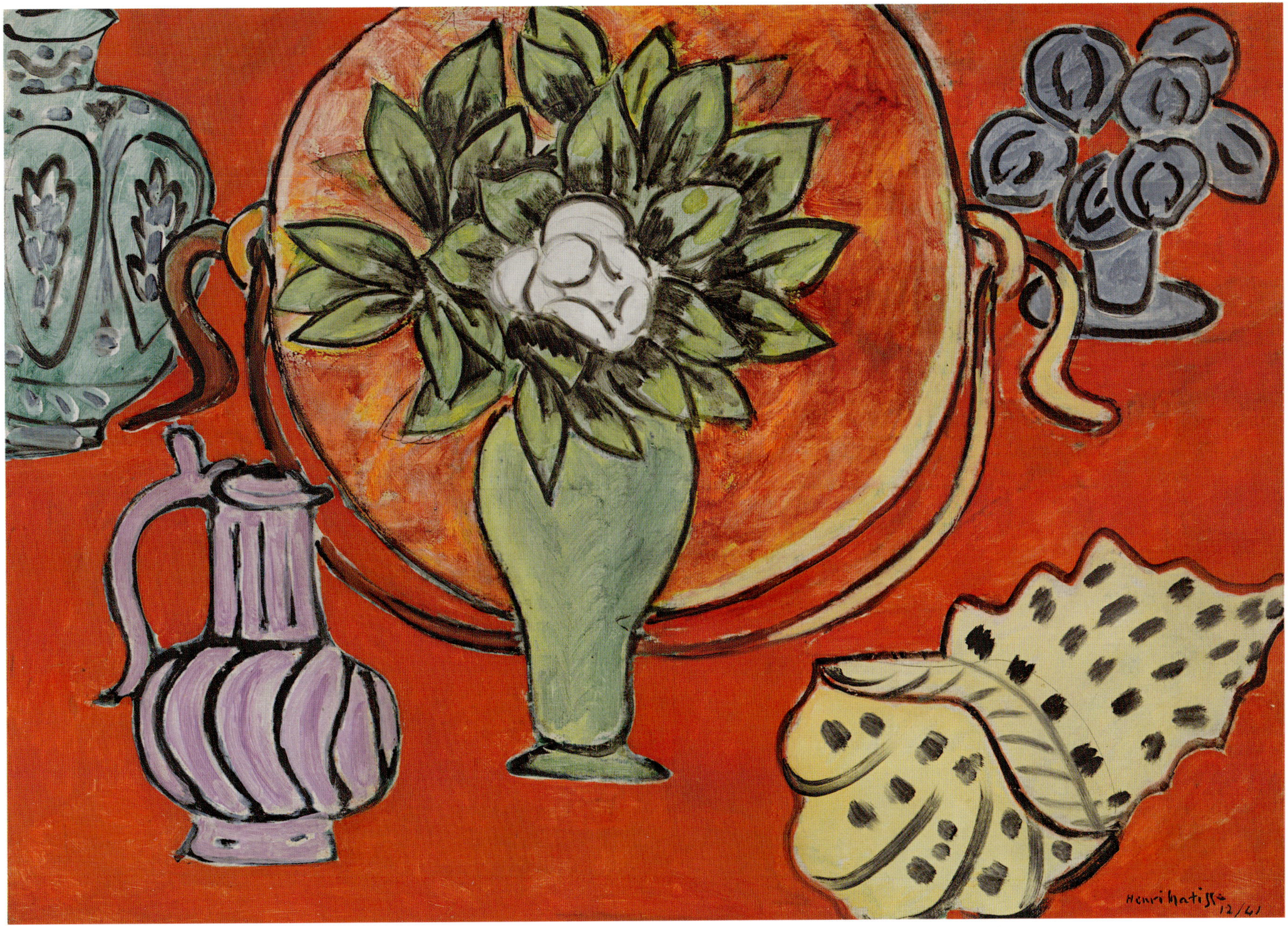
Henri Matisse 12/41

1948

INTERIOR WITH AN EGYPTIAN CURTAIN

The Phillips Collection, Washington, DC
Oil on canvas | 116.2 × 89.2cm (45¾ × 35⅛in)

Space is compressed and colour is explosive in *Interior with an Egyptian Curtain*. On the right, pressed up to the picture plane, hangs a black curtain overlaid with vibrant organic and geometric patterns of red, green, yellow, white and black. Adjacent to the curtain is a pink and yellow-orange table laden with pomegranates, which fairly dance in their pale blue bowl; alongside the bowl a solitary pomegranate perches on the table, while the bowl casts an opaque black shadow.

At a brief interval behind the table and occupying the largest portion of the pictorial field is a window divided into quadrants, offering a view of a pulsating palm tree. Like the interior space, exterior space is compressed: the green, yellow and black palm fronds push against the window, suppressing any view save the fragments of blue sky in its upper quadrants.

It is notable that in a work so energized by colour, black is the unifying element of the composition, playing the role of red in *Harmony in Red* (p. 63) and blue in *The Conversation* (p. 85). On the curtain, black is used both for geometric forms and for background; it is variously smooth, scumbled and applied as thick impasto. Black is balanced by white, both as contour and form. The most tactile portion of the curtain is the white impasto in its upper register. With its tactility and dynamic design, the curtain becomes a physical presence. Red and green arabesques descend from its upper register, joined by black arabesques in the central and lower registers, expanding in scale with their descent. The curtain, like the vibrating palm tree and the bountiful pomegranates, celebrates the renewable energy of spring. As if to emphasize the potency of such renewal, a phallic spear fragment lurches from its lower register, pointing to the artist's signature and date.

Interior with an Egyptian Curtain is as vital and energetic as any painting in Matisse's career. At the time of its creation he was in his seventy-ninth year and in the last decade of his life. It is one of his final statements in the medium of oil on canvas, coming at the conclusion of an extraordinary decade of artistic renewal. Yet some of his most original and influential artistic production lay ahead.

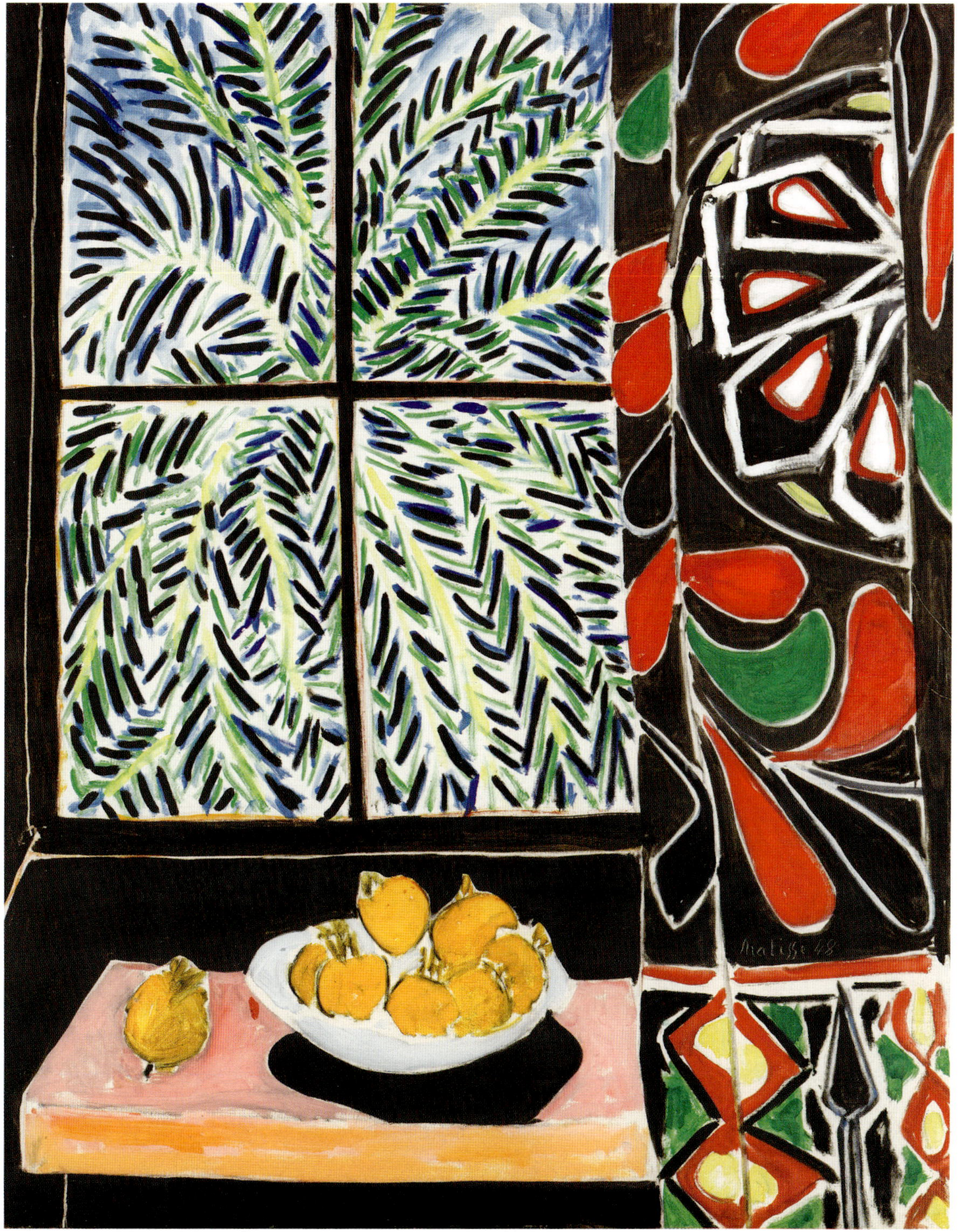

1951–2 MEMORY OF OCEANIA

The Museum of Modern Art, New York
Gouache on paper, cut and pasted, and charcoal on white paper | 284.4 × 286.4cm (112 × 112⅞in)

Memory of Oceania, a cut-out work in a square format on a large scale, combines rich colour with an austere composition, juxtaposing intensely hued rectilinear and curvilinear shapes, both architectonic and biomorphic. As in *The Swimming Pool* (pp. 131–3), the white ground plays an active role in the picture. The artist's freely rendered charcoal strokes activate the white ground of the canvas, imparting a pulse and buoyancy to the composition.

While *Memory of Oceania* verges on pure abstraction, like all of Matisse's works, from the least representational to the most descriptive, it conveys a heightened response to nature. Thus the blue shapes evoke sea and sky; the yellow and ochre shapes, sunlight; the green tilted rectangle, a sail; the black curved line and fuchsia rectangle, a tree or a mast; the ochre, white, and fuchsia shapes to the lower right, small boats; the three-part, yellow biomorphic shape suggests at once bananas and bathers; and the biomorphic blue shapes suggest bathers and fish or dolphins.

Lydia Delectorskaya, Matisse's assistant in his later years, had a precise reading of the work, perceiving it as 'a typical Tahitian landscape' which comprises 'a section of beach with a canoe, some tropical plants and coconut trees ... The rowboat (yellow shape) is at the right, as is the palm tree, the kind that bends close to the root and then becomes very straight (signified by the black curve extended by a stroke of purple).'[74]

Delectorskaya's description omits one salient element: the painted ochre and black frame that surrounds the picture, implying that the whole is meant to be read as a view through a window. Matisse painted window views wherever he lived, from his studio on quai Saint-Michel to hotel rooms in Nice. As a flat surface that indicates a realm beyond itself, the window was for Matisse a metaphor for the art of painting.[75]

Matisse had visited Tahiti two decades earlier, from late March to mid-June 1930. In a letter of 6 June 1930 to the painter Pierre Bonnard, he described 'pure light, pure air, pure colour; diamond sapphire emerald turquoise. Prodigious fish.'[76] The view from his room at the Hôtel Stuart in Tahiti made an indelible impression on him: it re-emerged, more than two decades later, with the abstracted imagery of this work. Just as *The Swimming Pool* looks back to Matisse's monumental dance decorations, *Memory of Oceania,* combining brilliant light and colour with formal rigour, recalls the structural power of earlier Cubist-influenced works such as *Goldfish and Palette* and *The Piano Lesson* (pp. 99 and 105).

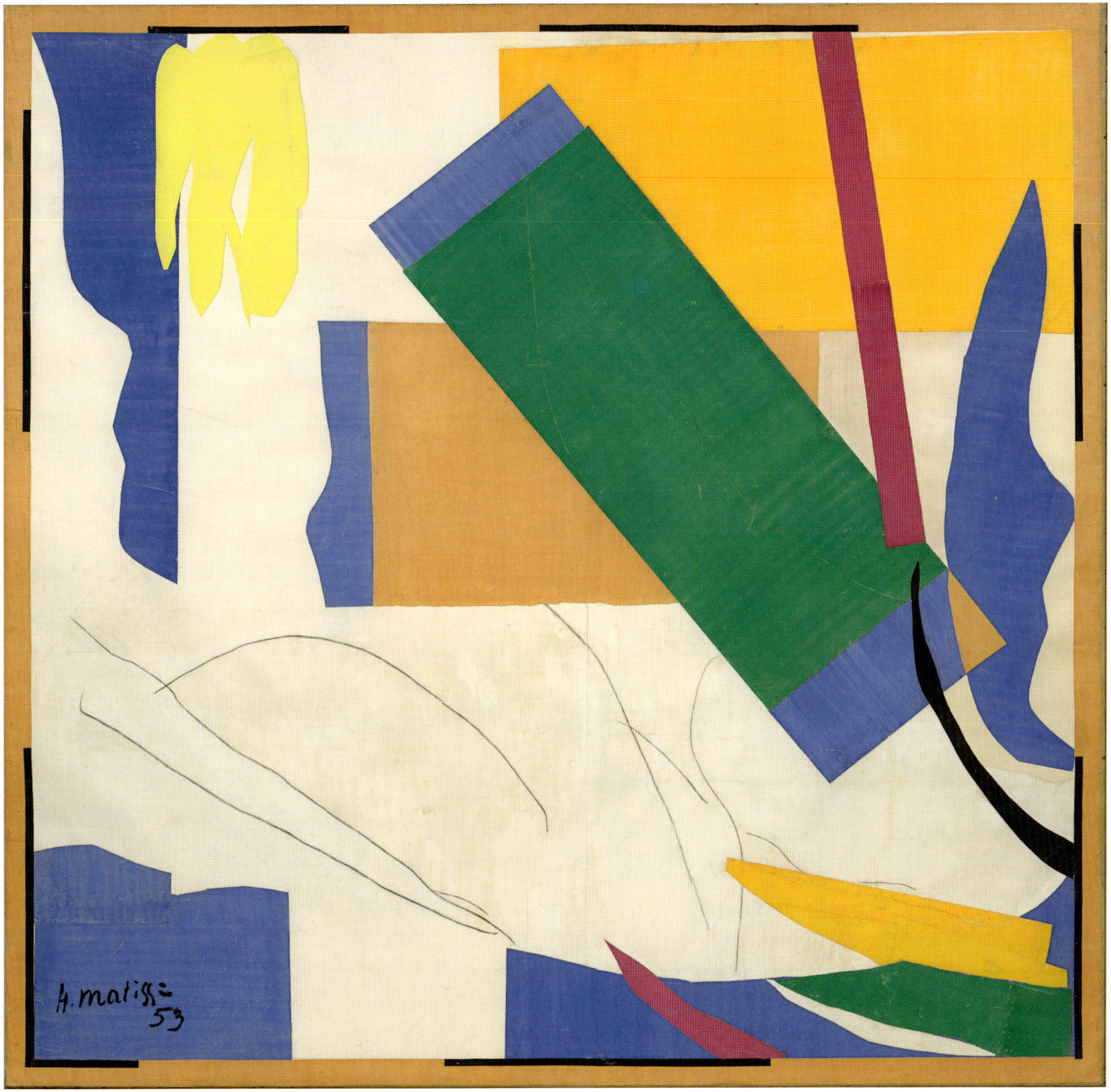
H. matisse
53

1952 THE SWIMMING POOL

The Museum of Modern Art, New York
Nine-panel mural in two parts: gouache on paper, cut and pasted, on white painted paper mounted on burlap
185.4 × 1643.3cm (73in × 53ft 11in)

The Swimming Pool is the largest and most ambitious of Matisse's late cut-outs. Its personal meaning to the artist is evident in the fact that it was made to decorate the walls of his apartment in Nice. The theme of aquatic motion was inspired by his visit to Tahiti two decades earlier. 'I have always adored the sea,' he told Margaret Scolari Barr, 'and now that I can no longer go for a swim, I have surrounded myself with it.'[77]

The frieze of cut blue shapes pasted onto white paper was initially attached to the beige wall fabric of the dining room of his apartment in the Hôtel Régina in Nice; it is now housed at The Museum of Modern Art in New York, where burlap mounting re-creates the colour and texture of the original setting. The sequence reads from right to left, punctuated, at beginning and end, with a single starfish. In the course of this sequence, the forms of the bathers decompose and reassemble, at times bursting the bounds of their white horizontal support; positive and negative forms reverse themselves; and the viewer's perspective shifts.

The sequence begins with five leaping and plunging figures. These figures are interspersed with forms suggesting other species of marine life – dolphins, jellyfish, algae. The first section concludes with a reclining figure with raised arms; the second begins with a splayed figure with intact contours. The forms of subsequent swimmers become progressively more fragmented, as positive form and negative space are transposed, to be reconstituted in the last figure. This final swimmer's form, cast in white silhouette, resembles Matisse's cut-out of *Venus* (p. 28), evoking the myth of the goddess's birth from the foam of the sea.

The theme of nudes in motion made its first appearance with the central ring of dancers in the *Le Bonheur de Vivre* (p. 53), and was developed further in his *Dance* murals of New York, St Petersburg and Philadelphia (pp. 65, 71 and 118-19). 'From *Bonheur de Vivre*,' Matisse declared, 'I was thirty-five then – to this cut-out – I am eighty-two – I have not changed … because all this time I have looked for the same things, which I have perhaps realized by different means.'[78]

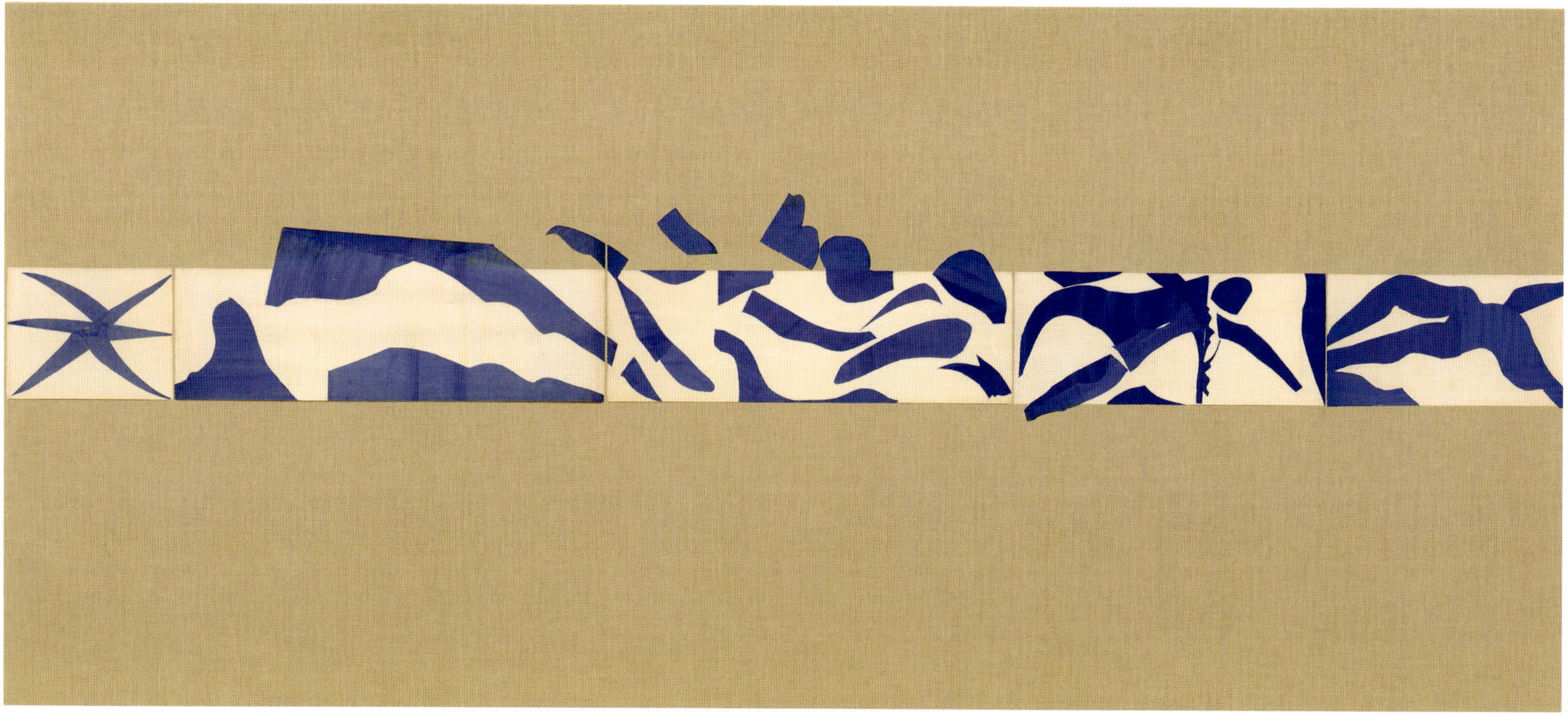

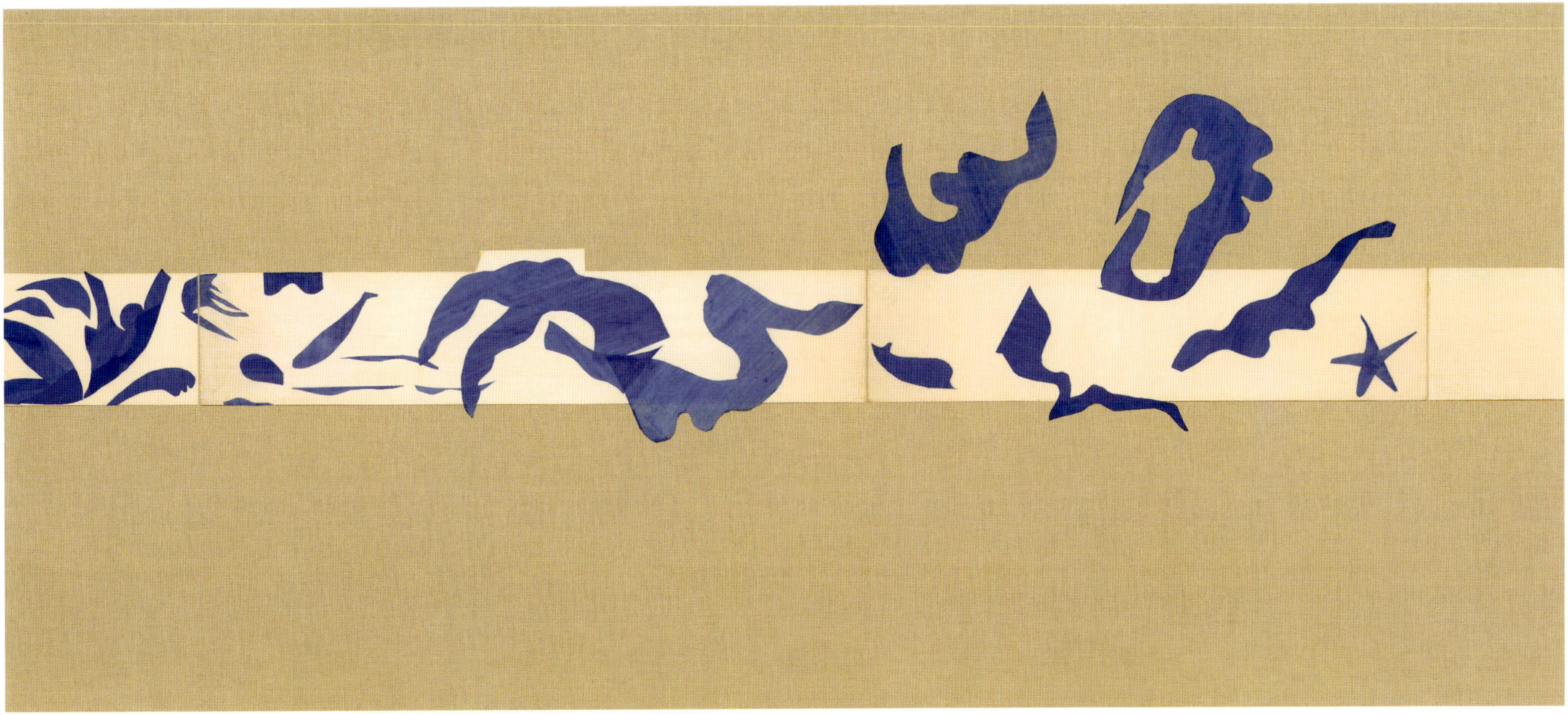

1953 THE SNAIL

Tate Modern, London
Gouache on paper, cut and pasted on paper mounted on canvas | 286.4 × 287cm (112¾ × 108in)

Even at its most abstract, Matisse's art never abandons nature. The artist acknowledged the abstract qualities of his cut-out *The Snail* with the secondary title *Chromatic Composition*. Yet it is not a work of pure abstraction: using abstract means, the artist creates an equivalent of a living creature found in the natural world.

Like *Memory of Oceania* (p. 129), *The Snail* is a large work in a square format. Within a jagged orange frame, angular and arched shapes are arranged on a white ground. Motion is evoked both by the spiralled arrangement of the shapes and by the vibrancy of the colours, whose full power is released through the juxtaposition of complementaries: red and green, blue and orange, yellow and violet.

The spiral shell of the snail is conveyed not by linear spirals, but by the arrangement of the coloured shapes on the pictorial field. This arrangement is a metaphor for universal movement, as found in nature, in music and in dance, as well as in visual art.

Matisse, more than any other European artist of his generation, spoke to a younger generation of painters. As a man in his eighties, he was producing works of extraordinary contemporaneity. *The Snail* anticipates works by the Colour Field painters of the 1960s, among them the British artist Richard Smith and the Americans Ellsworth Kelly, Kenneth Noland and Frank Stella.

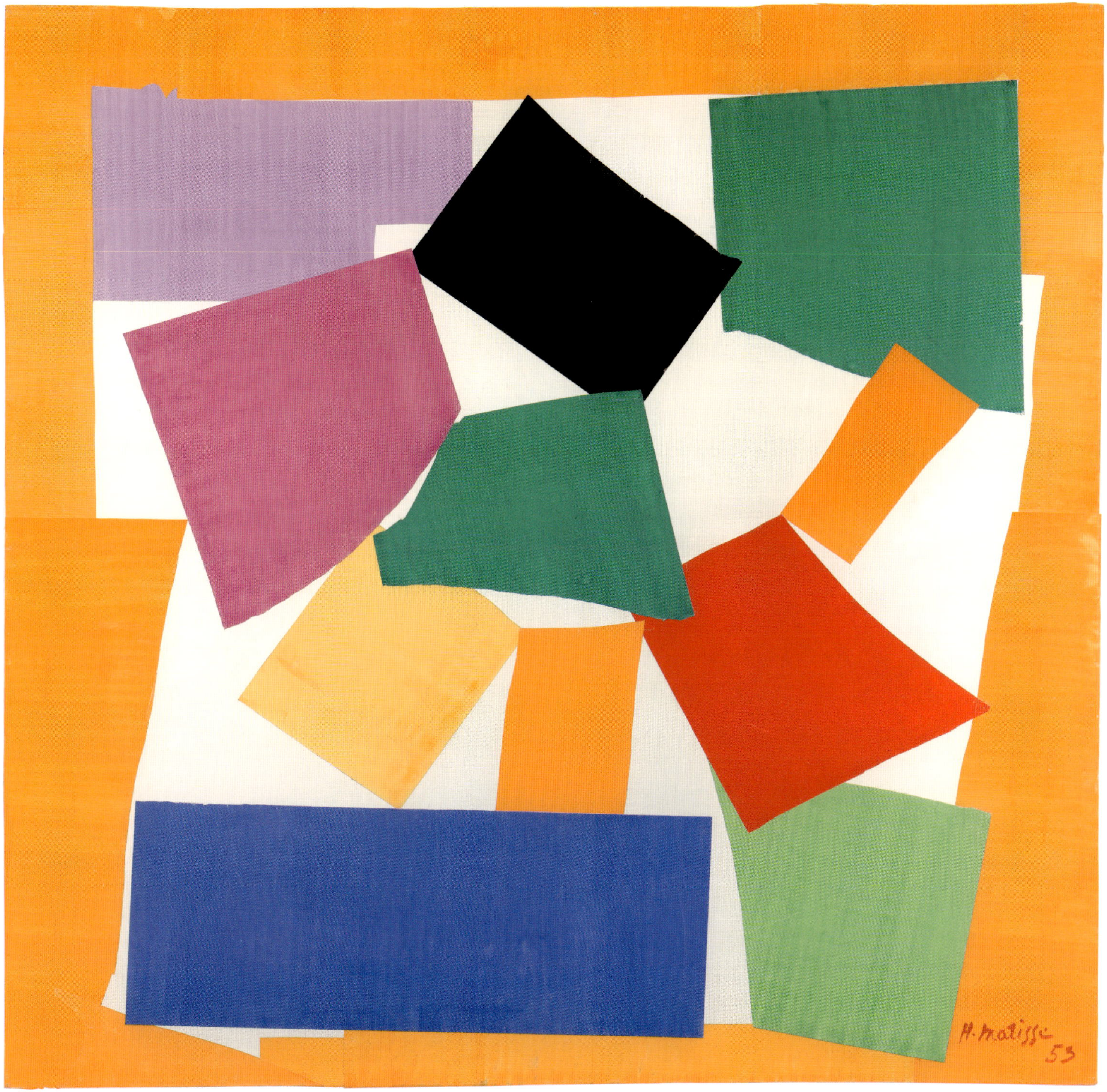
H. Matisse
53

NOTES ON WORKS

INTRODUCTION

1 Denys Sutton, ed., Letters of Roger Fry, New York: Random House, 1972, vol. 2, p. 534.
2 *Matisse's Radio Interviews, 1942*, in Flam 1995, p. 146.
3 *Interview with Jacques Guenne, 1925*, in Flam 1995, p. 79.
4 'Testimony against Gertrude Stein', *Transition,* supplement to no. 23 (February), Paris, 1935, p. 3.
5 *Interview with Jacques Guenne, 1925*, in Flam 1995, p. 80.
6 *Notes of a Painter, 1908*, in Flam 1995, pp. 37–8.
7 Barr 1951, p. 151.
8 *Statements to Tériade: Matisse Speaks, 1951*, in Flam 1995, p. 201.
9 Spurling 2005, pp. 141–4.
10 Spurling 2005, p. 154.
11 *Interview with Jacques Guenne, 1925*, in Flam 1995, p. 80.
12 *Statements to Tériade: On Fauvism and Colour, 1929*, in Flam 1995, p. 86.
13 Barr 1951, p. 243.
14 *Interview with Dorothy Dudley, 1933*, in Flam 1995, pp. 112–3.
15 Unsigned, 'Rivera's Views on Art Wrong, Matisse Thinks,' *New York Herald Tribune*, May 25, 1933, excerpted in Cauman 2000, p. 525.
16 Green 1953, p. 177.
17 Henri Matisse to Pierre Matisse, 1 September 1940, cited in Barr 1951, p. 256.
18 Russell 1999, p. 195.
19 Castleman 1985, p. xvii.
20 *Jazz, 1947*, in Flam 1995, p. 172.
21 See note 1.

THE PAINTINGS

22 *Statements to Tériade: Matisse Speaks, 1951*, in Flam 1995, p. 201.
23 *Interview with Jacques Guenne, 1925*, in Flam 1995, p. 80.
24 *Notes of a Painter, 1908*, in Flam 1995, p. 41.
25 Flam 1986, p. 79.
26 *On Cézanne's 'Three Bathers', 1936*, in Flam 1995, p. 124.
27 D'Alessandro and Elderfield 2010, p. 46.
28 *Statements to Tériade: Matisse Speaks, 1951*, in Flam 1995, p. 205.
29 Stein 1947, p. 158.
30 Stein 1947, p. 192.
31 Olivier 1965, p. 88.
32 'The Michael Steins of San Francisco: Art Patrons and Collectors' by Lucille M. Golson in Gordon, Golson, Katz, Cooper and Hirschland 1970, p. 43.
33 Courthion 2013, p. 138.
34 *Notes of a Painter, 1908*, in Flam 1995, pp. 37–8.
35 Courthion 2013, p. 73.
36 *New York Herald,* 12 February 1913; *Chicago Tribune,* 17 February 1913; *New York American*, 27 February 1913, cited in Cauman 2000, p. 193, n. 8.
37 *The Independent*, 6 March 1913, cited in Wattenmaker 1993, p. 308.
38 Pach 1938, pp. 116–7.
39 *Notes of a Painter, 1908*, in Flam 1995, pp. 41–2.
40 Stephanie D'Alessandro, 'Opportunity and Invention', in D'Alessandro and Elderfield 2010, p. 80.
41 *Letters to Alexander Romm, 1934*, in Flam 1995, p. 117.
42 *Statements to Tériade, 1929*, in Flam 1995, p. 85.

43 *The Role and Modalities of Colour, 1945*, in Flam 1995, p. 155.

44 See note 41.

45 *Interview with Clara T. MacChesney, 1912*, in Flam 1995, p. 66.

46 Elderfield 1978, p. 82.

47 Jean Puy, 'Souvenirs,' *Le Point* 21 (1939), p. 24, cited in Flam 2003, p. 239, n. 83.

48 Flam 1986, pp. 250–2.

49 Cited in Pierre Schneider, 'The Moroccan Binge,' in Cowart, Schneider, Elderfield and Kostenevich 1990, p. 56, n. 147 (author's translation).

50 Barr 1951, p. 159.

51 Henry Collins Walsh, 'The Rifs in Morocco,' *The Travel Magazine 14* (November 1908), p. 67, cited Jack Cowart, 'Matisse's Moroccan Sketchbooks and Drawings: Self-Discovery through Various Motifs,' in Cowart, Schneider, Elderfield and Kostenevich 1990, p. 130, and p. 151, n. 38.

52 See note 9.

53 Guillaume Apollinaire, 'Salon d'Automne: Henri Matisse', *Les Soirées de Paris,* 15 November 1913, p. 16, cited in Flam 1986, p. 372 and p. 501, n. 31; Apollinaire, *L'Intransigeant*, 14 November 1913, reprinted in Apollinaire, *Chroniques d'art* (1902–1918), Paris, 1960, cited in Flam 1986, p. 372 and p. 501, n. 30.

54 Caffin, 'Henri Matisse and Isadora Duncan', *Camera Work* 25 (January 1909), pp. 17–20, reprinted in Green, 1973, pp. 176–9.

55 Elderfield 1996, p. 76.

56 Spurling 2005, p. 154.

57 Gris to Kahnweiler [September or October 1914], cited in Barr 1951, p. 178.

58 Marmer 1966, p. 33.

59 Matisse to Camoin, December 1914, cited in D'Alessandro and Elderfield 2010, p. 241.

60 Matisse to Camoin, 22 November 1915, Archives Camoin, Saint-Mandé, cited in D'Alessandro and Elderfield, 2010, p. 261.

61 *Black is a Colour*, 1946, in Flam 1995, p. 166.

62 Barr Questionnaire I, Alfred Barr Papers, The Museum of Modern Art Archives, cited in Flam 1986, p. 405.

63 Barr Questionnaire I, Alfred Barr Papers, The Museum of Modern Art Archives, cited in Flam 1986, p. 405.

64 D'Alessandro and Elderfield 2010, p. 349.

65 Alfred Barr, *Henri Matisse*, exch. cat., New York: The Museum of Modern Art, 1931, p. 18; cited in D'Alessandro and Elderfield 2010, p. 23; and p. 31, n. 20.

66 See note 8.

67 'The Late Thirties in New York' in Greenberg 1961, p. 233.

68 *Interview with Ragnar Hoppe*, 1919, in Flam 1995, p. 75.

69 Jack Cowart, 'The Place of Silvered Light: An Expanded, Illustrated Chronology of Matisse in the South of France, 1916–1932', in Cowart and Fourcade 1987, p. 24.

70 Elderfield 1996, p. 149.

71 See *Conversations with Louis Aragon*, 1942, in Flam 1995, pp. 148–51.

72 Russell 1999, p. 195.

73 Monod-Fontaine 1989, p. 107 (author's translation).

74 Cited in Xavier Girard, et al., *Cahiers Henri Matisse*, vol. 1: 'Matisse et Tahiti', Musée Matisse, Nice, 1986, p. 150 (author's translation).

75 See *Statements to Tériade: Matisse Speaks, 1951*, in Flam 1995, p. 205.

76 *Bonnard/Matisse: Letters between Friends*, p. 41.

77 Elderfield 1978, p. 162 and p. 226, n. 3.

78 *Testimonial*, 1951 in Flam 1995, p. 207. In speaking of 'this cutout', Matisse was referring to *Chinese Fish*, 1951.

BIBLIOGRAPHY

Barr 1951: Barr, Alfred H., Jr., *Matisse: His Art and His Public*, New York: The Museum of Modern Art, 1951.

Bishop, Debray and Rabinow 2011: Bishop, Janet, Cécile Debray and Rebecca Rabinow, ed., *The Steins Collect: Matisse, Picasso, and the Parisian Avant-Garde*, exh. cat., San Francisco Museum of Modern Art, New Haven and London: Yale University Press, 2011.

Castleman 1985: Castleman, Riva, *Henri Matisse's Jazz*, New York: George Braziller, 1985.

Cauman 2000: Cauman, John, 'Matisse and America, 1905–1933', Ph.D. Dissertation, City University of New York, 2000.

Courthion 2013: Matisse, Henri with Pierre Courthion, *Chatting with Henri Matisse: The Lost 1941 Interview*, Serge Guilbaut, ed., Chris Miller, trans., London and Los Angeles, Tate Publishing, in association with the Getty Research Institute, 2013.

Cowart and Fourcade 1987: Cowart, Jack, and Dominique Fourcade, *Henri Matisse: The Early Years in Nice*, exh. cat., National Gallery of Art, Washington, New York: Harry N. Abrams, 1987.

Cowart, Schneider, Elderfield and Kostenevich 1990: Cowart, Jack, Pierre Schneider, John Elderfield and Albert Kostenevich, *Matisse in Morocco: The Paintings and Drawings 1912–1913*, exh. cat., National Gallery of Art, Washington, New York: Harry N. Abrams, 1990.

D'Alessandro and Elderfield 2010: D'Alessandro, Stephanie and John Elderfield, *Matisse: Radical Invention, 1913–1917*, exh. cat., The Art Institute of Chicago and The Museum of Modern Art, New Haven and London: Yale University Press, 2010.

Elderfield 1978: Elderfield, John, *Matisse in the Collection of the Museum of Modern Art,* New York: The Museum of Modern Art, 1978.

Elderfield 1996: Elderfield, John, *Masterworks from the Museum of Modern Art*, New York: The Museum of Modern Art, 1996.

Flam 1986: Flam, Jack, *Matisse: The Man and His Art, 1869–1918*, Ithaca and London: Cornell University Press, 1986.

Flam 1995: Flam, Jack, ed., *Matisse on Art*, second ed., Berkeley and Los Angeles: University of California Press, 1995.

Flam 2003: Flam, Jack, *Matisse and Picasso: The Story of Their Rivalry and Friendship*, Cambridge, MA: Westview Press, 2003.

Galerie des Ponchettes 1986: Galerie des Ponchettes, *Matisse et Tahiti*, exh. cat., Nice: Musée Matisse, 1986.

Gordon, Golson, Katz, Cooper and Hirschland 1970: Gordon, Irene, Lucille M. Golson, Leon Katz, Douglas Cooper and Ellen B. Hirschland, *Four Americans in Paris*, exh. cat., New York: The Museum of Modern Art, 1970.

Green 1973: Green, Jonathan, ed., *Camera Work: A Critical Anthology*, Millerton, NY: Aperture, Inc., 1973.

Greenberg 1961: Greenberg, Clement, *Art and Culture: Critical* Essays, Boston: Beacon Press, 1961.

Kostenevich and Semyonova 1993: Kostenevich, Albert and Natalya Semyonova, *Collecting Matisse*, Paris: Flammarion, 1993.

Marmer 1996: Marmer, Nancy, 'Matisse and the Strategy of Decoration', *Artforum* 4, 7 (March 1966): pp. 28–33.

Monod-Fontaine 1989: Monod-Fontaine, Isabelle, Anne Baldessari and Claude Laugier, *Œuvres de Henri Matisse*, Paris: Centre Georges Pompidou, Collections du Musée National d'Art Moderne, 1989.

Olivier 1965: Olivier, Fernande, *Picasso and His Friends,* trans. Jane Miller, New York: Appleton-Century, 1965.

Pach 1938: Pach, Walter, *Queer Thing, Painting: Forty Years in the World of Art*, New York: Harper & Brothers, 1938.

Russell 1999: Russell, John, *Matisse: Father & Son*, New York: Harry N. Abrams, 1999.

Spurling 2005: Spurling, Hilary, *Matisse the Master: A Life of Henri Matisse, Volume Two: The Conquest of Colour, 1909–1954*, London: Hamish Hamilton, 2005.

Stein 1947: Stein, Leo, *Appreciation: Painting, Poetry and Prose*, New York: Crown Publishers, 1947.

Terrasse 1991: Terrasse, Antoine, introduction and notes, *Bonnard/Matisse: Letters Between Friends*, trans. Richard Howard, New York: Harry N. Abrams, 1991.

Wattenmaker 1993: Wattenmaker, Richard J., ed., *Great French Paintings from the Barnes Collection*, New York: Alfred A. Knopf, 1993.

GLOSSARY

abstract art: The term usually employed to designate non-objective art, or the art of pure abstraction, in which forms are not meant to evoke objects in the visible world.

Abstract Expressionism: Also known as the New York School, American abstract art, c. 1945–60, as practised by such artists as Jackson Pollock, Willem de Kooning, Mark Rothko and Barnett Newman.

Analytic Cubism: The style of Cubism, c. 1908–12, as created by Georges Braque and Pablo Picasso. Inspired by Paul Cézanne, the artists re-created nature in a shallow, discontinuous relief space behind the picture plane; forms are reduced to geometric components; and different parts of a picture are painted from different points of view. In Analytic Cubist painting, colour plays a secondary role.

arabesque: Surface decoration of rhythmic, intertwined linear patterns of flowers, leaves or scrollwork.

architectonic: Relating to the use of architectural principles as a fundamental element of design, such as linear and grid forms.

avant-garde: Artistic movements characterized by innovative, experimental ideas.

cartoon: A full-size preliminary drawing for an artwork.

collage: An artwork formed by various elements glued to the pictorial surface, such as clippings, textiles, photographs or coloured papers.

Colour Field Painting: A style of abstract painting in Britain and the United States in the 1960s, as embodied by such artists as the British painter Richard Smith and the Americans Ellsworth Kelly, Kenneth Noland and Frank Stella. Paint tends to be applied thinly and in bright colours; an infinite space beyond the pictorial field is often evoked.

complementaries: The colour spectrum comprises primary and secondary colours. The primary colours are red, blue, and yellow; the secondary colours are green, orange, and violet. Each primary colour has a complementary secondary colour; the complementaries are red/green, blue/orange, and yellow/violet. When two complementaries are juxtaposed, they produce maximum colouristic intensity.

contrapuntal: A musical term; the adjectival form of 'counterpoint'. In music, counterpoint is created when two or more melodies are played simultaneously. By analogy, counterpoint in visual art is formed when two or more visual themes are simultaneously present.

Cubism: A style of painting inspired by Paul Cézanne that was invented by Pablo Picasso and Georges Braque in the first decade of the twentieth century. It began with Picasso's Proto-Cubism of 1907, inspired by Cézanne and African tribal art, followed by the Analytic Cubist style of Braque and Picasso in 1908, and then by the Synthetic Cubism of Braque, Picasso and Juan Gris, beginning c. 1912, which attracted many artists in Europe and the United States in subsequent years. Cubism is characterized by near abstraction, flattened space, geometric reductionism and multiple points of view.

cuneiform: Literally, 'wedge-shaped'; the wedged-shaped characters of the writing systems of ancient Mesopotamia, which survive primarily in clay tablets.

curvilinearity: Characterized by a curved line or lines.

distemper: A paint medium formed by pigment and water with a glue binder that produces a matte effect.

Divisionism: See Neo-Impressionism.

écorché: A statuette of a human figure with skin removed, displaying its musculature, used by artists for studying anatomical structure.

en plein air: 'In the open air'; for artists, the act of painting figures and landscapes outdoors.

Fauvism: A style of painting in France, c. 1905–06, led by Matisse, and including Derain, Vlaminck, Rouault, Braque, Dufy, Camoin, Manguin and Marquet. The style employed bold colour, violent distortions and loose brushwork. It was the first avant-garde artistic style of the twentieth century.

fresco: A technique of mural painting employing water-based paint on wet plaster.

Futurism: A style of art stressing dynamism and glorifying the machine. As practised by such Italian artists as Marinetti, Severini, Boccioni and Carrà, it came to adopt an Analytic Cubist style with the added element of motion.

Golden Age: A mythical, idealized past of peace, harmony and prosperity.

impasto: The technique of applying paint thickly so that it is raised from the surface and its texture is visible to the viewer.

in situ (Latin): Literally, 'on the site'; a work of art that is done *in situ* is made entirely on the site, rather than the studio, based on sketches.

iridescence: Of colour which is luminous, lustrous.

luminosity: The degree to which an object appears to radiate light.

lunette: In architecture, a semi-circular structure.

Neo-Impressionism: Founded by Georges Seurat and Paul Signac and also known as Divisionism or Pointillism, it was an outgrowth of Impressionism. More systematic than its parent style, it breaks up colour into small dots or points, separated on the canvas surface, but intended to blend in the viewer's eye to re-create the effects of the brilliant colours of nature.

organisé: Literally, 'organized'; a term employed by Matisse for the final, more abstract stage of a work which was representational in its preliminary stages.

odalisque: A depiction of a woman, often reclining, in a Near Eastern interior.

orthogonals: Lines which intersect at right angles; since the Renaissance, they have been used by artists in their depiction of three-dimensional perspective.

passage (French term): Pioneered by Paul Cézanne, a technique of applying parallel brushstrokes to depict angled planes which fuse solid form and negative space, foreground and background, evoking three-dimensionality without violating the flatness of the pictorial surface.

pentimenti: Plural of pentimento, an alteration made by an artist while a painting is in progress which shows through in the final work.

plastic signs: In Matisse's later work, the artist's work became more abstract, and objects were re-created less by the artist's direct observation than by his concept of the object. He employed the term 'plastic signs' to designate the abstract forms that he created to evoke the original objects.

Pointillism: See Neo-Impressionism.

Post-Impressionism: The late nineteenth-century style that followed Impressionism, as practised by such artists as Cézanne, Gauguin and Van Gogh. These artists employed the brilliant colours of Impressionists, but sought, in various ways, to create artworks that were at once more subjective and more structurally permanent.

rectilinear: Characterized by a straight line or lines which meet at right angles.

representation: As opposed to 'abstraction', the depiction of forms and figures as they appear to the eye.

scumble: To apply a thin layer of opaque paint over another layer so that, seen together, the layers produce a softened effect.

still life: A work of art that depicts inanimate or motionless objects, such as fruit, flowers, dead animals, skulls, plants, rocks, shells, pipes, books, plates, glassware or vases.

Symbolism: A movement in art and literature in the last three decades of the nineteenth century. Symbolism was a reaction against Realism, with a tendency to look inward, and with an interest in myth and mysticism. Among its literary practitioners were Stéphane Mallarmé, Charles Baudelaire and Edgar Allan Poe. Symbolist painters included Gustave Moreau, Odilon Redon and Pierre Puvis de Chavannes.

Synthetic Cubism: A more readable and less monochromatic style than Analytic Cubism, this style is less fragmented, and colour and texture play a greater part. Flattened forms are depicted in front of, rather than behind, the picture plane. Collage is introduced, and Synthetic Cubist paintings re-create the effects of collage.

INDEX

Note: Page numbers in *italics* refer to illustration titles/captions.

CREDITS

Every effort has been made to trace the copyright holders and obtain permission to reproduce this material. However, the publishers will be glad to rectify in future editions any inadvertent omissions brought to their attention.

The publisher would like to thank the following collections for their kind permission to reproduce the illustrations in this book:

Page 3, The Barnes Foundation, Philadelphia, Pennsylvania, USA / Bridgeman Images; **5,** Gamma-Keystone via Getty Images; **9**, courtesy of Matisse Archives, Issy; **10**, courtesy of Matisse Archives, Issy; **11**, courtesy of Matisse Archives, Issy; **12**, Photograph © The State Hermitage Museum/photo by Vladimir Terebenin; **13**, courtesy of Matisse Archives, Issy; **15**, State Hermitage Museum, St. Petersburg, Russia / Bridgeman Images; **16**,: Photo Josse/Scala**;** **17**, Philadelphia Museum of Art, The Louise and Walter Arensberg Collection, 1950, 1950-134-59, © Association Marcel Duchamp / ADAGP, Paris and DACS, London 2018**;** **19**, Private Collection / Bridgeman Images; **21**, Kunstmuseum Solothurn, Dübi-Müller-Stiftung; **23**, courtesy of Matisse Archives, Issy; **27**, Thannhauser Collection, Gift, Justin K. Thannhauser, 1978. Photo: © 2018. The Solomon R. Guggenheim Foundation/Art Resource, NY/ Scala, Florence. Artwork: © Succession Picasso/ DACS, London 2018; **28** Courtesy the National Gallery of Art, Washington; **33**, Private Collection / Bridgeman Images; **35,** The Baltimore Museum of Art: The Cone Collection, formed by Dr. Claribel Cone and Miss Etta Cone of Baltimore, Maryland, BMA 1950.225; **37**, Kay Sage Tanguy and Abby Aldrich Rockefeller Funds. Acc. n.: 377.1975.© 2018. Digital image, The Museum of Modern Art, New York/Scala, Florence; **39**, Tompkins Collection - Arthur Gordon Tompkins Fund. Acc.n.: RES.32.14© 2018. Museum of Fine Arts, Boston. All rights reserved/Scala, Florence; **41** Photo ©RMN-Grand Palais (musée d'Orsay) / Hervé Lewandowski © Succession H. Matisse; **43,** Courtesy the National Gallery of Art, Washington**;** **45,** San Francisco Museum of Modern Art, bequest of Elise S. Haas. Photograph: Ben Blackwell; **47,** The National Gallery of Denmark, Copenhagen, © SMK Photo; **49** Jacques and Natasha Gelman Collection, 1998. Acc.n.: 1999.363.41.© 2018. Image copyright The Metropolitan Museum of Art/Art Resource/Scala, Florence; **51,** The National Gallery of Denmark, Copenhagen, © SMK Photo; **53**, The Barnes Foundation, Philadelphia, Pennsylvania, USA / Bridgeman Images; **55**, The Baltimore Museum of Art: The Cone Collection, formed by Dr. Claribel Cone and Miss Etta Cone of Baltimore, Maryland, BMA 1950.228; **57**, The Barnes Foundation, Philadelphia, Pennsylvania, USA / Bridgeman Images; **59,** The National Gallery of Denmark, Copenhagen, © SMK Photo; **61**, Saint Louis Art Museum, Missouri, USA / Gift of Mr. and Mrs. Joseph Pulitzer Jr. / Bridgeman Images; **63**, Photograph © The State Hermitage Museum/photo by Vladimir Terebenin; **65**, Gift of Nelson A. Rockefeller in honor of Alfred H. Barr,Jr. 201.1963.© 2018. Digital image, The Museum of Modern Art, New York/Scala, Florence; **67**, The State Hermitage Museum, St. Petersburg. Photograph © The State Hermitage Museum/ photo by Vladimir Terebenin; **69**, The State Hermitage Museum, St. Petersburg. Photograph © The State Hermitage Museum/photo by Vladimir Terebenin; **71**, The State Hermitage Museum, St. Petersburg. Photograph © The State Hermitage Museum/photo by Vladimir Terebenin; **73**, The Pushkin State Museum of Fine Arts, Moscow; **75**, The State Hermitage Museum, St. Petersburg. Photograph © The State Hermitage Museum/photo by Vladimir Terebenin; **77**, Ville de Grenoble / Musée de Grenoble – photo: J.L. Lacroixnce ; **79**, Mrs. Simon Guggenheim Fund. Acc. n.: 8.1949.© 2018. Digital image, The Museum of Modern Art, New York/Scala, Florence; **81**, The Pushkin State Museum of Fine Arts, Moscow; **83** Gift of Mr. and Mrs. John Hay Whitney. Acc. n.: 199.1955.© 2018. Digital image, The Museum of Modern Art, New York/Scala, Florence; **85**, The State Hermitage Museum, St. Petersburg. Photograph © The State Hermitage Museum/photo by Vladimir Tereben; **87**, The Barnes Foundation, Philadelphia, Pennsylvania, USA / Bridgeman Images; **89** St. Petersburg, Hermitage Museum. © 2018. Photo Scala, Florence; **91**, The State Hermitage Museum, St. Petersburg. Photograph © The State Hermitage Museum/photo by Vladimir Terebenin; **93**, Acquired through the Lillie P. Bliss Bequest and the Henry Ittleson, A. Conger Goodyear, Mr. and Mrs. Robert Sinclair Funds, and the Anna Erickson Levene Bequest given in memory of her husband, Dr. Phoebus Aaron Theodor Levene. Acc. n.: 116.1975. © 2018. Digital image, The Museum of Modern Art, New York/Scala, Florence; **95**, Philadelphia Museum of Art, The Louise and Walter Arensberg Collection, 1950-134-130; **97**, Photo © Centre Pompidou, MNAM-CCI, Dist. RMN-Grand Palais / Philippe Migeat**;** **99**, Gift and Bequest of Florene M. Schoenborn and Samuel A. Marx. Acc n.: 507.1964. © 2018. Digital image, The Museum of Modern Art, New York/Scala, Florence; **101**, Gift of Mr. and Mrs. Samuel A. Marx. Acc. n.: 386.1955.© 2018. Digital image, The Museum of Modern Art, New York/Scala, Florence; **103**, Mrs. Simon Guggenheim Fund. Acc. n.: 109.1935.© 2018. Digital image, The Museum of Modern Art, New York/Scala, Florence; **105**, Mrs. Simon Guggenheim Fund. Acc. n.: 125.1946. © 2018. Digital image, The Museum of Modern Art, New York/Scala, Florence; **107**, The Art Institute of Chicago, IL, USA / Charles H. and Mary F. S. Worcester Collection / Bridgeman Images; **109**, Lillie P. Bliss Collection. Acc. n.: 86.1934.© 2018. Digital image, The Museum of Modern Art, New York/Scala, Florence; **111,** Courtesy the National Gallery of Art, Washington**;** **113**, Paris, Musèe National d'Art Moderne - Centre Pompidou. © 2018. Photo Josse/Scala, Florence; **115**, The William S. Paley Collection. Acc. n.: SPC22.1990. © 2018. Digital image, The Museum of Modern Art, New York/Scala, Florence; **118 and 119**, The Barnes Foundation, Philadelphia, Pennsylvania, USA / Bridgeman Images; **121,** The Baltimore Museum of Art: The Cone Collection, formed by Dr. Claribel Cone and Miss Etta Cone of Baltimore, Maryland, BMA 1950.258; **123**, courtesy of Matisse Archives, Issy; **125**, Photo (C) Centre Pompidou, MNAM-CCI, Dist. RMN-Grand Palais / Philippe Migeat © Succession H. Matisse; **127,** The Phillips Collection, Washington, DC, Acquired 1950**;** **129,** Mrs. Simon Guggenheim Fund. Acc. n.: 224.1968.© 2018. Digital image, The Museum of Modern Art, New York/Scala, Florence; **132 and 133** Mrs. Bernard F. Gimbel Fund.302.1975.a-i.© 2018. Digital image, The Museum of Modern Art, New York/Scala, Florence; **135** ©Tate, London 2018.

Cover Photograph © The State Hermitage Museum, Dance II

ACKNOWLEDGEMENTS

This book was made possible by a legacy of Matisse research. Credit should be given to the pioneers of Matisse scholarship, of which the following is an incomplete list: the late Alfred H. Barr, Jr.; the late Pierre Schneider; Jack Flam; Dominique Fourcade; and John Elderfield.

I am grateful to Georges Matisse and Wanda de Guébriant of the Archives Matisse for their help in making this book possible.

I thank my friend, art historian Francis Naumann, for his moral support and editorial suggestions while this book was in progress.

Finally, I thank the management and staff of Pavilion Books, London: Polly Powell, publisher, who first suggested *Matisse in 50 Works*; my editor, Bella Cockrell; Victoria Nairn, who was editor in the book's early stages; Katie Cowan, publishing director; Michelle Mac and James Boast, designers; Anne Hildyard, copy editor; Emily Hedges, picture researcher; and Diana Vowles, proofreader.

First published in the United Kingdom in 2019
Pavilion
An imprint of HarperCollins*Publishers*
1 London Bridge Street
London SE1 9GF

www.harpercollins.co.uk

HarperCollins*Publishers*
Macken House
39/40 Mayor Street Upper
Dublin 1
D01 C9W8
Ireland

ISBN 978-1-91159-513-7

A CIP catalogue record for this book is available from the British Library.

10 9 8 7 6 5 4 3 2

Reproduction by Rival Colour Ltd, UK
Printed and bound in China by RR Donnelley APS

MIX
Paper | Supporting responsible forestry
FSC www.fsc.org FSC™ C007454

This book is produced from independently certified FSC™ paper to ensure responsible forest management.

For more information visit: www.harpercollins.co.uk/green